The RHP Companion to

Outdoor Education

Edited by

Peter Barnes and Bob Sharp

RHP

Russell House Publishing

First published in 2004 by:
Russell House Publishing Ltd.
4 St. George's House
Uplyme Road
Lyme Regis
Dorset DT7 3LS

Tel: 01297-443948
Fax: 01297-442722
e-mail: help@russellhouse.co.uk
www.russellhouse.co.uk

Cover photograph by Nina Saunders

British Library Cataloguing-in-publication Data:
A catalogue record for this book is available from the British Library.

ISBN: 978-1-903855-36-2

Typeset by TW Typesetting, Plymouth, Devon

Printed by Cromwell Press, Trowbridge

About Russell House Publishing

RHP is a group of social work, probation, education and youth and community work practitioners and academics working in collaboration with a professional publishing team.
Our aim is to work closely with the field to produce innovative and valuable materials to help managers, trainers, practitioners and students. We are keen to receive feedback on publications and new ideas for future projects.
For details of our other publications please visit our website or ask us for a catalogue. Contact details are on this page.

Contents

About the Authors

Marcus Bailie was the first Head of Inspection of the Adventure Activities Licensing Authority when it was formed in 1996. At the time of writing he is still in post. His background is adventure activities, not Health and Safety. He is a qualified teacher and has been delivering activities, in and out of school for over 20 years, including as head of mountain leadership at Plas y Brenin, The National Mountaineering Centre. He has been the Director of two centres including Tiglin, The National Adventure Centre of Ireland. He has always questioned and probed at conventional thinking and has written on alternative approaches to the learning and teaching of canoeing and kayaking. His qualifications include the BCU level 5 Coach Award, and the Mountain Instructor Certificate, both of which he has trained and assessed. He has been involved in kayaking expeditions on a regular basis since 1978.

Peter Barnes is the coordinator for the BA Outdoor Education in the Community programme at the Jordanhill Campus of the University of Strathclyde. He has had a wide and varied career including youth work, military service, radar systems design and many years of outdoor work with Outward Bound and others in a variety of countries. He was also responsible for the instigation and development of outdoor education at the University of Central Lancashire. His PhD research was in 'The Motivation of Staff Working in the Outdoor Industry' and current research issues include the content and viability of outdoor degrees. He has been the chair for the Northern and Scottish regions of the Institute for Outdoor Learning and is a Fellow of the Royal Geographical Society. Peter has published widely in a diverse range of subjects revolving around leadership and the outdoors as well as caving, mountain biking and mountaineering. He lives with his wife, Sue, and a manic household of cats, dogs and children in Paisley near Glasgow.

Geoff Cooper is head of Wigan LEA's two outdoor education centres in the Lake District. He has introduced many young people to the outdoors through a range of experiences based on adventure, field studies, problem solving, conservation and the arts and regularly runs training courses for youth leaders and countryside staff. He has organised workshops on environmental education for teachers and leaders in Britain and across the rest of Europe. He is author of *Outdoors with Young People: A Leader's Guide to Outdoor Activities, the Environment and Sustainability* (Russell House Publishing, 1998) and co-author of *In Touch: Environmental Education for Europe*. He is secretary of the Adventure and Environmental Awareness Group.

Bertie Everard has chaired the Development Training Advisory (now Employers') Group (DTAG/ DTEG) since 1982 and was Vice-chair of the National Association for Values in Education and Training (NAVET). He was a founder trustee of the Foundation for Outdoor Adventure. He now chairs the Welwyn Hatfield YMCA and the Christ and the Cosmos Initiative and is a trustee of the Brathay Hall Trust. His research in schools was published in *Developing Management in Schools* (Blackwell 1986) and he co-authored *Effective School Management* (Paul Chapman Publishing 1985), now in its fourth edition.

Roger Greenaway trained and worked as a teacher of outdoor education and has a PhD in outdoor management development. He discovered 'reviewing' during his six years as a 'develop- ment trainer' at Brathay where he worked with young people, with managers and with trainers. Roger continues to retain an active interest in both youth development and management development and has travelled to many countries to provide trainer-training events in reviewing skills and the transfer of learning. He has written several books and articles on the subject and maintains an encyclopaedic website on reviewing and outdoor education topics at http://reviewing.co.uk

Nick Halls began as a temporary instructor at Ogwen Cottage, and Plas Gwynant in 1962. He studied at Chester College gaining a BEd degree encompassing; Physical Education, Geography and Moral Education. From 1969 he worked at Benmore Centre, Argyll, for Edinburgh Corporation, where he was working at the time of the Cairngorm Tragedy. From 1973 to 1990 he worked for Renfrewshire Council as Deputy Principal of Ardentinny Centre. He was then appointed as Regional Adviser for Outdoor Education for the former Strathclyde Regional Council. He took early retirement in 1994 and now works as a mountaineering instructor and risk management consultant.

Adrian Ibbetson is a Senior Lecturer in Sport and Recreation Management at the University of Central Lancashire, Preston. His interest in management development programmes that use the outdoors as the learning medium was stimulated during his Masters degree at Dalhousie University, Canada, where he investigated the efficacy of adventure-based, experimental training. Adrian undertook his PhD evaluating the effectiveness of outdoor management development (OMD) at the University of Birmingham, where he had earlier done his undergraduate studies in Sport and Recreation Studies. Adrian is a keen outdoor enthusiast whose activities have been curtailed of late due to the joys of fatherhood. Adrian periodically facilitates OMD programmes but likes to reflect critically upon practice.

Patrick Keighley is a 'freelance education consultant' and author of *Learning through First Hand Experience Out of Doors*. Before becoming an independent consultant he was Inspector/Adviser of Schools (Outdoor and Environmental Education) for Northumberland LEA and an Ofsted Inspector. As a former teacher he held various senior posts both in schools, outdoor education centres and in local government. He is currently external examiner to the I. M. Marsh College. B.Sc (Hons) course. Outdoor and Environmental Education and is the Hon. Chair of an outdoor charity for disadvantaged and disaffected young people, Mobex Network UK. He lives in the Northumberland National Park.

Steve Lenartowicz first worked in the outdoors as a student, at the Travellers Trust on Loch Nevis, and the Ridgway Adventure School. He became a 'Sparklet', having trained as a teacher with Barbara Spark at Bangor. He taught for three years in Moss Side, Manchester, before sailing in the Whitbread Round the World Race and then moving to Ghyll Head Outdoor Education Centre. He spent two years teacher training for VSO, returned to work at Outward Bound, ran hotel-based youth and management training courses for Central Manchester College, and worked at Derwent Hill Outdoor Education Centre. He is now Youth Development Director at Brathay.

Angus McWilliam began his career as a botanist and ecologist drawing and describing flowers and communities but then moved into the area of environmental interpretation and countryside management working with the National Trust for Scotland. Moving into formal education he developed outdoor curricula for children with social and emotional needs and became part of the Central Region's team of instructors delivering activities to primary and secondary students. Now in higher education he lectures on experiential learning, environmental ethics and the aesthetics of outdoor experience and is competent (but not skilled!) in a wide variety of outdoor pursuits.

Geoff Nichols has been a lecturer in Leisure Management at Sheffield University Management School since 1990. His current research interests include evaluations of local government programmes using sport as a medium to reduce youth crime, and volunteers in sport. He worked for Outward Bound in the UK for five years during the 1980s, and for three years as an Outdoor Pursuits Development Officer for local government.

Kate O'Brien is the youngest contributor to this book. She originally comes from Inverness and is currently working towards an Honours degree in 'Outdoor Education in the Community' at Strathclyde University. Kate loves working with young people and has worked as a mentor for the Summer Academy at Strathclyde University. She enjoys many different outdoor activities including mountain biking, walking and snow sports and hopes to pursue a career in the outdoor industry when she graduates.

Roger Putnam has had a long and distinguished career in the outdoors. He was Principal of Outward Bound Eskdale from 1968 to 1988. Roger compiled the Hunt Report *In Search of Adventure* (1988-1989) and was co-author (with David Hopkins) of *Personal Growth Through Adventure*. He is a former chairman of the Mountain Leader Training Board, the National Association for Outdoor Education and the English Outdoor Council. He is also a member of the Climbers Club. In 2000, Roger was awarded the MBE for services to sport.

Nina Saunders is a full time PhD student at the Scottish School of Sport Studies (University of Strathclyde) in Glasgow. Her current research explores the role of female leaders working in overseas expedition environments. She has completed a BA (Honours) in Outdoor Education in the Community at the same institution and currently works part time at the Glasgow Climbing Centre. She holds a variety of national governing body awards and has over 10 years of experience working in outdoor education both in the UK and overseas. Her interest and enthusiasm for travel and mountaineering has taken her to numerous countries worldwide. Nina is a keen photographer, and in her spare time can be found wandering around the Scottish Highlands.

Bob Sharp has been a University lecturer for 30 years and is presently a Reader in Sport Studies in the Scottish School of Sport Studies at Strathclyde University. His interest in the outdoors (particularly skiing, climbing and open canoeing) was awakened when he lived in the Canadian Rockies in the late 1960s. Since then he has instructed at the National Outdoor Training Centre, various local authority outdoor centres and also delivered technical courses to teachers and the public at large through the University. He is Team Leader of one of Scotland's mountain rescue teams and also Secretary to the Mountain Rescue Committee of Scotland. He is a former Vice President of the Mountaineering Council of Scotland and Chair of the Scottish Mountain Safety Forum. In his professional work he delivers courses in skill acquisition, safety management, statistics and research methods to sport and outdoor education students. He was recently elected as a Fellow of the Royal Geographical Society and awarded the Queen's Golden Jubilee Medal for services to mountain rescue.

Janet Shepherd trained as a teacher and taught Maths and Physical Education in Gloucestershire. She was seconded to attend the Outdoor Education course at Plas y Brenin in 1975. From then until taking up her present employment she worked in Outdoor Education Centres in England, Scotland and Wales. This included serving as warden of a centre and senior tutor responsible for adult training and leader validation schemes in one council area. For the last 12 years Janet has been with The Duke of Edinburgh's Award and is currently responsible for the Award in Scotland. She is a Board member of Mountain Leader Training (Scotland) and has been a representative for Youthlink, which is the National Youth Agency in Scotland on a number of outdoor issues.

Alan Smith now works as a supply teacher in Derbyshire. He was previously Head of Geography at a comprehensive school in Nottinghamshire where he was also responsible for outdoor education. His first book, *Working Out Of Doors With Young People*, was published by the Scottish Intermediate Treatment Resource Centre in 1987. This book was later extended and updated to become *Creative Outdoor Work With Young People*, published by Russell House Publishing Ltd. in 1994.

Archie Waters originally trained as a Youth and Community worker at Jordanhill College and subsequently achieved a BSc (Hons) degree in psychology with the Open University. A keen outdoor enthusiast, with a particular passion for sea kayaking, he began work as an outdoor education instructor for Strathclyde Regional Council in 1976. After 12 years working at a variety of the council's residential education centres he took up his current position of Project Leader of Drumchapel Adventure Group. Over the past 15 years he has developed a reputation as a successful 'social entrepreneur', bringing the project long-term stability and recognition as a centre of best practice.

Randall Williams graduated from Oxford with a degree in physics. He worked for Outward Bound in the UK for five years and then became Warden of Outward Bound Zambia. After a master's degree in management, he became Director of Bowles Outdoor Centre, a post which he has held for 25 years. He has been President of the English Ski Council, Chair of the English Outdoor Council and was centrally involved in the formation of the Institute for Outdoor Learning. Over the years, his enthusiasms have included climbing, canoeing, caving, sailing and skiing. His current passion is gliding.

Judy Ling Wong FRSA, OBE is the Director of Black Environment Network, an organisation with an international reputation as the pioneer in the field of ethnic environmental participation. She has worked extensively in various sectors – in the arts, in psychotherapy and in community involvement. This multiple background means that she is uniquely placed to take forward the development of an integrated approach to environmental participation, bringing together different fields and sharing cultural visions. She was made a Fellow of the Royal Society of Arts in 1997 in recognition of her contribution to contemporary environmental thinking. In June 2000 she was awarded the OBE as part of the Queen's Birthday Honours, in recognition of her outstanding contribution to ethnic environmental participation.

Phil Woodyer is Head of Centre at Low Mill Outdoor Centre where he started in 1993, after eight years as a teacher in Blackpool and four years as Deputy Warden of Lancashire Education Authority's Prior House Centre. He has been consistently active in the outdoors with expeditions to Norway, Iceland and the Alps as well as serving as Secretary to the Northern Council for Outdoor Education, Training and Recreation. Phil also acts as a technical advisor for the Adventure Activities Licensing Authority scheme and is an assessor and trainer for the Local Cave Leader Award. He has published widely on working with special needs groups.

Foreword

Roger Putnam

Progress in any field requires a combination of competence and enterprise. One without the other is never enough. There is a need for vision and imagination, but also for down-to-earth attention to detail; any successful entrepreneur has to anticipate the needs of the future whilst continuing to meet the practical needs of the present. This is true in most areas of human activity, including what, for the purpose of this book, is identified as outdoor education, but which many may choose to approach more widely as learning through the outdoors.

The RHP Companion to Outdoor Education, notable for the breadth of its content, will contribute both to today's practice and also to our attempts to identify and meet future needs. The book provides a comprehensive analysis by leading practitioners of up-to-date thinking in the diverse and fascinating arena of outdoor learning, whilst signalling what may become the priorities of outdoor work in the years ahead. The authors collectively provide a lucid and helpful assessment of the state of outdoor education today, with an important focus on how differing individuals and groups may learn from outdoor experience. From their contributions we may gain a clearer picture of the directions in which we will travel in the future.

Looking back to the Hunt Report in search of adventure

I am tempted to look back to consider an earlier attempt to take stock of outdoor education and anticipate future priorities. I had the privilege in the late 1980s of working under the direction of a team led by Lord Hunt which set out to assess the state of play at that time in the outdoor adventure field. The production of the Hunt report *In Search of Adventure* (1989) was a fascinating exercise. Perhaps for the first time, the report revealed the diversity and the significance of many of the outdoor experiences on offer to young people in that already distant era, as well as the sheer enthusiasm and commitment of the people who created those earlier programmes. The Hunt report set out quite deliberately to propose an agenda for future action, which drew a surprisingly positive response from those to whom it was addressed. It also threw up many difficulties, of scope, of terminology and of philosophy. How could we encompass the great range of outdoor experiences available; describe the rationale behind each programme; and decide where the outer boundaries of outdoor adventure lie? And how might the work conducted at that time be linked to the profound social and economic changes taking place towards the end of the 1980s? Of course the report was essentially a snapshot, by no means comprehensive, of what was going on at that time. The aspiration we set out then was to seek to ensure that all young people had the opportunity for the stimulus and the adventure of challenging outdoor activities, and this was backed by a wide range of practical proposals to improve quality and access.

Getting the balance right

This new book identifies many similar themes and problems but addresses them in a different way. By challenging leading practitioners in the many facets of outdoor work to describe their own current priorities and best practice, the book harnesses massive reservoirs of energy, imagination and expertise. At the same time it indicates how such practice is relevant to the emerging social themes of the 21st century. In many respects, although there have been important advances in working practice, these underlying themes have not changed much from the time of the Hunt report. We are still seeking answers to the environmental challenges which confronted us then; indeed as research into global warming demonstrates, the problems may now be even greater than in the 1980s. We are still grappling with wide concerns about inclusivity, gender and race issues; women are still under-represented in many spheres and the growth of overt racism has not yet been halted. We are still little closer to a settled consensus about the correct balance of educational provision; the debate continues about a curriculum relevant to our times; an appropriate qualifications structure for the future, or the best balance between academic and vocational provision.

However, there have been important developments since 1989. One of the most significant is the extent to which experienced practitioners have begun to write authoritatively about their work. Fifteen years ago, the outdoor field was strong on practice, providing a range of experiences which generally gave important developmental and value-forming experiences for young people. However it fell seriously short when it came to discussing and understanding the learning processes at play in outdoor education. I am confident that many if not most outdoor leaders, teachers and instructors thought hard about the work they were engaged in; they were indeed 'reflective practitioners'. However, with some notable exceptions, they signally failed to share their thinking widely and this impoverished the whole field. That this has changed is to be greatly welcomed. Many more outdoor programmes have been researched, linked to broader learning theory and to experimental work in other fields such as the arts, with the results published for the benefit of all. Overseas experience has been written up and published in Britain. The influence of *Horizons* magazine under Chris Loynes and Chris Reed and the *Journal of Adventure Education and Outdoor Learning* published by the Institute for Outdoor Learning has been particularly beneficial.

The rich debate and other issues

Another current issue much in the headlines and directly relevant to work in the outdoors is the keen debate on the appropriate balance between safety and adventure. It is impossible to be complacent about the safety of young people when we learn about the extent of child abuse, particularly within the family, or even the scale of casualties on our roads. The truth of course is that, despite occasional major tragedies such as the events in the Cairngorm mountains in 1971 or the Lyme Bay disaster in 1993, outdoor programmes have always been relatively safe. It has often been said that the journey to the course, the activity or the camp is more dangerous than the activities themselves. It is no surprise to those involved in outdoor work that the Health and Safety Executive have in 2003 repeated their view that, whatever the other merits of the scheme, on a normal cost/benefit analysis there is scant justification for the ALAA licensing regime for outdoor centres.

It is generally accepted that a systematic process of risk assessment is important, and should be applied in outdoor work as in other fields. Yet if taken too far and applied too rigidly and unimaginatively it will have a damaging effect on all exploratory or innovative work. There is already some disturbing evidence that teachers may be more reluctant to venture beyond the safety of the classroom in fear of possible consequences arising from anticipated hazards or possible subsequent litigation should anything go amiss. If this happens it will be a great setback and not simply for outdoor work; for the education process as a whole should be flexible and outward-looking – the classroom and the curriculum may sometimes serve to narrow rather than widen the perspective of the learner.

Another trend which arouses concern is the move to a culture in which 'cost-effectiveness' becomes a priority, and 'best value' an all-pervading slogan. This is fine where outcomes can be measured in cash terms, but we have to recognise this is not easily possible in education, at least beyond the simple acquisition of measurable skills. What price do we place on curiosity, confidence or the propensity to care for others or the environment? What value do we attach to the beauty of a sunrise in the hills; the dappled shadows of a mature forest; the elemental power of a wild seascape? What long-term pleasures and benefits arise from companionship and the sharing of ideas and experiences? Robert Graves once said, 'If there is no money in poetry, neither is there poetry in money.' There is a poetry available for all in the outdoors, and this surely should be the birthright for every child from every background, even if that value cannot readily be assessed in cash terms.

Another trend developing over the past 15 years, perhaps itself arising from the 'cost-effectiveness culture', has been the increasing reluctance of the public to commit themselves to communal enterprises which do not bring immediate material reward. There has been a reduction in donations to charities. Voluntary bodies find it more difficult to identify new active volunteers for the future. There is widespread disengagement, cynicism even, about the political process, whether exercised at the level of the local community or of the major international organisations. People in many western societies are increasingly inclined not to exercise hard-won democratic rights; they choose not to cast their vote, even when they have the opportunity. Yet young people are still strongly committed to idealistic causes; marches over animal welfare issues and protests at the globalisation of the world economy are constantly in the news, with young people at the forefront. We have to find new ways of organising our society which encourage a greater sense of empowerment and engagement in place of the prevailing disillusion and even cynicism about political and community or-ganisations.

It is in this context that governments of differing colours have sought, relatively unsuccessfully, to promote the ideal of active citizenship. Why have these efforts made so little impact? Is it because they are advanced by those who are themselves seen as part of the failed structures that require change? Is it because educational philosophies and approaches have not been modified nor resources made available which might achieve better understanding and commitment? Might it be because the best form of training for citizenship has rarely been attempted for most young people; by which I mean the active practice of citizenship skills in a context where practical actions do make a difference and where enterprise, initiative and effective teamwork can be seen to effect outcomes directly and immediately? It would be facile to suggest that the outdoors by itself can provide the context in which these issues may be comprehensively addressed. However, the outdoor environment, indeed any real life environ-ment, transports us immediately from theoretical problem-solving to an active arena in which real decisions and actions have to be taken; where cause and effect are directly linked.

I believe that *The RHP Companion to Outdoor Education* will be much more than a summary of the differing approaches to the use of the outdoor environment for different learning needs and purposes, important though that role will be. This book should, in addition, create powerful impetus for future movement and change, providing a catalyst for further experiment and innovation in outdoor education. For there is always a danger that the practitioners of this important work, the teachers, leaders and instructors of the future, may feel so constrained by the wider emphases on risk avoidance and the misguided quest for short-term cost-effectiveness that they will work only within known and familiar boundaries rather than trying new, more ambitious and less readily quantifiable alternatives.

Looking forward

Whether one surveys the fields of science, medicine, commerce, industry, the arts or sport, one thing is clear; progress stems from the willingness to take risks, to try new approaches, to think the unthinkable, 'to go boldly where no man has gone before'. Without such creativity, innovation and enterprise, we are faced with stagnation. There can be no progress without risk. I believe that one of the fundamental values and benefits of challenging outdoor education programmes may be that such programmes positively encourage recognition that life is hazardous, that although prudence is important risks must be taken, and that making the all-important judgements about how and when to do this is an all-important skill. And this is where outdoor education has a major part to play, in showing that the innate curiosity, creativity and enterprise of humankind, the fact that our reach can and should exceed our grasp, is what entitles us to optimism.

Preface

The idea for this book arose from the recognition that a comprehensive text about outdoor education which is appropriate to the UK market, does not exist. Whilst there are numerous American books written by highly respected authors there are only a small number of relevant texts written explicitly for the UK market. Some of these might be coined 'classics' and they are written by very credible outdoor educationalists. But few, if any, aim to present a complete overview of all the issues relevant to outdoor education today. The aim of this book is to present readers with outlines of current topics and issues that are central to outdoor education in the UK. A major intention is to provide information about outdoor education in its many and varied guises. The editors managed to persuade (without too much difficulty) an impressive array of authors from diverse backgrounds in outdoor education – professional, academic, commercial and voluntary sectors – to provide a current perspective 'in their area' which would not only give readers an up-to-date picture, but also a feel for the kinds of issues and problems pertinent to their area of work. We feel that one of the book's particular strengths is the varied manner in which the chapters are presented. Readers will not find themselves bogged down with comprehensive detail from scientific documents and esoteric journals. Some do have an 'academic' ring where the text is well supported by extensive literature reviews. Readers should find a lot of highly valuable information in some of the key references. Others have been written from the perspective of practice and application. In these, readers will appreciate the wisdom and reality that can only come from extensive years of practical experience. Other chapters tend to straddle both of these end points.

Clearly, the reader's background, experience and professional viewpoint will dictate how much is taken from the book. However, the intention is to change the reader's thinking in one or more of three ways. For some readers, the book will introduce ideas and topics they have not encountered before. For others, it will remind them of methods, principles or issues which have been forgotten. And we suspect that for many readers, the book will reinforce principles which are currently used. The book will have achieved its overall aim if it makes the reader a more informed (and therefore better) outdoor educationalist. To do this, the reader will have to take ideas from the book, dwell on their merits, perhaps experiment with them in practice where appropriate and also embark on discussion with colleagues. The authors recognise only too well that books by themselves do not make people better practitioners, researchers or thinkers. Ideas have to be considered and principles tested in practice. We expect that whilst readers may disagree with some aspects of what they read, they will also digest others that allow them to move forwards as practitioners or theorists.

This book is aimed at all scholars of outdoor education, whether they be students in tertiary or higher education, practitioners working in the field or academics involved in research at university. We are confident that the wide array of subjects included in the book combined with the varied manner in which chapters have been written, will mean readers from such diverse backgrounds will find the book beneficial. To give structure to the many topics, we have located each chapter in one of four major sections – Context, Users, Practice and Issues. The sections are reasonably independent but readers will find many topics span more than one section. Of course, this simply recognises the interactive nature of outdoor education.

We hope the book will find its way to library bookshelves and also be adopted as a personal source of reference. We both feel that outdoor education still has a long way to go in terms of its acceptance by educational organisations and the public at large. Many important issues such as licensing and the safety culture need to be fully explored; and the meaning of outdoor education also requires ongoing scrutiny. Hopefully, this book will go some way to clarifying the aims, purposes and practice of outdoor education in today's society.

Bob Sharp and Peter Barnes, January 2004

Acknowledgements

First and foremost we would like to thank all the authors who have contributed chapters to this book.

Secondly, we must thank Geoffrey Mann and Russell House Publishing for their support and the decision to back this project.

Finally, of course, we must thank our wives, Sue and Guyda, for their continuing support in our outdoor and academic endeavours.

Introduction: Some Thoughts on the Nature of Outdoor Education

Peter Barnes and Bob Sharp

There is no doubt that 'outdoor education' means different things to different people, although it is likely that outdoor educationalists would agree with many of the claims listed below (adapted from Higgins, 1997):

- *Outdoor education provides opportunities for children (especially at primary level) to integrate knowledge and experience from a wide variety of subject areas – history, geography, English, mathematics and so on.*
- *Outdoor education permits individuals to develop intellectual, physical, emotional, aesthetic and spiritual aspects of their personality – holistic learning.*
- *Outdoor education has the capability to improve health and fitness of pupils thorough physical activity and the potential to develop positive, long-term attitudes to an active lifestyle.*
- *Outdoor education provides an outlet for children to exercise their natural instinct to play and seek adventure.*
- *Outdoor education contributes to personal and social development. Pupils who find themselves in novel environments where new skills have to be learned, sometimes in harmony with others, will invariably learn more about themselves and the need to adopt strategies essential to group cohesion. This is probably the single most important claim made for outdoor education within the school context.*
- *Outdoor education promotes an understanding and awareness of the environment. Direct contact with and travel through the environment can not only lead to the acquisition of knowledge about the land and its use and history but also facilitate the development of values such as sustainability, aesthetic appreciation and respect for the outdoors.*
- *Outdoor education has the potential to inculcate a sense of belonging and place within the landscape; viewing the countryside from a mountain top or canoeing down a wide river helps generates a sense of perspective and importance within a much wider world.*

- *Outdoor education provides young people with opportunities to discover the importance of decision-making and resulting consequences. For example, placing tent pegs in the correct location may well have a key bearing on the comfort level of a night's sleep. Simple judgements like this help to bring home the importance of decisions and their consequences and the need to take and develop responsibility for personal actions.*
- *Outdoor education has the potential to develop citizenship by creating opportunities for pupils to take responsibility for themselves, others and the environment.*
- *Outdoor education – through residential experiences – forces children to reflect on the coping strategies they employ under (sometimes) conditions of hardship, their emotions during times of pleasure and stress, and their involvement when living with others. Reflecting, changing and discussing with others such experiences can be a salient part of the 'growing up' process.*
- *Outdoor education provides scope for the development a wide array of abilities and interests and therefore serves as a medium for pupils with differing abilities and interests to excel and achieve potentials that might otherwise go unnoticed.*

Such a wide list of aims, purposes and claims is one of the key reasons why there is still difficulty deciding what exactly is outdoor education and especially conveying meaning to outside bodies. There have been many definitions over the years and as many alternative names put forward, but somehow, many outdoor educators are still not quite comfortable with who they are, what they do and why they do it. Hopkins and Putnam (1993: 16) refer to this issue by commenting:

> . . . *the effectiveness of [outdoor] education depends upon: a clear specification of the [outdoor] education process, and the relating of this process to specific individual needs. We are not confident that these two desiderata are*

always met. It is an unfortunate tendency of outdoor educators that their rationales tend towards obfuscation and mystification.

This debate is discussed in more detail by Peter Barnes in Chapter 1, whilst Geoff Nichols addresses the issue of research within outdoor education in Chapter 4.

The traditional definition, as used by the National Association for Outdoor Education (NAOE – before it became part of the Institute for Outdoor Learning, OL) is:

> *. . . a means of approaching educational objectives through direct experience in the environment using its resources as learning materials.*
>
> (Hunt, 1989: 17)

It can easily be seen how this definition defines the potential outcomes of outdoor education and the vehicle by which these are achieved. It is less clear, however, on the nature of the actual activity involved, how the environment is utilised and what specific educational objectives are proposed. A more comprehensive, although rather dated, definition (as used by Cumbria Local Education Authority, 1974) provides much more detail:

> *. . . the term to describe all learning, social development and the acquisition of skills associated with living and journeying in the outdoors. In addition to physical endeavour, it embraces environmental and ecological understanding. Outdoor Education is not a subject but an integrated approach to learning; to decision making and the solution of problems . . . [it] stimulates the development of self-reliance, self-discipline, judgement, responsibility, relationships and the capacity for sustained practical endeavours.*

This definition highlights the significance of self-development as a key educational component of outdoor education. In Chapter 18, Pat Keighley takes this educational component and discusses its role within the national curriculum. The definition also includes notions of skill development and environmental understanding; areas which, to some people, would be better described as outdoor activity training and environmental education. As with the NAOE the Cumbria definition describes outdoor education as an integrated process rather than a subject – an

idea that is returned to later. Central to the idea of process is the whole area of values and ethics as discussed by Bertie Everard in Chapter 2.

Another often reported definition stems from the so-called Dartington Conference of 1975 (Department of Education and Science, 1975: 1–3). At that time, outdoor education was viewed as:

> *. . . those activities concerned with living, moving and learning in the outdoors.*

The Conference went on to outline the three most important aims of outdoor education. It proposed that outdoor education heightened awareness and respect for:

- *Self: through the meeting of challenge.*
- *Others: through group experiences and the sharing of decisions.*
- *The natural environment: through direct experience.*

These aims are, perhaps, more recognisable to us today than the Dartington definition, which focuses strongly on activities rather than processes. A more recent approach proposed by Higgins and Loynes (1997: 6) and developed further by Higgins and Sharp (2003) suggests that outdoor education is the common ground, or overlap, between three sectors, viz., 'outdoor activities', 'environmental education' and 'personal and social development' (Figure 1).

It can be seen that this model leans heavily on the Dartington definition and aims. Higgins and Loynes argue that most practitioners would agree that outdoor education must encompass:

- An educational element which stimulates personal and social development.
- An experience which includes themes of 'outdoor', 'adventure' and 'education'.
- Learning as an experiential process which utilises direct experience.
- An increased self and social awareness plus increased awareness of community and environment.

They comment that:

> *. . . outdoor education provides opportunities for individuals to develop personal and social skills, to become active, safe and skilled in the outdoors, and to protect and care about the environment.*
>
> (1997: 6)

Figure 1   The range and scope of outdoor education

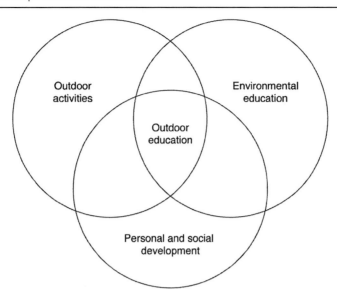

Their model is clearer about what is involved in outdoor education but it could also be argued that it encompasses areas that are not strictly outdoor education. For example, is it essential that outdoor education use outdoor activities? This begs a further question, about what actually is an outdoor activity? In Chapter 14 on creative outdoor work, Alan Smith suggests that an outdoor activity need not necessarily be one of the traditional outdoor 'sports' such as climbing, canoeing and so on; areas such as art and drama are increasingly being incorporated into outdoor programmes.

'Adventure Therapy', for example, is a relatively new field which combines traditional and new ways of working. Higgins and Loynes, as part of their discussion above, also focus on the importance of adventure which Hopkins and Putnam (1993: 6) describe as '. . . an experience that involves uncertainty of outcome'. Many of today's practitioners would argue that adventure is largely precluded from the tightly controlled outdoor education field. Bob Sharp in Chapter 13 discusses the nature of risk in the outdoors and in Chapter 20 Marcus Bailie, using his unique perspective as head of the Adventure Activity Licensing Authority looks at how outdoor activities have become regulated, largely due to society's attitude to risk. In addition Nick Halls, in Chapter 17, examines how the duty of care is implemented

and in Chapter 12 Peter Barnes looks at the significance of outdoor leadership in this modern context.

The model proposed by Higgins and Loynes (1997) includes the idea that outdoor education should lead to an increased awareness of the environment; although it could be argued that this is an ideal that often only has lip service paid to it. Geoff Cooper suggests ways, in Chapter 21, in which outdoor education can be used to pass on lessons regarding environmental awareness and sustainability. By way of contrast he also highlights, in Chapter 22, some of the issues faced by outdoor education in its sustainable use of the environment. Strongly linked to environmental issues, Angus McWilliam, in Chapter 3, looks at the role of aesthetics in outdoor education and in Chapter 11 Nina Saunders looks at a situation where the environment is likely to have one of its biggest impacts; leadership and expedition work

A particularly contentious issue is whether or not areas such as management training and development, discussed by Adrian Ibbetson in Chapter 8, which are often based exclusively within a training centre or hotel, are included within a definition of outdoor education. Many of the activities contained within these courses are certainly grounded in outdoor education, but does that justify their inclusion within outdoor education? Hunt (1989: 16) underlines this difficulty and suggests that outdoor education is best approached by highlighting key themes; these include:

- *Development of skills, whether technical, intellectual or social.*
- *Scientific or aesthetic appreciation of the outdoor environment.*
- *The concept of service, to society, the community, the environment or the activity.*
- *Personal development.*

This idea finds favour amongst many writers; Cooper (1998) and Hopkins and Putnam (1993) both include similar suggestions. It would appear that practitioners might be more comfortable talking about the process of what they do rather than trying to come to any agreed definition.

Cooper (1998) agrees with the idea that outdoor education is multi-faceted, but he suggests a much broader definition including areas such as outdoor pursuits, field studies, development training, outdoor recreation and environmental education. This contrasts with the idea that outdoor education is actually the overlap between diverse areas. Cooper believes outdoor education is used as a 'catch-all' expression that includes a variety of approaches or types and he urges that:

> It is important that outdoor leaders are aware of the distinctions between outdoor sport, outdoor recreation and outdoor education.
>
> (1998: 42)

A major difficulty with any attempt to examine the nature of outdoor education arises from the nature of the field itself. Far from being discrete and homogeneous it is made up of a wide and diverse variety of employment sectors. These range from personal development centres to outdoor management development organisations to technical skills centres such as the national centres. There are also private multi-activity organisations and a (decreasing) number of local authority centres. In addition, charities are widely represented, as are individuals (sole traders) such as mountain guides and freelance instructors. Many suggest that voluntary organisations such as the Scouts, Guides, and Boy's Brigade also have a strong link to outdoor education. This subject is discussed in Chapter 9 where Janet Shepherd talks about how the voluntary sector makes use of outdoor education. One of the

complications is that many of these sectors overlap to a large degree. For example, management centres may offer multi-activity breaks during quiet periods whilst many multi-activity centres will also offer corporate courses. The expressions used to describe these organisations have aroused heated debate in some quarters. No truer example of this can be found than the recent, and highly contentious, expression, which has come into popular use, that of the 'outdoor industry' (Humberstone, 1995). This expression implies that the outdoor field has moved into a professional era of 'clients and providers'. It is questionable whether this expression appropriately describes those involved in the voluntary or educational sectors. Randall Williams discusses the issue of the professional era and the market place in Chapter 24 and in Chapter 25 Bob Sharp examines another current and contentious issue, the use of technology in the outdoors.

Even the term 'outdoor education' has been questioned by some as it implies that the only true providers are those in mainstream education. Some have argued that expressions such as 'outdoor learning' or 'learning out of doors' are more appropriate. One viewpoint proposes that 'learning out of doors' is more accurate since it places the focus on the learner rather than the environment, i.e. learning through the outdoors rather than about the outdoors. The expression 'outdoor learning' has greater prominence today as it emphasises the learning involved rather than merely the form of delivery. Most radically, it has been argued that the use of the word 'outdoor' itself is outmoded particularly when so many activities take place in the grounds of centres and hotels or indoor or urban settings. Reed (2002) suggests there is a need to reconsider what is meant by the outdoors and outdoor activities. He questions whether this includes urban and controlled settings and suggests that any definition should contain a wilderness-related element. Archie Waters, who leads an 'urban' project, discusses this issue in Chapter 23 and suggests ways in which urban projects can move forward.

Despite the many differences mentioned in this introduction, there are some common threads. The outdoors is usually considered a vital component of outdoor education; even though some activities may not take place, strictly speaking, in the outdoors. Many people see a physical, adventurous activity as a central defining feature; even though not all activities will be adventurous or physical all of the time. Personal and social development is an important feature of outdoor education, as highlighted by Geoff Nichols in Chapter 5. There is also a long-held view that service and a respect and love for others and the environment are essential, even though an increasing number of modern outdoor activities (e.g. bungee jumping) are essentially selfish and hedonistic in nature. Despite this, there is little doubt that practical, interactive learning through experience (experiential education) is a central feature. Experiential learning, an area which Angus McWilliam looks at in Chapter 19, has indeed become synonymous with outdoor education. Involvement is not mediated or simulated; it is active and explicit. This is a principle that views the teacher as a facilitator where learners are encouraged to take a high degree of responsibility for their own learning. There seems little doubt that direct, personal encounters provide powerful and memorable learning experiences. As part of this process Bob Sharp looks at teaching strategies in Chapter 16 and in Chapter 15 Roger Greenaway discusses the significance of facilitation and reviewing.

It is very important to accept that outdoor education, if that is what people choose to call it, can and does mean different things to different people. As long as people can justify what they do on moral, ethical and educational grounds, their viewpoint is valid in its own right; even though to an outsider each may be completely different. This multi-faceted view is reflected in the words of Steve Lenartowicz in Chapter 6, Phil Woodyer in Chapter 7, Judy Ling Wong, in Chapter 10 and Kate O'Brien and Nina Saunders in Chapter 26 who discuss how young people, special needs students, those from ethnic communities and women, respectively interact with outdoor education. The key is that the view and experience of each person is unique to the individual and subject to development and change, although it must also be recognised how the perspective of each individual is coloured and influenced by their cultural and social upbringing and norms.

In conclusion, however, the authors of this introduction have no problem with the term outdoor education. They take it to be concerned with 'helping educate people about themselves and others through the use of the outdoors, or linked to the outdoors'. This is a very broad definition, which encompasses all the subjects, processes and organisations identified in this introduction. Some readers may see this as an 'opt out' and others will agree wholeheartedly. Given that the only certainty about outdoor education is that it is continuing to evolve, accept new practices and new ideas, perhaps the time has come for a new debate on what is the nature and identity of outdoor education. We expect this book to make a contribution to that debate.

References

Cooper, G. (1998) *Outdoors with Young People*. Lyme Regis: Russell House Publishing.

Department of Education and Science (1975) *Report on the Dartington Hall Conference*. Outdoor Education Study Conference N496.

Higgins, P. (1997) Why Educate Out of Doors? In Higgins, P., Loynes, C., and Crowther, N. (Eds.) *A Guide for Outdoor Educators in Scotland*. Penrith: Adventure Education.

Higgins, P. and Loynes, C. (1997) On the Nature of Outdoor Education. In Higgins, P., Loynes, C. and Crowther, N. (Eds.) *A Guide for Outdoor Educators in Scotland*. Penrith: Adventure Education.

Hopkins, D. and Putnam, R. (1993) *Personal Growth Through Adventure*. London: David Fulton Publishers.

Humberstone, B. (1995) The Commercialisation of Outdoor Adventure: Profit and Loss in Adventure! In Lawrence, L. et al. *Professional and Development Issues in Leisure, Sport and Education*. LSA pub no: 56.

Hunt, J. (Ed.) (1989) *In Search of Adventure*. Guildford: Talbot Adair Press.

Reed, C. (2002) *Horizons*. Editorial. 20: (Autumn).

Higgins, P. and Sharp, R. H. (2003) Outdoor Education. In Hulmes, W. and Bryce, T. (Eds.) *Scottish Education*. Edinburgh: Edinburgh University Press.

Section 1:
The Context of Outdoor Education

1   Debate and Cliché: A Philosophy for Outdoor Education?

Peter Barnes

Abstract

This chapter discusses the underpinning philosophy for outdoor education. It does not attempt to define or present a definitive philosophy but discusses how various internal and external influences have led to the outdoor field we know today. Initially, it presents a brief overview of how mainstream outdoor philosophy has developed. However, it is argued that this view of philosophy is largely the preserve of the academic world and an overview of external influences acting on the modern outdoor field is presented in order to discuss a more pragmatically oriented viewpoint.

There is a surprising, if little realised, dichotomy in the field of outdoor education. On the one hand we talk about the field being based on strong philosophical principles; which many academics can discuss *ad nauseam*. On the other hand however, this philosophical grounding is frequently broken down into a series of clichéd sound-bites, which when fully examined fall short of reality. Nowhere is this dichotomy more apparent than when the parents of nervous children, about to go on their first outdoor course, are soothed by the public face of an outdoor organisation – often the principal or centre manager. The 'spiel' will almost certainly contain expressions such as 'no-one is forced to do anything; everyone can refuse to take part if they wish', 'it's not about the activity; it's what we can learn about ourselves by doing the activity' and 'at no time will anybody be placed in any danger' or 'we are strictly non-competitive'. Whether these statements, or statements such as these, are grounded in theory or philosophy is debatable, if not contentious. This chapter will show it is apparent that there is a gulf between the academic concept of an outdoor philosophy and that being practiced in the field.

Historical perspectives

It would be fair to say that outdoor education, as a whole, lacks a current and coherent philosophy, which can readily be put over to an outside audience. Hopkins and Putnam (1993: 19) go so far as to say:

It is our contention that the failure to develop a plausible conceptual basis for this work has led to a failure on the part of educators and others to give [outdoor] education the importance it deserves.

The debate must, therefore, be whether the cliché sound-bites prevalent in modern outdoor education relate to an established philosophy or whether a new philosophy is being engendered by ongoing changes and new requirements. In order to take this debate forward it is necessary to do two things; establish what a 'traditional' view of an outdoor education philosophy might consist of and relate it to the demands of modern outdoor education.

Whilst it is very hard to generalise about an area as broad and diverse as outdoor education there are some common traits in philosophy which readily lend themselves to examination. Perhaps in many ways the most widely acknowledged of these traits is the influence and ethos of Kurt Hahn (1886–1974) and through him the Outward Bound movement. In many ways the philosophy of outdoor education reflects and follows the ethos and philosophy of Outward Bound itself; a fact reflected in this chapter. This ethos traditionally centred on the idea of physical challenge and competition, not so much against others but against one's self or within nature. Kurt Hahn (1957: 1) spoke of the 'continuity of purposeful athletic training'. Such physical activity was linked directly to 'the restoration of spiritual health' (ibid: 5) and to strong communal values; the values which Hahn saw as constituting a 'moral' character. With Britain being in the midst of a global war (Outward Bound was founded in 1941) the emphasis at the first Outward Bound school, at Aberdovey in Wales, was very much on fitness, duty, dedication and sacrifice to the greater good. Hahn believed that students 'should learn to discipline their own needs and desires for the good of the community. They should realise, through their own experience, the connection between self-discovery and service' (James, 1995a: 35). This ethos still prevails, in some measure, at Outward Bound through its concentration on the individual being part of a group or team.

Hahn's ideas were not as original as many people might believe; indeed Hahn himself said that his approach was built entirely on the ideas of others. It was, however, in his re-formulation and implementation of these ideas as well as his passion for education of the 'whole-person', that Hahn had his greatest impact. To look at the true and earliest origin of an outdoor education philosophy it is necessary to go back to the early Greek philosophers – notably Socrates (470–399 BC), Plato (427–347 BC) and Aristotle (384–322 BC). Socrates was one of the first, if not the first, philosopher to suggest that it was the process of education that was important, rather than the end result. Education was, therefore, better approached through questioning rather than rote learning; in other words he encouraged his students to think for themselves. One of Socrates' students and perhaps the greatest of the Greek philosophers was Plato who in his best known work, *The Republic,* a discussion on society, put forward the idea of young men learning virtue from taking part in risky activities. Kurt Hahn drew heavily on principles outlined in *The Republic* when developing his ideas of education for a just and moral society. Carrying on in turn from Plato, his student Aristotle worked on the process of education in developing virtues or, as we would say today, values. Most notably, he put forward the idea which sits at the very heart of outdoor education, that:

> . . . in our transactions with other men it is by action that some become just and others unjust, and it is by acting in the face of danger and by developing the habits of feeling fear or confidence that some become brave men and others cowards.
>
> (cited in Wurdinger, 1994: 5)

Aristotle thus lays the foundation of action, rather than ideas alone, as being the route to education.

Interestingly, he also shows in the quote above how action, can be mis-educative just as it can be educative. At the time of the Greek philosophers the most notable risky activity was following the army to war and to learn by observing, although not participating in the fighting, war at first hand. Warfare was thus considered to inculcate the virtues required by society at that time. This idea was built on much later by William James who wrote of the 'moral equivalent of war' (1949) as the way to teach the military virtues such as heroism, tenacity and conscience. James was concerned with the virtues to be found in a time of war, rather than in war *per se*; indeed he spoke of the need to fight a war against war; although he also commented that 'war has been the only force that can discipline a whole community' (1949: 325). By learning the military virtues, including discipline, he saw a way in which people would reject war itself. Hahn himself adopted this idea and suggested that Outward Bound could be considered as a moral equivalent of war with a carefully structured programme of activities providing the self-discipline and virtues to be found in soldiers in battle. However, Hahn, partly because of his experiences with Nazism and Fascism also emphasised the ideals of justice and compassion. In a similar way to James he saw that the learning of these virtues could provide an antidote to war. Virtue was not, however, generally seen in the context of the individual. In a similar vein to Plato before him, a prime concern of Hahn was that each individual in society fulfilled their allotted role in life to the best of their ability – not only for their own sake but for the greater good. The military virtues were needed to first, prevent young people from becoming a menace to society and, secondly, to encourage them to play an active and worthwhile part in society's function. This approach to the education of young people has long been prevalent in the UK; a prime example being the Scouting movement, founded by Lord Baden-Powell.

The Scouting Association and, later, Outward Bound were both strongly influenced by the values of their time. In particular, these revolved around notions of self-denial, particularly with regard to such 'vices' as smoking and drinking and the muscular Christian ethos of *mens sana in corpore sano,* 'a healthy mind in a healthy body'. The Christian ethos, in general, has had a strong influence on outdoor education, one which is still at the core of many organisations today. Notably this influence has been felt in areas such as self-denial, duty to others and aestheticism. It can also be argued that the Christian influence has also been at least partly responsible for the notion of the journey or voyage of discovery, perhaps best exemplified by Bunyan's *Pilgrim's Progress* and the concept of the 'solo' experience, or contemplation.

Following a parallel route it was the French-Swiss writer, Jean Jacques Rousseau (1712–1778) who put forward the idea of using nature as an educational tool in the way we know it today. Himself a solitary man, in his work *Emile* (1762) he maintained that education is most effective when approached through first-hand activities and experience. In particular, he suggested that experiencing nature was the most powerful form of education. It was the ideas of Rousseau that influenced the philosophy of many of the European Progressive schools in the late 19th and early 20th centuries. Almost certainly Kurt Hahn would have picked up on this influence. Linked to Rousseau's 'romantic' view of nature is one of his most enduring legacies, that of the 'noble savage'. Although Rousseau saw the 'noble savage' idea as being flawed, the idea of 'primitive' people having higher codes of morality and values through being both closer to nature and at the same time distanced from the ills of 'civilisation' is one which still influences many people today. Most significantly however, where Rousseau deviated from the Greek ideals was that he saw the individual as being free and fulfilled in their own right; with society being a collection of moral individuals rather than a collective binding force.

Central to the whole process of understanding a traditional outdoor education philosophy are the ideas of John Dewey (1859–1952). In *Democracy and Education*, Dewey (1916) developed the concepts of Plato and Rousseau together with his ideas on the role of the individual within society. Dewey saw the role of education as expanding ideas and celebrating a diversity of individuals. In this way society is served, as in Plato, as well as the individual, as in Rousseau. Dewey's most famous work, *Experience and Education,* expands on the Aristotelian ideas of experience as a way of education and says that 'education . . . must be based upon experience – which is always the life experience of some individual' (Dewey, 1938: 89). Dewey took these ideas further by looking at the significant features of experience. Most importantly, in experiential education terms, he wrote, 'experience as trying involves change, but change is meaningless transition unless it is consciously connected with the return wave of consequences which flow from it' (Dewey, 1916: 139). Dewey maintained that lessons learnt from experience could be applied to the everyday world of the student; a core belief of outdoor education today.

Current thinking

Modern outdoor education, while it still retains many of the Greek and Christian ideals has moved further towards the ideas of Rousseau and Dewey in its teaching. There is now a much stronger emphasis on allowing the 'student' to initiate and then to make their own discoveries at their own pace. Interestingly it could be argued that this contradicts much of Outward Bound's early philosophy, which was to impel students into experience (Hogan, 1968). Although Kurt Hahn saw it as wrong for anyone to force their opinion onto others he saw it as morally legitimate, even essential, to impel people into new and valuable experiences, whether they were inclined to or not. Rousseau, and later Dewey, recognised that student learning is far more effective if it is voluntary rather than forced and, furthermore, that the student is actively engaged in their own learning. This is now generally regarded as the fundamental, and underpinning philosophy behind experiential education; which is not to say that this is synonymous with an outdoor education philosophy, although it usually is.

The philosophy of outdoor education, far from remaining in thrall to the ideas espoused by Plato and Kurt Hahn, continues to grow and develop. In recent years ideas from North America have played a strong part in shaping ideas in Britain. These new ideas have largely centred, to an even greater extent, around beliefs in the power of nature and the wilderness environment. Philosophers such as John Muir and Henry David Thoreau, long regarded in the USA, have started to play an increasingly important role in thinking in this country. Thoreau's most famous work *Walden* discusses his ideas of living an idea, particularly within nature, as a vital part of the learning process, notably he says, 'How could youths better learn than by at once trying the experiment of living?' (Thoreau, 1973: 51). The difference in the typical British and American approach can be seen in the structure of the solo experience. In Britain this might revolve around ideas of survival together with escape from the pressures of society. In America there has been a much stronger emphasis on 'opening up' to nature and experiencing it rather than merely surviving, or utilising, it. Likewise, 'friluftsliv', the Norwegian concept of feeling at home with nature, is being recognised more in the UK. This opening up, or interaction, with the environment is despite a mainstream move towards high adrenaline, confrontational, outdoor sports such as mountain biking and extreme skiing. This trend can be recognised in Vanreusel's (1995) 'Rambo' approach to the outdoors; a critique of how modern outdoor sport relates to nature. Further to this environmental aspect, Rousseau's 'noble savage' has been re-born in the guise of the Native American and the Aborigines of Australia whose philosophy supposedly holds many of the answers to western society's problems. Eastern philosophy such as Buddhism has also started to have an impact on the thinking and values of outdoor educators. How much of this new thinking is largely a matter of trends is difficult to say but it is certain that cracks are starting to appear in the Hahnian tradition that has typified outdoor education in Britain since the Second World War. Despite this, the largely white male, Anglo-centric values, which have traditionally dominated outdoor education in this country, are only just starting to be questioned.

Impact of risk

Many of the recent developments discussed above are, however, taking place largely in the academic or 'intellectual' spheres of outdoor education. More fundamental, if less profound, changes in philosophy are happening at practitioner or 'root' level. One of the more significant questions facing outdoor education is the use of risk. An early virtue, dating back to the time of Plato and Aristotle, is that of courage. This

was usually, if not always, taken to mean physical courage, which could be developed through the use of physical adventure. This did not always mean, as many believe, blind courage. Indeed, Aristotle saw recklessness as a great a vice as cowardice. William Unsoeld (1926–1979), a noted American outdoor educator and Outward Bound stalwart, wrote that safety should be emphasised as much as risk because true risk is always approached with safety in mind. However, Unsoeld (1976) also wrote:

> You emphasize safety, but you don't kill the risk. You emphasize safety as a rational man's effort at survival, but we're going to go right ahead and stick our head in the noose . . . that's the game.

> (cited in Hunt, 1995: 120)

This is not to say that the risk is negated, rather that it is not approached in a reckless manner. Since the Lyme Bay canoeing tragedy of 1993, however, risk has been a 'dirty word' within outdoor education in the UK. Much to the chagrin of purists, new legislation and an increased need for certification, qualification and risk-management policies has stifled much of the adventure element within the outdoor field. Dewey however, expanded on the idea that risk is not always physical and suggested that 'It also follows that all thinking involves a risk. Certainty cannot be guaranteed in advance' (Dewey, 1916: 148). Modern outdoor education has seized on this idea and through the use of such mediums as art and drama is now teaching the values that previously had been thought only possible to teach through physical adventure. Values such as compassion and understanding as well as self-evaluation and emotional courage can all be successfully approached through these mediums.

Influence of consumerism

In recent years outdoor education has also had to struggle with other of its core philosophies. Typical of these struggles is the notion of the 'the outdoor industry' (Humberstone, 1995: 137). Although this term has only been used in recent years it is now widely adopted, if contentious. Much of this contention stems from the concept of an industry, which infers, directly or indirectly, a notion of commercialism and thus of consumerism. By working to consumerist values, centres and organisations, the providers, are increasingly being forced to supply what the customer wants; even if the provider's own philosophy disagrees with what is being asked for. Consumerism has meant that large parts of the industry have been forced to take a subtle move away from being led by principles and beliefs to being led by the need to survive in a competitive market place.

Some writers have been noted for their attacks on the new face of the 'outdoor industry'. Perrin, for example, in referring to commercialism, comments that 'philosophical principles are readily forsaken and become subordinate to the profit motive' (1997: 16). Loynes (1996: 54) in his turn, agrees with this argument and notes that the outdoor education movement has 'core values . . . that are not amenable to exploitation'. Whether these arguments hold true for centre managers trying to survive in an increasingly difficult market is debatable.

Influence of professionalism

Strongly linked to the idea of commercialism is the idea of professionalism, which also brings with it a question of inherent philosophy. Professionalism can be taken as synonymous with, not only commercialism but with an industry driven not by social ideals but market demands. However, professionalism also implies an exemplary level of practice and the status accorded to it. In this sense the need to be professional is seen in a positive light. It is worthwhile, however, to bear in mind the underlying cause for much of this debate. Beames (1996: 9), for example, writes that:

Being an outdoor leader in the 1990s means being a practitioner who upholds the accepted standards of the profession, since instructing has evolved into just that – a profession, a practice. The conduct of outdoor instructors is increasingly coming under . . . scrutiny.

When this scrutiny is taken together with the debate on safety the role of the professional becomes even more problematic. In one possible scenario, the professional instructor could be expected to not only protect their client from harm but also to absolve that client from taking any responsibility for their own well-being. A central feature of outdoor education has always been the idea that it teaches people to take responsibility for their own actions. The authenticity involved in

outdoor activities is seen as a powerful tool in this process. Professionalism is seen, by some, as removing this facility. In this manner it 'dis-empowers the people it is intended to serve' (Reynolds, 1991, cited in Loynes, 1996: 56).

In our own times, the philosophy of a sub-culture can be affected by the wider society; as outdoor education is currently finding in its interaction with a consumer-oriented mass culture. A notable change in the values of outdoor education has been in the move away from a duty to society to concern for the individual while the value of courage has started to veer away from the act of physical courage to that of emotional courage. In modern society we are seeing more and more how hectic lifestyles, hedonism and self-interest have eroded the barriers of a traditional philosophy such as that espoused by the early Outward Bound Schools. A poignant example of this is that when time constraints, bought about as a financial necessity meant Outward Bound courses had to be reduced from their traditional length of 28 days it was the community service element that was removed in order to maintain the level of adventure activities.

A great irony is present when the Platonic ideal is followed through Kurt Hahn and the Outward Bound movement:

Plato was a political reformer who sought to recall the Athenians to the old civic virtues eroded . . . by democratic enthusiasm and soft living. His aim was . . . to regenerate society . . . It takes little digging to find precisely the same intentions in the founding of Outward Bound in 1941.

(James, 1995b: 86)

Later, in 1962, Outward Bound in Colorado was moved to act by the same concerns during the Korean War when 'Americans were overweight, deluged by material goods and technology; the young [were] increasingly apathetic and often violently self-centred' (James, 1995b: 87). Today Outward Bound, together with much of the outdoor education field, faced with profound financial incentives has been forced to embrace many of the traits which Kurt Hahn was opposed to, courses are shorter, self-denial and self-discipline are no longer seen as core virtues, risk and adventure are strictly controlled and regulated and there is a greater emphasis on enjoyment and comfort. This is not to say, of course, that outdoor education has 'sold-out' or abandoned its entire ethos; rather it has been compelled by a wider society to adapt to survive. The irony mentioned above is, of course, that Plato and Kurt Hahn saw the influence working in the other direction.

Conclusion

Far from presenting a coherent philosophy for outdoor education this chapter has raised the spectre that any philosophy is in danger of being diluted, not only by other philosophical developments and movements, but by outside pressures, constraints and concerns. Whilst academics and intellectuals may debate the content and nature of a coherent and 'purist' philosophy it must be asked whether this is a luxury that the field simply can't afford at the present time. Controversially, as far as the outdoor field is concerned, the way forward in this debate may be to re-visit the whole of Kurt Hahn's influence. As Brookes (2002) says:

> I argue that discarding the intuitively appealing but fallacious foundations of neo-Hahnism can clear the way for approaches to understanding outdoor education that are better engaged with broader intellectual endeavours.

It may be that the field needs to look to broader, and more academically established, philosophies if it is to survive as outdoor education, rather than outdoor activity. How this would sit with the fundamental and under-pinning ethos and values of outdoor education is problematic and difficult.

References

Beames, S. (1996) So You Want to be an Outdoor Adventure Instructor..? *The Journal of Adventure Education and Outdoor Leadership*. 13: 3, 9–10.

Brookes, A. (2002) *Adventure Programming and The Fundamental Attribution Error. A Critique of Neo-Hahnian Outdoor Education Theory*. Workshop Presentation at 'Whose Journeys?' Conference, High Wycombe.

Davis, B. (1986) *Threatening Youth*. Milton Keynes: Open University Press.

Dewey, J. (1916) *Democracy and Education*. New York: The Free Press.

Dewey, J. (1938) *Experience and Education*. New York: Macmillan Publishing Co.

Friere, P. (1972) *Cultural Action for Freedom*. Harmondsworth: Penguin Education.

Hahn, K. (1957) Origins of the Outward Bound Trust, in James, D. (Ed.) *Outward Bound*. London: Routledge and Kegan Paul.

Hogan, J. M. (1968) *Impelled Into Experiences*. Wakefield: Educational Productions Ltd.

Hopkins, D. and Putnam, R. (1993) *Personal Growth Through Adventure*. London: David Fulton Publishers.

Hunt, J. S. (1990) Philosophy of Adventure Education, in Warren, K., Sakofs, M. and Hunt, J.S. (Eds.) *The Theory of Experiential Education*. Dubuque, IO: Kendall Hunt Publishing Company.

Humberstone, B. (1995) The Commercialisation of Outdoor Adventure: Profit and Loss in Adventure! in Lawrence, L. et al., *Professional and Development Issues in Leisure, Sport and Education*. LSA Pub No; 56.

James, T. (1995a) Kurt Hahn and The Aims of Education, in Warren, K., Sakofs, M. and Hunt, J.S. (Eds.) *The Theory of Experiential Education*. Dubuque, IO: Kendall Hunt Publishing Company.

James, T. (1995b) Sketch of a Moving Spirit: Kurt Hahn. in Warren, K., Sakofs, M. and Hunt J.S. (Eds.) *The Theory of Experiential Education*. Dubuque, IO: Kendall Hunt Publishing Company.

James, W. (1949) *Essays on Faith and Morals*. New York: Longmans, Green and Company.

Loynes, C. (1996) Adventure in a Bun. *Journal of Adventure Education and Outdoor Leadership*. 13:2, 52–7.

Perrin, J. (1997) Instructors, Skillmongers, Fiscal Pimps. *Climber*. February, 16–7.

Rousseau, J, J. (1762) *Emile*. Trans., Foxley, B. (1974) London: Dent Publishing.

Thoreau, H, D. (1973) *Walden*. Princeton, NJ: Princeton University Press.

Vanreusel, B. (1995) From Bambi to Rambo: Towards a Socio-ecological Approach to the Pursuit of Outdoor Sports, in Weiss, O. and Schulz, W. (Eds.) *Sport in Space and Time*. Vienna: Vienna University Press.

Wurdinger, S. (1994) *Philosophical Issues in Adventure Education*. Dubuque, IO: Kendall Hunt Publishing Company.

2 Values and Ethics in Outdoor Education

Bertie Everard

Abstract

Outdoor education has a long history in developing values in young people and is applied for this purpose in both the English National Curriculum and in vocational training based on the experiential learning cycle. Its own special values fit well into the context of values generally, which have been collected from various sources and categorised in a hierarchy. Activities and processes in outdoor programmes which promote values development are described and the processes that deal specifically with values issues are scoped.

Introduction

Values are central to outdoor education for two reasons. Firstly, outdoor education has a long-established and well-developed philosophy characterised by values that are often deeply held and intentionally transmitted. Secondly, an outdoor setting often evokes a sense of values and facilitates their exploration. Moreover, at the heart of outdoor education is a profound ethical dilemma: how to balance risk and benefit. In few other educational settings is this dilemma so stark.

The roots of some outdoor education values stretch back for centuries; the theme of self-discovery leading to self-knowledge through the experience of adventure and the endurance of hardship inspired much Graeco-Roman, Christian and Eastern religious teaching, but is not exclusive to literate societies. The physical journey without serves as a metaphor for the spiritual journey within. The theme was taken up in the rise a century ago of the boys' movements such as the Scouts, in which the development of a set of values was a central aim. More recently, the widespread application of the Kolb learning cycle (Kolb, 1984) connects active experience and experimentation with reflective observation and abstract conceptualisation. Kolb writes that 'appreciation of apprehended reality is the source of values' (Kolb, 1984: 104) and he regards integrity as the master virtue combining value and fact, love as the link between value and meaning and courage as the link between value and relevance (Kolb, 1984: 228).

Everard (1990) offers another working model depicting the relationships between and the meanings of beliefs, values, opinions, attitudes and behaviour (Figure 1).

Values are closely linked to spirituality (not to be confused with religion) and recently the Bramha Kumaris World Spiritual University has worked closely with outdoor education bodies in clarifying the links. Spiritual development is an integral part of 'whole person development' (body, mind and spirit) and is enshrined not only in the definition of the school curriculum in the Education Reform Act 1988 and successive legislation, but also in the values of vocational education (Sport and Recreation Industry Lead Body, 1992: 20; Paulo, 2003).

When the National Curriculum was developed for England and Wales, outdoor education was subsumed in physical education (PE) and the PE Working Party produced reports and guidance documents that clearly expected outdoor education to help pupils to re-appraise personal attitudes, values and beliefs while learning and living with others. The rationale specifically mentions:

> *The development of qualities such as commitment, integrity, fairness, enthusiasm and concern for quality as well as success . . . self-reliance, self-discipline, a spirit of enterprise, a sense of social responsibility, the ability to work alone and with others, a value for and sensitivity towards individual differences . . . opportunities to learn to distinguish between the good, bad and anti-social, including cheating . . . which will help them to develop a personal value system.*
>
> (quoted in Everard, 1992a)

Grimmitt argues that 'human spirituality is not merely a core value among others but the source of the human capacity "to value" ' (quoted in

Figure 1   A working model of relationships

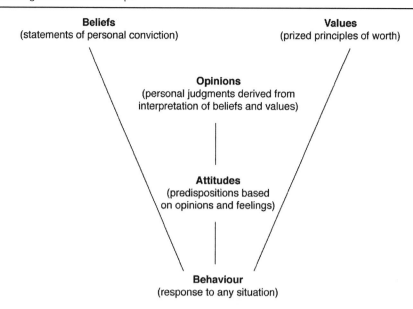

Plunkett, 1990: 86). In other words values are part of what it is to be human. Plunkett describes values as 'either preferred ways of being or behaving, or purposes that are considered of vital importance, but which are not necessarily provable by logic or by measurable outcomes'. Collier (1997) attaches to values a sense of obligation and defines them existentially in terms of the tacit, often unverbalised driving forces in people's lives, which determine where they will direct their effort and energies, and to which in their inner selves they attach the greatest value or importance – summed up in the biblical saying: 'Where your treasure is, there will your heart be also'. Values are an integral part of individual personhood and collectively of a culture; both have a major effect on individual, organisational and societal behaviour.

The values of outdoor education in the context of generic values categories

There are several organising principles for setting out values. Lewis (2002) uses a hierarchy on which I have built, using a taxonomy devised by Beck (1990) and examples from several value sets identified below. The result is shown in Table 1 (sources are appended to this chapter). Values

and their sources with an outdoor education provenance are italicised if listed in the sources specified and are emboldened if mentioned elsewhere in an outdoor education context; the rest are general.

Values are expressed as abstract, philosophical concepts each of which may use a variety of words and phrases. By pulling together value sets from various sources in a comparative table, it is possible to cross-map them and thereby identify a surprising degree of consistency whatever their provenance (Everard 1999; Lewis, 2002). It may be that agreement on a universal set of values is beyond our reach, but there is much more to unite than divide. Consequently, when outdoor education is used for values education, the risk of 'indoctrination' with an idiosyncratic set of values is less than is sometimes feared by moral relativists or those who worry that the attempted inculcation of common values is incompatible with a plural, inclusive society. This was the conclusion of the former Schools Curriculum and Assessment Authority (SCAA) which in 1990 set up a National Forum for Values in Education and the Community, bringing together 150 people with different backgrounds, including one from the outdoor sector (Tate, 1997).

This comparison shows that the values of outdoor education have much in common not only

Table 1   Hierarchy of values

Spiritual
Self-transcendence, *serenity*, higher purpose,
acceptance, **wonder**, gratitude, hope, *humility*,
gentleness, wisdom, *commitment*, self-motivation

Socio-political
Peace, **harmony**, *justice, equality, freedom, due process,*
tolerance, participation, co-operation, community, service, loyalty,
citizenship, stewardship, sustainability

Moral
Responsibility, courage, self-discipline, reliability, truthfulness, honesty,
fidelity, integrity, fairness, trust, **unselfishness**, *kindness, generosity*

Personal capability
Leadership, teamwork, decision-making, endeavour, challenge, dealing with the
unknown, self-development

Human
Self-awareness, happiness, sense of humour, *friendship, love, compassion, caring,*
respect for others, belonging

Basic
Survival, *health, self-respect*

Foundation
Free will, self-responsibility, freedom to choose one's own values

with the values of mainstream education but also with values from a much wider provenance, whilst the values of adventure education are similar to those espoused by the military. The differences are largely to do with emphasis and nuance. Environmental values such as sustainability, the specific value of endeavour, adventure and challenge, a particular care for emotional and physical well-being, confidence in dealing with the unknown and unfamiliar, the value of risk acceptance as a source of benefits and the salience of personal capability are usually emphasised in outdoor education.

Some of the contemporary values problems faced by society in general impinge particularly on outdoor education. Ecological deterioration can be hastened as the increasing use of the outdoors by learning groups causes more pollution and erosion. Child protection measures, necessary

also for the protection of staff, limit the scope for the intergenerational intimacy and close personal interaction that used to be a valued feature of camping, which often provided young people with a vivid personal experience and a veritable adventure in human relationships (Everard 1993: 10–1). Worst of all, the culture of fear and litigation has led to the 'sanitisation' of adventure, as statutory inspection of outdoor centres takes its toll. There is a particular set of values associated with mountaineers, the flavour of which has been vividly captured by McDonald (1997). Whilst many of these values are shared with outdoor education, the 'physical' focus subordinates the rest.

Outdoor education activities and processes leading to values development

The systematic use of outdoor education for developing values, once known as 'character-building', is often an ingredient of outdoor programmes, and none more so than in dealing with young people deemed to be 'at risk' (e.g. of social exclusion or offending). Many programmes are explicitly intended to transmit, instil, inculcate, nurture or shape values, and indeed this is one of the overt principles of development training, a subset of outdoor education. The foundation values and those associated with personal capability are frequently emphasised to participants. Others like this are respect for others, tolerance, responsibility (especially as regards safety), self-awareness, co-operation, due process, environmental sustainability and commitment. Working outdoors as a group is an activity conducive to the development of these values, especially when the allotted task is challenging.

The choice of activity influences whether and which values are likely to be developed, as does the method and quality of the teaching, and the underpinning ideology and learning emphasis of the educator. The spiritual values usually need a deep experience with 'magic moments', such as being on a mountain at sunrise or in solitude under the stars, although adventures of the spirit can also be created in activities involving self-revelation. Paffard, in a survey of 220 young people, has identified the factors most effective in triggering a transcendental experience (Everard, 1999).

The socio-political category of values can be highlighted in overseas expeditions or in acts of service that form an integral part of the Duke of Edinburgh Award or Prince's Trust Volunteers schemes. The Moral category requires sensitive treatment if it is not to be experienced and rejected as 'moralising'. It is here that process reviews of activities can be particularly useful, because a skilled tutor can often draw out from a group a reflective observation that exemplifies the application of a moral value, which may well have contributed to the successful completion of a task. It is even more powerful when a sequence of well-chosen experiences reinforces the same

value. How much nicer it feels to belong to a group whose members value, and are habitually kind to, one another! This can build a group culture that members can seek to emulate when they plan to transfer their outdoor learning to other settings. The very formation of a group with a common aim can help to bring out the values in the human category, but it will be up to the tutor to draw attention to what is happening, celebrate it and help the group to identify the conditions that lead to it. Towards the end of a common group experience will be an opportunity to return to the basic value of self-respect and the foundation value of freedom to choose one's own values. Many an outdoor programme ends with the participants feeling seven feet tall, with an enhanced sense of self-worth and a feeling that the group 'did it themselves', thus awakening the sense of self-responsibility. Some programmes end with individual action plans or resolutions to work on 'back at the ranch'. This can be a powerful way of consolidating the re-shaping of value sets which took place during the programme and it becomes even more effective if it embodies a follow-up monitoring process.

Of all the stages in the process of outdoor education, the review is usually the best time to bring values issues into the arena of conscious discussion and verbalisation. Tutors need to be very skilful to make the most of this opportunity. A national standard of occupational competence (B.1) has been written for the youth work standards framework which provides a useful benchmark (Paulo, 2003).

The valuing of safety is also the subject of an occupational standard in the Sport, Recreation and Allied Occupations framework (SPRITO, 1997) – in 'Promote a culture of health and safety'. So too is environmental sustainability in 'Promote the conservation of the environment'. Both are mandatory units in the outdoor education NVQ, as is 'Deliver education in the outdoors' which requires candidates to know 'how to shape values and attitudes without moralising', 'how to choose activities that lead to desired learning outcomes' and understand 'the benefits and values of Outdoor Education'. There is also a mandatory unit entitled 'Promote the transfer of learning from outdoor experiences' which requires candidates to show how they encourage enduring changes in particular value sets.

Insofar as such national standards are benchmarks of good professional practice, there is clearly an expectation that outdoor education tutors will be adept at handling values issues purposefully and designing experiences that enable this to be done. Approaches that usually work include:

- Making it clear that values are to be lived and owned, not just treated cognitively or philosophically.
- Posing ethical dilemmas can provoke intense discussion: discussion is the anvil on which values are often shaped.
- Exploring the behavioural consequences of alternative value sets illustrates the influence that values have on our lives.
- Creating opportunities in which it feels natural and right to articulate and share one's own values is an antecedent to shaping them.
- Helping people to find meaning and purpose in their lives (what it is to be human) exposes their values; the outdoors, under the stars or atop a mountain, is just right for this purpose.
- Evoking a sense of humility and a feeling that there is a world above and beyond the conscious rational self helps people to explore their innermost values.

Values and processes

Values are not just static concepts kept in the back of one's mind; they need to be lived and applied. This means that they must form part of a process. Since outdoor education is generally focused on experiential learning, practitioners tend to think in process terms more often than the general run of educators. So what processes can be identified in which values are central (Everard, 1992b):

- **Valuing**: probably the most important process. It consists of reflecting on, identifying, articulating and perhaps asserting and celebrating values.
- **Value consciousness-raising**: the process, common in outdoor education, of enhancing people's readiness and ability to engage in valuing.
- **Values clarification**: a well-established process in mainstream education and business which seeks to expose and understand the values people say they hold, or which are inferred from their behaviour to hold, but makes no overt attempt to influence or judge these values. It sometimes reveals inconsistencies between actual behaviour and hypocritically declared values.
- **Values decision-making**: the process that enables one to choose between two or more values or to rank them in order of priority. In outdoor education for example, sometimes the needs of an individual clash with those of the group, as in the parable of the lost sheep.
- **Values shaping**: a large constellation of processes that aim to change people's value sets and hence their behaviour. Reward and punishment systems, advertising, image-building, legislation and political propaganda are among those with which education competes.
- **Adaptation to cultural change in society or organisations**: refers to the way in which people respond to societal trends or changing cultures (such as the youth or the litigation culture), whether planned or unplanned. They may steadfastly resist the change, secure in their own values, or move with the times.
- **Connecting values to beliefs and behaviour**: the process that elucidates and builds on the causal and sequential connection, in a particular context, between fundamental beliefs, values, attitudes and behaviour. It is an important part of leadership.
- **Values reconciliation**: the process whereby a conflict (real or apparent) in values is constructively resolved, with the aim of getting the best of both worlds (a 'win-win' situation). It usually entails an appeal to a superordinate value in the hierarchy.
- **Values confrontation**: By contrast, in this process people react to values conflict by enhancing the difference, single-mindedly espousing one value set at the expense of another and seeking uncompromisingly to gain for it dominant ascendancy (a 'win-lose' situation). Fundamentalists and extremists prefer this approach. It has a place in education, if only to expose diversity, but it tends to entrench value sets.
- **Value selling**: is the use of techniques of persuasion to sell a product not on the basis of fitness for use or effectiveness, but of a

particular character such as its provenance or supposed inherent goodness. It has been known for outdoor education to be 'sold' on this basis. The denigration of the value of commercial providers on the grounds that they are corrupted by the profit motive, compared with the supposed occupation of the moral high ground by educational institutions, has led to a regulatory regime that is plainly biased.

- **Measuring value**: often called for when outdoor education providers are expected to demonstrate 'value added' by comparing the worth (e.g. in terms of employability) of an individual before and after an outdoor education programme.
- **Values competence development**: By this is meant the pedagogical processes that teachers and trainers use to help their clients to manage any of the afore-mentioned processes.

This list is not exhaustive, but is intended to scope the types of processes that may be encountered in dealing with values in an outdoor education context.

References

Barnes, P. (2000) *Values and Outdoor Learning*. Penrith: Association for Outdoor Learning.

Beck, C. (1990) *Better Schools*. Lewes: Falmer Press.

Collier, G. (1997) Learning Moral Commitment in Higher Education. *Journal of Moral Education*. 26: 73–83.

Cranfield, I. (2002) *Inspiring Achievement: The Life and Work of John Hunt*. Penrith: Institute for Outdoor Learning with The Foundation for Outdoor Adventure.

Everard, K.B. (1990) *Values, Beliefs, Education and Training and Developing Competence in Dealing With Values*. Aberdeen: A NAVET Occasional Paper.

Everard, K.B. (1992a) *Values and Ethics in Outdoor Education*. NAVET Papers, VII 5.

Everard, K.B. (1992b) *A Guide to Handling Some Values Issues*. Aberdeen: A NAVET Occasional Paper.

Everard, K.B. (1993) *The History of Development Training*. Welwyn Garden City: DTAG.

Everard, K.B. (1999) *Spiritual Development in the Outdoors*. Penrith: Address to The AGM of The Association for Outdoor Learning, 3 July.

Exeter, D.J. (Ed.) (2001) *Outward Bound: Learning in the Outdoors*. London: The Outward Bound Trust.

Kidder, R. (1999) Global Ethics is an Individual Responsibility. *Royal Society of Arts Journal*. 1: 4, 39–43.

Kolb, D.A. (1984) *Experiential Learning: Experience as the Source of Learning and Development*. Englewood Cliffs: Prentice-Hall.

Lewis, I. (2002) *The Values of Being*. Paper Presented to The 2002 Geneva Conference on *Youth and Human Values*. UNESCO.

McDonald, P. (1997) *Climbing Lessons: Inside Outdoor Education*. Northland, New Zealand: Pete McDonald.

Paulo. (2003) Raising the Standards in Community-Based Learning and Development. www.paulo.org.uk.

Plunkett, D. (1990) *Secular and Spiritual Values: Grounds for Hope in Education*. London: Routledge.

Robb, W.M. (1996) *Values Education: The Contribution of Some Voluntary Youth Organisations*. Aberdeen: Centre for Alleviating Social Problems Through Values Education (CAVE).

SCCC. (1991) *Values in Education*. Dundee: Scottish Consultative Council on The Curriculum.

Sport and Recreation Lead Body (1992) *A Guide to The Qualifications Framework: Leading The Way in Vocational Qualifications*. London: Sport and Recreation Lead Body.

SPRITO. (1997) Outdoor Education Development Training and Recreation Level 3. National Occupational Standards and S/NVQ Guide, C214.

Tate, N. (1997) Values in the Curriculum. *Royal Society of Arts Journal*. Aug–Sept, 9–12.

Other literature

A useful, well-referenced booklet on values education has been published by the Centre for Alleviating Social Problems through Values Education (Robb, 1996). It describes the work of the Scout Association, the Boys' Brigade, the Scottish YMCA, the DTAG organisations and others, concluding that 'the role of voluntary youth organisations in effecting values education has been vastly underestimated'. It quotes from HM

The Queen's Commonwealth Day Message, 1993: I am asking you all to think about human values . . . The young people of the Commonwealth have the future in their hands. May they keep their vision of human values alive and their determination to achieve them undiminished'? The outdoor sector has an important part to play in realising these aspirations.

The Association for Outdoor Learning published a book, 'Values and Outdoor Learning' – a collection of papers reflecting some contemporary thinking (Barnes, 2000).

Appendix

Institute of Global Ethics: State of the World Forum (Kidder 1999).

Institute of Global Studies: 24 moral exemplars in 16 countries (Kidder 1999).

SCAA Values (see above). For values in the Scottish curriculum see SCCC (1991).

The NAVET (National Association for Values in Education and Training) Guide is an aid to introducing values into the curriculum (Everard, 1992b).

The Values and Standards in the British Army were issued in 2000.

The values by which Nelson Mandela lived his life (quoted from his authorised biography) are included because he is widely accepted as a role model throughout the world.

The Values of Being are taken from Lewis (2002).

The Living Values Workshop (1999). It was organised by the Bramha Kumaris World Spiritual University in conjunction with the English Outdoor Council, the Foundation for Outdoor Adventure, Youth Clubs UK, the Rank Foundation and others.

The SPRITO (Sport, Recreation and Allied Occupations National Training Organisation) value statements were developed in 1991–1992 as an adjunct to the National Standards of Occupational Competence. There is a generic set and one specific to Outdoor Education (SRLB 1992).

The Outward Bound Trust Values Base – see Exeter (2001)

The Lindley Educational Trust Values were derived from 2.Peter, Ephesians 4–5 and Galatians 5–6.

The IOL Code of Conduct was revised from that developed by the Association for Outdoor Learning.

The National Youth Agency's Statement of Values and Principles was developed by S Banks.

The value set contributed by Denys Brunsden is based on the 1986 St George's House Consultation on 'Outdoor Adventure and Challenge for Youth' (Cranfield, 2002: 129).

3 Aesthetics and the Outdoor Experience

Angus McWilliam

Abstract

There are those, and I would not disagree with them who argue that the 'outdoor' in outdoor education is a misnomer; that outdoor education can occur in urban, in artificial and indeed even in indoor areas. In this essay I wish to propose that there is a quality unique to the outdoor experience that is both motivationally important and educationally useful.

I further wish to argue that it is important for creators of outdoor experiences, whether recreational or educational, to be aware of the impact which environments have on their clients and to understand why they are attracted to, repelled by or attach value to certain environments. Educators may then more effectively help their clients create the experiences they seek and develop an aesthetic language allowing them to celebrate, reflect and make sense of the events they encounter.

Introduction

Outdoor education creates opportunities for individuals to explore natural environments, to live and move in ways which are in harmony with that landscape and to get close to and feel a part of a natural world which is complex, uncertain and demanding. Participants seek experiences in which their senses are bombarded with colour, form, movement, texture, sounds, taste and touch. Outdoor education is for sensation seekers! These are powerful aesthetic experiences which envelop the individual and awaken feelings of awe, wonder, fear, and empathy. Some of these may be associated with the activity, the speed, effort, vertigo, whilst others arise from a prospect or view. Others arise from the surprise encounters with fellow creatures of great beauty and alien-ness and yet still others from a greater awareness of one's self in relation to where one is. But experiences are ephemeral, transient and cannot be repeated. That is a part of their attraction but perhaps that is also part of the reason why events in the natural world have been so often the focus of artistic creativity. From representational arts such as landscape painting or travel writing to abstract sculpture and poetry, the artist has tried to capture the moment and express the feelings encountered. We experience the environment in which we live not directly but through the filter of our senses. Our brains interpret the cascade of information which we receive identifying shapes, sounds and smells and arranging the objects perceived (e.g. trees, rivers, hills) in the three dimensional space which is the place in which we are. But our brains do more than this. They make qualified judgments about these objects and places ascribing value to them. They categorise objects as useful, ugly, beautiful or dangerous and feelings are stimulated such as curiosity, wonder or loathing as a result of that value. What are these values? How have we acquired or learnt them? Some are clear and obvious. For example, we value, are attracted to and take pleasure in objects and places which are useful and which satisfy our needs for example water, food, shelter. Others however are less obvious. Why do we delight in the colours of the sunset, marvel at the spectacle of a waterfall, or stand in awe at the view from a high cliff top? What is even more interesting is the observation that for each individual the experience is unique. Wilson (1993) presents evidence which suggests that we all tend to be attracted or repelled by the same aesthetic experiences and suggests in turn that there may be a rational explanation for these responses.

Aesthetics

The word aesthetic is derived from the Greek word 'aisthanomai' which means to perceive. Thus aesthetic pleasure means literally pleasure associated with or deriving from perception and an aesthetic response is one in which the perception of an object or an environment results in the arousal of emotions or feelings. All experiences to a greater or lesser degree will stimulate an aesthetic response but most of the time our familiarity with the events or concern about other matters means that we hardly notice. Aesthetic experiences are ones in which the emotional arousal which results from our perception commands our attention. Not all events that result in an emotional response can be described as aesthetic. Aesthetic experiences have certain characteristics which set them apart from others. Botzler (1993) describes seven key characteristics of the aesthetic experience:

- Aesthetic experiences are valued or responded to for their own sake rather than for their potential use or the satisfaction of the observers needs.
- Aesthetic experiences are receptive experiences in which the observer lets the event or object be itself and seeks to relate to it or understand it on its own terms.
- Aesthetic experiences are centred on the present on the object as it is rather than how it came to be or what it might lead to.
- Aesthetic experiences focus attention on the uniqueness of the object or experience rather than it as an example of a class of experiences.
- Aesthetic experiences may entail a delight in the beauty harmony or complex unity of an event but may also stimulate fear loathing or disgust.
- Aesthetic experiences can involve both emotive and intellectual responses, spontaneous feelings and a reflection on their meaning.
- Finally aesthetic experiences can occur in the presence of any kind of object or event and involve one or all of the senses or be apprehended only with the mind.

From this list it appears hard to express in words precisely what an aesthetic experience is except that each is immediate and unique. However, we all know when we have had one; for example, the sense of wonder when the light from a sinking sun turns the sky to a blaze of pinks and violets or the gasp when turning a corner a prospect of distant hills opens out. But why do we experience such emotions and in particular why do nature, wilderness and outdoor experiences specifically seem to arouse such emotions? There seem to be two arguments for the development of such attractions, the cultural and the socio-biological.

Socio-biological root of environmental aesthetics

The socio-biological argument simply states that in the course of evolution there have been certain survival advantages in being attracted towards particular aspects of nature and being repelled by others and that these are not learned, but genetically burnt into our psyche. What evidence is there for this? Ulrich (1983) surveyed research literature in landscape aesthetics and found that people irrespective of who they were or where they came from consistently preferred natural scenes over built views. Wilson and Kellert (1993) proposed the 'Biophilia Hypothesis' claiming 'that there is a human dependence on nature that extends far beyond the simple issues of material and physical sustenance to encompass as well a craving for the aesthetic satisfaction which results from encounters with life and lifelike processes'. They argued that holding these aesthetic preferences at some time during our evolutionary history must have held strong survival advantages. They cite examples such as the universal fear of snakes that seems to occur even amongst those who have no prior knowledge or encounter with them. They argued from this and other observations that the emotional arousal which results from direct contact with nature had value as it stimulated and encouraged man to seek out and explore habitats conducive to human survival.

Iltis (1980) supported this idea claiming that there is a genetic need for natural pattern, beauty and harmony which is developed by selection over evolutionary time. Heerwagen and Orians (1993) goes on to explain this by arguing that a crucial step in the lives of most organisms including humans is the selection of a habitat or home and that aesthetic responses are initially emotional feelings that lead to rejection or exploration of a certain environment. Good habitats that have the potential to support life and growth therefore evoke strong positive responses. Psychologists and landscape architects have taken these ideas further trying to discover the characteristics of natural landscapes that arouse an aesthetic appreciation. Appleton (1975) suggested that places to which people felt attracted were ones in which they felt safe and supported. Being safe encompassed being able to see dangers (hazards) such as wild animals or enemies from a distance

Table 1   Criteria for aesthetic preference

Level of interpretation	Making sense/easy to characterise to map out or summarise	Involvement/the need to figure out/learn or be stimulated
Immediate	Coherence	Complexity
Inferred	Legibility	Mystery

and being able to identify places to which they could retreat if danger threatened (a refuge). Thus, an elevated position with a view out over a landscape in which there were open spaces and clumps of vegetation was expected to be aesthetically pleasing. Outdoor educators will not be surprised to hear that such places are indeed sought after but this of course does not in itself mean that hard wiring of landscape types to aesthetic responses is necessarily true. Kaplan (1987) following a similar line of reasoning, claimed that aesthetic preference is not based on an irrational whim but a set of inclinations that direct choices which are functional and have evolutionary significance. He proposed that places which are attractive firstly need to be understandable and have a simplicity based on order and pattern with distinct recognisable features. These would be places where you will not get lost, or even if you do, you will be able to find out where you are. Secondly, they are places that are complex, displaying variety and the potential for finding the kinds of resources needed for support. He further suggested that such places need to have characteristics which make them immediately attractive and characteristics which arouse curiosity and invite deeper study. From these ideas Kaplan constructed the hypothesis that aesthetic preference is based on the following criteria (also see Table 1):

- **Coherence:** the degree to which the scene hangs together through repetition of elements, textures, colours (which facilitate comprehension).
- **Complexity:** the degree to which they display variety or diversity in space.
- **Legibility:** the degree to which the scene can be explored without getting lost and its composition described.
- **Mystery:** the degree to which you can gain more information by proceeding into the scene.

Cultural root of environmental aesthetics

While empirical studies have been carried out which demonstrate the ability of both Appleton's and Kaplan's theories to predict locations and landscapes that are attractive, this does not infer that the assumption of a genetic evolutionary basis is the whole truth. Indeed personal experience, history and cultural comparisons all demonstrate differences in what people find attractive. When we look at history and archaeology we can find evidence of the value people have placed on the aesthetic qualities of objects they have surrounded themselves with and the places they have lived. The pots they made and the buildings they lived in are not only functional but they are also decorated. It would appear that a desire for beauty existed even as far back as the drawings of prehistoric cave dwellers. It may be argued that the drawings and decorations were functional; a signature which identified the owner; a record of events and places which needed to be remembered; a way of establishing one's importance. It may even be that they had mystical or ritual significance in a way we can no longer appreciate, but the care and skill devoted seems to suggest that delight was taken in these creations. That natural creatures and features often formed a part of these decorations may suggest that even in the past, people took aesthetic delight from nature.

When we look closely however, we tend to find that in such early art the landscape and animals are seldom represented as such, but as a background for human activity. The appreciation or at least the celebration of outdoor natural environments as being beautiful in themselves is according to writers such as Nash (1982) and Oeschlaegear (1991) a relatively recent phenomena. They describe how classical philosophers such as Plato and Aristotle drew attention to nature's abundance and the human place in nature's hierarchical system. They indicate how Virgil and Horace introduced the notion that nature exists as a retreat from the artificiality of the city; how during the middle ages, authors from Augustine to Aquinas proposed a Christian view that nature was primarily significant as evidence of God's design; how in medieval and renaissance art, nature in art was stylised and civilised. Nature here was still considered as what man had escaped from; it was dangerous, unknowable, and unpleasant. It was, these authors argue, only with the coming age of enlightenment, the age of science and commerce that in reaction against the squalor of industrialisation and commercialisation of life that the aesthetic qualities of the natural world came to be valued for themselves. They describe how in the early 17th-century, writers such as Bacon and Descartes introduced a modernist world view praising human control over natural forces. As a counter point Robert Burns's poetry and Gilbert White's natural history helped to re-establish more sympathetic and congenial attitudes toward nature and lead to the 19th century, when romantic literature across the western world from Goethe to Wordsworth to Emerson criticised the prevailing industrial view of nature as mere commodity. Finally in the 20th century, the most eloquent voices for an ecologically integrative vision of nature have come from such authors as D. H. Lawrence, Aldous Huxley, John Muir and Edward Abbey. Not only from history but an anecdotal analysis of how people live around the world seems to suggest that different aspects of nature attract them. So, just as there is variety in buildings and objects of art which is particular to cultures and people so there does appear to be aspects of the appreciation of nature that are culturally created.

Aesthetics: learned

The argument that appreciation is as much or more dependent on culture as genetics is even further strengthened by the observation that aesthetic appreciation can be learnt. As we mature, our taste in the arts develops. We find more satisfaction in objects as we become aware of the complexity and skill of their creation and the subtlety in the meanings and stories they tell. This is certainly true of music, books and pictures. Exploring our own childhood show clearly how much the media and fashion industries have taught us and moulded our tastes. If this is true of works of art it is reasonable to suggest that it may also be true of our appreciation of nature and that as we mature and collect aesthetic experiences in natural areas our tastes may grow and become more discerning.

Key questions are – can we teach, learn to delight and appreciate nature. And is there a point in doing so. When we read authors such as Thoreau (1862), Abbey (1968) and Dillard (1975), what becomes increasingly evident is how their delight in nature and places increases with encounter. What is surprising to the modern reader is that these were not global tourists who searched the world for novelty and sensation but spent most of their lives exploring the places they lived in. Dillard (1975) describes Pilgrims Creek and how she came to learn to perceive it in all its splendour, in all its changes and seasons and how that seeing was a revealing of the coherence and complexity of the environment. The aesthetic satisfaction was enhanced by the developing ability to read that complexity and be aware of the mysterious depths undiscovered. In all these writers what is clear is that if aesthetics is as we said at the beginning, pleasure derived from perception involving our senses and intellect, then it is more than just seeing. Perception is looking into; it takes time and requires attention. Perception requires that we take time to allow sensations to impinge on our senses, revealing the form and diversity of the places we visit. Perception in addition requires time for the interplay of the senses with our accumulation of experience, expectations, reflection on the meaning and impact of these sensations This is not so different from other forms of learning or at least experiential learning, for as we are constantly reminded, experience without reflection is unlikely to lead to learning and reflection itself is an art that needs to be learnt. So, to develop a natural aesthetic, we need to be exposed to nature and natural environments and we need to reflect on our experience of them. We need to become aware of how our emotions are aroused and explore why we feel the way we do. And to reflect, we need to develop a language of reflection appropriate to the subject. This may be through words, music or images and it may be analytical and argumentative or it may be intuitive and creative. But in this way we will deepen our understanding of ourselves and our relationships with the places we inhabit and the objects and creatures we share it with.

There is an urgency about this. Kohak (1992) asks how we can expect people to defend nature if it is not first seen as good. Leopold (1949) suggests that without the development of a love of the land, an environmental ethic is a 'dry concept which touches no-one'. Aesthetics is about delight and anger at ugliness. Outdoor experiences need to foster delight in places and engender anger at their removal.

References

Abber, E. (1968) *Desert Solitaire*. New York: Ballantine Publishing Group.

Appleton, J. (1975) *The Experience of Landscape*. London: John Wiley and Sons.

Armstrong, S.J. and Botzler, R.G. (1993) in Kellert, S.R. and Wilson, E.O. (Eds.) *The Biophilia Hypothesis*. Washington: Island Press.

Dillard, A. (1974) *Pilgrim at Tinker Creek*. New York: Harper's Magazine Press.

Heerwagen, J.H. and Orians, G.H. (1993) Human Habitats and Aesthetics, in Kellert, S.R. and Wilson, E.O. (Eds.) *The Biophilia Hypothesis*. Washington: Island Press.

Iltis, H. (1967) To the Taxonomist and the Ecologist, Whose Fight is the Preservation of Nature. *Bio-Science*. December, 887.

Kaplan, S. and Kaplan, R. (1982) *Cognition and Environment: Functioning in an Uncertain World*. New York: Praeger.

Kaplan, S. (1987) Aesthetics, Affect, and Cognition: Environmental Preference From an Evolutionary Perspective. *Environment and Behavior*. 19: 3–32.

Kellert, S.R. (1993) The Biological Basis for Human Values of Nature, in Kellert, S.R. and Wilson, E. (Eds.) *The Biophilia Hypothesis*. Washington: Island Press.

Kohak, E. (1992) Perceiving the Good, in Oelschlaeger, M. (Ed.) *The Idea of Wilderness*. Washington: Island Press.

Leopold, A. (1949) *A Sand County Almanac*. Oxford: Oxford University Press.

Nash, R. (1882) *Wilderness and the American mind*. Newhaven: Yale University Press.

Oeschlaegear, M. (1991) *The Idea of Wilderness*. Newhaven: Yale University Press.

Thoreau, H.D. (1862) Walking in Environmental Ethics, in Kellert, S.R. and Wilson, E.O. (Eds.) *The Biophilia Hypothesis*. Washington: Island Press.

Ulrich, R.S. (1993) Biophilia Biophobia and Natural Landscapes, in Kellert, S.R. and Wilson, E.O. (Eds.) *The Biophilia Hypothesis*. Washington: Island Press.

Wilson, E.O. (1993) Biophilia and the Conservation Ethic, in Kellert, S.R. and Wilson, E.O. (Eds.) *The Biophilia Hypothesis*. Washington: Island Press.

Watson, S. (1997) A theoretical Approach. http://www.sli.unimelb.edu.au/LSP/Lit82revs.html

4 Research Methods in Outdoor Education

Geoff Nichols

Abstract

This chapter gives an introduction to the issues involved in choosing research methods in outdoor education. It will argue that selection of methods depends on: philosophical assumptions about the nature of knowledge and how we discover it; the research audience; and the practicalities of implementation. It describes research approaches of positivism, interpretivism, scientific realism and use of the 'theory of change'. References are given to supporting research methods texts and examples. In their review, Barrett and Greenaway (1995) concluded research into outdoor adventure in the UK was inconclusive, hampered by methodological problems, uncritical and of a low standard. This chapter might at least draw attention to the issues in choosing research methods.

Philosophical positions

An excellent and readable introduction to the philosophy of research is Bryman (2001). I have drawn from this and for consistency have used the same terms he uses to describe research. Slightly different terms are used in other texts. Epistemology is concerned with how we generate knowledge about the world, and thus what is, (or should be) regarded as valid knowledge. Ontology is concerned with the nature of reality. The two 'ologies' are linked. Conflicting views on both of them help explain disputes over which research methods to use and how validity is defined.

Positivism

The epistemological position, often termed positivism, maintains that we have to apply the same methods as are normally associated with the natural sciences to the social sciences. To summarise Bryman (2001), positivism implies certain principles and only if we apply these will we generate 'valid' knowledge. Knowledge is confirmed by our senses (so it is not just abstract concepts). Theory is used to generate hypotheses that can be tested and this allows general explanations (laws) to be assessed. Thus we can deduce if a law is valid. By gathering facts we can provide the basis for laws; thus laws can be induced from these facts. There is an emphasis on the value free application of scientific methods. Causality is thought of as a simple relation of cause and effect: I hit a pool ball and it goes in a certain direction; and if I am any good, it will go in the pocket.

Interpretivism

In contrast, the epistemological position of interpretivism maintains that understanding of social situations requires us to understand the subjective perception of social actors. To understand why a person does something I have to understand the conceptual map of the world that person has in their head; their own system of logic. I may not share that logic, but it helps me understand the way it has caused that person to act in a particular way. A good example is religious belief. A friend stood for a long time at a motorway junction trying to hitch a lift, and then decided to walk back to a station just to find that a convenient train was about to arrive. She told me she had responded to God's will, who had first directed her to wait at the junction, and then return to the station. I may not share this interpretation of divine intervention, but in order to understand my friend, I have to understand the way she sees the world: her conceptual map which determines her own system of logic.

Objectivism

These two epistemological positions are related to ontology; philosophical positions on the nature of reality. The ontological position of 'objectivism' believes that there is an external reality independent of the observer and of social actors.

Figure 1 The classic experimental design (Pawson and Tilley, 1997)

	Pre-test	Treatment	Post-test
Experimental group	O1	X	O2
Control group	O1		O2

Reality is, 'out there' somewhere, and it will not be affected by our attempts to observe it. This fits well with the principles of positivistic method as above. Therefore we do experiments which mimic the methods of the natural sciences to reveal this reality. Bryman (2001) gives the social science example of researching an organisation. Let's take this a step further and consider researching an outdoor education centre. We might describe its rules and procedures; who does what job when; the job hierarchy. We are describing a reality external to the staff member working in it or the course participant. They experience the centre as an external reality to which they react; like the pool ball after it has been hit in the previous example. As an example: in the context of an outdoor centre, if course members or staff do not comply with rules specifying they must not use illegal drugs, they will be sent home or fired. The rules are experienced as an external reality.

Arising from positivism and objectivism is what Pawson and Tilley (1997: 5) have described as the classic experimental design (See Figure 1). Figure 1 illustrates that 'classic experimental research' design starts with two identical groups. One group is given the treatment and one group is not. Research is looking for measurable outcomes of a programme in the experimental group and comparing them to the control group who has not experienced the same programme. If the group that had the treatment changes and the control group do not, it is deduced that the treatment caused the change. If numbers in the two groups are large enough it can be ascertained whether the evidence of a causal relationship is statistically significant. Causation between the programme and intermediate effects, or the final outcome, is inferred from the repeated succession of similar effects after similar programmes. This will be referred back to when we consider some practical problems of research in outdoor education.

Constructionism

In contrast, the ontological position of 'constructionism' asserts that the social world is constructed by social interaction. We all have different world views and as a result of interaction we generate shared meanings. Reality is socially constructed. The implications for researching an outdoor education centre would be that we needed to understand it not as a reality external to the actors but as a result of shared and negotiated meanings; a socially constructed reality. The different staff members, and course members, might have different perceptions. A 'rule' might be regarded by objectivism as existing externally from the actor, but constructionism would emphasise the way its understanding was the result of shared meanings and was continually being renegotiated. For example, Outward Bound Ullswater once refused me employment on the basis that I had a beard and Outward Bound only employed people who were clean shaven. A few years later this 'rule' had been renegotiated to the extent that I was considered suitable for employment (I still had the beard). A sociologist might have researched firstly, what was meant by 'having a beard', the degree to which facial hair was acceptable; and secondly, how this 'rule' was renegotiated, reflecting the 'shared' and changing meanings of particular centre heads, and possibly the market for hairy staff. Similarly, to relate back to the previous example of centre rules and acceptable behaviour, the interpretation of rules will be the result of negotiated meanings and will change as they are renegotiated. Constructionism can lead to research which explores differences in perception. A good example was Greenaway's research of participants on a management training course at Brathay who had a very different perception of the course to those held by the course staff: the participants saw it more as a holiday. This helped understand participants' reactions to the course.

* * *

So far I have described one version of constructivism, which implies the social scientist has to understand the conceptual frameworks through which individuals themselves understand their worlds. These pre-exist the research. For example, Outward Bound's 'rules' on beards existed before the researcher attempted to reveal them by research. However this position can be extended to a second version of constructivism applied to the social scientist's own world view; in which case social scientists 'always present a specific view of social reality, rather than one that can be regarded as definitive' (Bryman, 2001: 18). The social scientist cannot escape their own set of meanings within which their research is constructed. They will only ask certain questions because of their own set of values and those questions only 'make sense' within their own system of logic. This second version of constructivism implies that all knowledge is indeterminate. This complete social relativism is not useful if one wants to use research to inform policy. It is reflected in the position of postmodernism.

Thus the epistemological and ontological positions, above, have different implications for how we do research. Positivism and objectivism typically lead to a quantitative approach where a large number of observations are collected to test theory by seeking statistically significant regularities. Interpretivism and constructionism are typically associated with a qualitative approach; often a small number of qualitative interviews, or participant observation. This can lead to generalisations from which theory is generated (Bryman, 2001: 20).

So, why not use both approaches? Some might say a combination of quantitative and qualitative methods give a better grasp of reality: it might show us what people do and why they do it. This pragmatic approach has been advocated (Tashakkori and Teddlie, 1998). However, as noted in the introduction, one factor determining the choice of methods is the research audience. If you are working for a PhD a philosophical fudge is not acceptable: so you need to chose one approach or the other. In other circumstances you may be guided by pragmatism, what is most practical, and the preferences of research funders and policy makers; as discussed later.

Scientific realism

An approach which appears to achieve a philosophically coherent compromise is scientific realism. Influential proponents of this approach are Pawson and Tilley (1997) who have applied it to criminology and particularly in researching the effectiveness of crime reduction programmes. Although I am not aware of applications in outdoor education there is a lot of common ground as in both fields much research is concerned to evaluate the effectiveness of programmes at achieving objectives, such as personal development, or perhaps a shared objective of crime reduction (Nichols, 1998).

The epistemological position is that causation in a programme cannot be understood through deducing how a programme works just through statistical regularities (as in positivism and objectivism). One has to understand why actors involved in the programmes chose to change the way they act. This is called 'generative causality'. Causality has to be understood as a combination of human agency and its reaction to new opportunities and resources. For example, to understand the impact of an outdoor education course, one would need to understand not only the new range of opportunities offered by the course, but also the resources and attitudes the participants brought with them, and how these changed as the course developed. As involvement progresses, the participant may be able to take advantage of a greater range of opportunities offered by the programme, and may in fact only see them as opportunities after some period of involvement. For example, a timid participant might initially perceive group work as a challenging situation in which they feel they have little to contribute. As their confidence grows they might become more assertive and see the same situations as an opportunity to express themselves and to develop new skills. The way they make sense of their situation and the meanings they give it have changed. This accords with the process of personal development through the medium of an outdoors based course, as described in Chapter 5 in this book. The interaction between programme and participants is termed, 'generative causality', in contrast to positivism, where causality is a one way process.

Figure 2 A context, mechanism, regularity configuration (source, Pawson and Tilley, 1997)

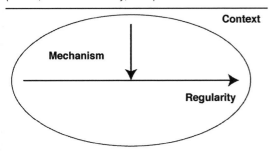

This tells us why a programme has a particular impact. For example, why an outdoor education programme increases self-esteem (if it did). However, we still need to know how often or how much a programme causes a particular effect, and in what circumstances. How much has the self-esteem of participants changed and for how many has this effect been observed? In what circumstances does this happen? Pawson and Tilley (1997) use the concepts of 'regularity' and a 'context' to incorporate these questions.

The three elements of mechanism, context and regularity are drawn together in Figure 2.

The mechanism causes regularity, but this is contingent on a particular context. Some programmes will work with some participants, in some contexts, but not in others. An example is from research (Nichols, 1999) into the place adventure activities took in the rehabilitation of long-term drug addicts. It was found that a key to successful rehabilitation was the ability to start a new life among new peers in a new geographical area. The area could be thought of as the context. If, having gone through rehabilitation (a process as long as 12 months) a former addict moved back to their former home area, then the pressures and opportunities to become trapped in a cycle of drug taking and crime were often too hard to resist. In this example, the rehabilitation programme and the role of adventure activities was the mechanism, the regularity (not measured in this research) was the rehabilitation rate and the context was the area in which the participant found themselves after the rehabilitation process. The general 'CMR' model informs hypothesis generation about context, mechanism, regularity configurations. These hypotheses can be tested with a combination of quantitative and qualitative

methods, the combination of which is justified by the epistemological position described above; that causation in a programme has to be understood both through statistical regularities and by understanding why actors involved in the programmes chose to change the way they act. This is in contrast to the pragmatic avocation of mixed methodologies (e.g. Tashakkori and Teddlie, 1998) where quantitative and qualitative methods are used, but without a philosophical justification. Pawson and Tilley (1997) want to explain the mechanism by which a programme 'works', but they still want to measure regularities; or outcomes. Thus while we might interview participants to see how their perceptions changed while on the programme, and how this can help us understand the programme mechanism (how it works) we still want to measure outcomes. For example; we might want to measure a quality such as self-esteem before and after a programme, or we might be interested in reconviction rates of participants against a control group.

The ontological position of scientific realism is that, as in positivism, 'there is an external reality to which scientists directs their attention' (Bryman, 2001: 13) but unlike positivism, 'scientist's conceptualisation is simply one way of knowing that reality'. Bryman quotes Bhaskar (1975: 250) the philosopher who founded this approach, 'science then is the systematic attempt to express in thought the structures and ways of acting of things that exist and act independently of thought'. Scientific knowledge has a particular status because of the systematic way in which data is collected. But we still need to understand the different levels of social reality. Any mechanism has to be understood as embedded in its particular level of social reality. This provides a context on which it is contingent. This is common with interpretivism and constructionism: we need to understand the system of logic the actor uses to understand the world, so as we can understand their own rationality within this.

There has been fierce debate over the validity of scientific realism applied to criminology; mainly with advocates of more positivistic methods (Pawson and Tilley, 1998a, 1998b; Farrington, 1998) and Pawson and Tilleys' work is a response to the prevailing positivism in criminology. However, one might equally well make a criticism from the interpretivist tradition that Pawson and Tilley assume that there is some sort of reality that the researcher can get closer to than the actor. This is implied in their use of the word 'stratified' reality, in that the researcher is implied to understand a 'level of reality' superior to that of the actor, rather than just alternative to that of the actor. This may seem a reasonable view, given the researcher's superior knowledge of theory, but, from the second constructionist view, one could argue that Pawson and Tilley's' understanding of 'reality' may be no nearer to some ideal ultimate reality than the view of the actor: it is just an alternative. Other difficulties in scientific realism are that it is not clear what constitutes regularity and how one defines a context. Secondly, while this approach starts from theory, which forms the basis of a 'CMR' model from which hypotheses are derived, how different from the hypothesised position does a result have to be to challenge the original theory (Nichols, 2001a)?

Is any approach more valid?

So, is any one approach more valid? This is a philosophical question, so it depends which philosophical position you take, and if you take one at all! If you are doing a PhD you can stick to one philosophical position or another and as long as you are logically consistent that's fine. You can argue your case and defend your position logically. The differences can often lead to acrimonious academic exchanges, as noted above.

The positivist approach emphasises that research must be conducted in a value free and objective manner and from this standpoint criticisms have been made of interpretivist research in that it is too easily influenced by the values of the researchers. For example, interviewers might lead interviewees in particular ways and interpret them according to their own value laden frame of reference. This general criticism is misplaced. Firstly, qualitative research can be just as rigorous as quantitative (Mason, 2002). Secondly, while quantitative results might appear objective, the questions asked to generate them might themselves reflect the researcher's values. While positivism maintains that we must do value free science, interpretivism, which has its roots in the sociologist Weber, maintains that

everything we do is directed by values and the best we can do is be aware of them.

The influence of research funders, politicians and policy makers

So far we have just considered debates between academics, which may be based on philosophical grounds, and sometimes on professional rivalry. But research funders, politicians and policy makers; all have an influence, whether they conduct the research themselves or more commonly commission others to do it. All of these groups have their preferences for particular methods, but these are more likely to be just that, rather than based on philosophical arguments about epistemology and ontology. For example, the 'Evaluation of pilot summer activities for 16 year olds: summer 2000', commissioned by the Department for Education and Employment (Nichols, 2001b; Hutchinson, Henderson and Francis, 2001) attempted to quantify changes in self-esteem using two questions, both administered at the beginning and end of a five day course. This quantitative approach probably reflected the preference of the funder, the Department for Education and Employment. One can see how this was close to the classic experimental design but did not include a control group.

The 'theory of change'

An approach which puts explicit emphasis on the perceptions of policy makers and has been used in evaluation research is the 'theory of change' (Connell and Kubish, 1998). This neatly sidesteps some of the epistemological and ontological questions above. The 'theory of change' approach starts by identifying 'a set of beliefs that underlie action' (Weiss, 1998: 55). This is, 'a set of hypotheses upon which people build their program plans. It is an explanation of the causal links that tie program inputs to expected program outputs', and will include both the activities and the mechanisms of change. This corresponds to Pawson and Tilley's CMR configuration but does not arise from previous theory. In researching the impact of an outdoor education programme the hypotheses would be derived from interviewing programme staff and managers. They would describe the type of participants they worked with, the outcomes of the programme, and how they thought their programme contributed to these.

The focus of the theory of change approach is to change policy and practice. To do this it identifies key stakeholders in the policy community. These stakeholders are the most important judges of the validity of the research methods and results although advice is still sought from academics. The key stakeholders are consulted, both to agree the initial hypothesis, but also on how the research must be conducted to provide valid results. Jim Connell, who introduced the theory of change to the UK, made the following points in discussion in 1998, with Rowan Astbury at the Charities Evaluation Services:

> . . . the theory of change is a prediction about what leads to what; plausibility to relevant people is critical. They validate in advance; face validity is always important but especially where change [produced by the intervention] is likely to be small. Credibility of results is related to stakeholders having agreed not only ultimate outcomes, but also interim ones – i.e. if they agree at the start that activities abc, properly done, should lead to outcomes xyz – then if abc and xyz all occur as expected, they will have confidence that the outcomes are due to the interventions. Stakeholders agree in advance the standard of evidence which will convince them.

Thus the theory of change helps to circumvent the philosophical debates on methodology, especially in evaluation research, by recognising that the most important judges of validity are the stakeholders who are going to use the results. If these stakeholders are pragmatists rather than philosophers they will be less interested in questions of ontology and epistemology; although they will still have views on validity. The theory of change approach is presently (1999–2003) being applied in a study of the Fairbridge organisation in the UK (publications forthcoming).

Research practicalities and problems

A further consideration in choosing research methods is the practicality of conducting research and this may be the determining factor. It is extremely difficult to conduct research in outdoor education which meets all the ideal criteria of the classic experimental framework (Figure 1).

Gibson (1979) made a critical review of 21 previous research projects into 'wilderness programmes' in the United States. Comparing the methods used with the ideal criteria he found the following limitations:

- Bias in sample selection.
- Small sample size.
- Lack of adequate control group.
- Questionable validity of assessment instrument (for example, a questionnaire may not have been validated as measuring a phenomena; its construction may have been ad hoc).
- Insufficient description of outcome criteria (poor definition of outcomes).
- Inadequate statistical analysis of data (to show a significant relationship).
- Lack of follow-up investigation (monitoring outcomes over a longer period than just after the programme).

Of the 21 research projects only three had two or less of the limitations above. Of course the validity of all these criticisms only holds if one accepts the classical experimental design, arising from positivism and objectivism, however it does illustrate how hard it is to attain such standards.

The problem of a small sample size, incapable of producing statistically significant results, is inherent in this type of research as often programmes have relatively small numbers. I recently conducted a comparative reconviction study on an initial sample of 94 'offenders' who had attended an outdoor pursuits programme, but the small size of relevant sub-samples, once those ineligible to be included for various technical reasons had been removed, meant that most results were statistically insignificant (Nichols, 2001d). In attempts to apply the classical experimental design it is also extremely difficult to eliminate the problem of bias in sample or control group. In any programme where there is voluntary participation those on a programme might be more likely to gain benefit from it, not because of the programme itself, but because of their own attributes which led them to volunteer.

One way of generating a larger sample is to use a meta-analysis by pulling together independent empirical research results to produce big enough samples to provide statistically significant results, overall, and for specific variables. But within this, it is still extremely difficult to isolate the individual causal variables. This is illustrated by Hattie, Marsh, Neill and Richards's (1997) aggregated results from 96 studies of Outward Bound courses. One criticism of this analysis is that it was attempting to 'add up' results from dissimilar programmes (Glass, McGraw and Smith, 1981). They ranged from a one-day abseiling course for adults to a 42 day long course for 'low achievers' run by Outward Bound Australia. Another assumption is that all the programmes had the same objectives. Both Barrett and Greenaway's (1995: 54) review and Hattie et. al's (1997: 78) meta-analysis of evaluations concluded that research had revealed little about the process of adventure education, and this is a further limitation of the positivist research paradigm.

In addition to the problems of generating a sample size large enough to produce significant results, the nature of some programmes may make it impossible to conduct before and after measures or to construct a control group (Nichols, 2001c).

An interpretivist approach might more simply lead to results showing how and why a programme had a particular impact. It has the attraction that it is easier to obtain a small sample and conduct interviews with them, and perhaps also programme staff. As noted above, this approach can be criticised as being more open to researcher bias. It is possible to conduct it in a rigorous manner (Mason, 2002) but this is not always apparent from the way the research is written up. There is probably a greater danger of bias in interpreting results when the theoretical framework used is both an explanation of social action and an agenda for political change: for example, Marxism or feminism. A limitation of this approach is that it can not answer 'how many' or 'how much' questions. The outdoor education programme might have made a significant impact on the few participants studied in depth, but for how many did it make this difference?

Scientific realism appears to offer the possibility of doing a set of small case studies; each their own CMR configuration; and adding them up cumulatively (Pawson and Tilley, 1997: 115). This is not the same as the meta analysis used by a positivist approach. This option maintains philosophical purity, however, from a more pragmatic perspective, one could just conduct a case study juxtaposing qualitative and quantitative

methods, according to one's research resources (Yin, 1994).

The theory of change approach has an advantage that inherent difficulties in the research can be overcome by persuading the relevant stakeholders that this is really the best one can do in a specific situation. It does however require the establishment and maintenance of a stakeholder group. It also has the considerable advantage that the methods are developed to test the internally generated hypothesis and as a consequence the research process is recognised and valued by key stakeholders, including programme staff. This contributes to the ability to generate the research data. Evaluations which impose methods based on an externally generated hypothesis (as in the positivist approach) have often produced poor results. For example, an extensive survey of the impact of physically demanding programmes on probationers (Taylor, Crow, Irving and Nichols, 1999) had very poor response rates to pre and post programme questionnaires. One reason for this was that the programme workers felt no commitment to administering the questionnaires and completing them interfered with the important initial contact with young participants (Nichols, Taylor, Crow and Irvine, 2000).

Conclusion

The selection of research methods depends on: philosophical assumptions about the nature of knowledge and how we discover it; the research audience; and the practicalities of implementation. The contrasting philosophical positions will be more important in pure academic research. In other cases the preferences of key stakeholders; those who have funded the research and policy makers they seek to influence; will be more important. From a pragmatic point of view the choice of methods is also limited by what is possible, given the constraints of the research situation and resources. This has been particularly so in attempts to evaluate the impact of outdoor education.

References

Barrett, J. and Greenaway, R. (1995) *Why Adventure?* Coventry: Foundation for Outdoor Adventure.

Bhaskar, R. (1975) *A Realist Theory of Science*. Leeds: Leeds Books.

Bryman, A. (2001) *Social Research Methods*. Oxford: Oxford University Press.

Connell, J.P. and Kubish, A.C. (1998) Applying a Theories of Change Approach to the Evaluation of Comprehensive Community Initiatives: Progress, Prospects and Problems, in Fullbright-Anderson, K., Connell, J.P. and Kubish, A.C. (Eds.) *New Approaches to Evaluating Community Initiatives: Theory, Measurement and Analysis*. Washington, DC: Aspen Institute.

Farrington, D. (1998) Evaluating 'Communities That care'. *Evaluation*. 4: 2, 204–10.

Gibson, M. (1979) Therapeutic Aspects of Wilderness Programs: A Comprehensive Literature Review. *Therapeutic Recreation Journal*. Second quarter, 21–33.

Glass, G.V., McGraw, B. and Smith, M.L. (1981) *Meta-analysis in Social Research*. London: Sage.

Hattie, J. et al. (1997) Adventure Education and Outward Bound: Out-of-Class Experiences That Make a Lasting Difference. *Review of Educational Research*. 67: 1, 43–87.

Hutchinson, J., Henderson, D. and Francis, S. (2001) *Evaluation of Pilot Summer Activities for 16 Year Olds*. London: DfEE.

Mason, J. (2002) *Qualitative Researching*. London: Sage.

Nichols, G. (1998) Would You Like to Step Outside for a Moment? A Consideration of the Place of Outdoor Adventurous Activities in Programmes to Change Offending Behaviour. *Vista*. 4: 1, 37–49.

Nichols, G. (1999) Is Risk a Valuable Component of Outdoor Adventure Programmes for Young Offenders Undergoing Drug Rehabilitation? *The Journal of Youth Studies*. 2: 1, 101–16. (Reproduced in Cieslik, M. and Pollock, G. (Eds.) (2002) *Young People in Risk Society: The Restructuring of Youth Identities and Transitions in Late Modernity*. Aldershot: Ashgate Press.

Nichols, G. (2001a) A Realist Approach to Evaluating the Impact of Sports Programmes on Crime Reduction, in McPherson, G. and Reid, G. (Eds.) *Leisure and Social Inclusion, New Challenges for Policy and Provision*. Eastbourne: LSA publication no. 73.

Nichols, G. (2001b) A Review of Evaluation of Pilot Summer Activities for 16 Year Olds (Summer 2000). *Horizons*. 14: Summer, 23–5.

Nichols, G. (2001c) The Difficulties of Justifying Local Authority Sports and Leisure Programmes for Young People With Reference to an Objective of Crime Reduction. *Vista*. 6: 2, 152–63.

Nichols, G. (2001d) The Use and Limitations of Reconviction Rate Analysis to Evaluate an Outdoor Pursuits Programme for Probationers. *Vista*. 6: 3, 280–8.

Nichols, G. et al. (2000) Methodological Considerations in Evaluating Physical Activity Programmes for Young Offenders. *World Leisure and Recreation*. 42: 1, 10–7.

Pawson, R. and Tilley, N. (1997) *Realistic Evaluation*. London: Sage.

Pawson, R. and Tilley, N. (1998a) Caring Communities, Paradigms Polemics, Design Debates. *Evaluation*. 4: 1, 73–90.

Pawson, R. and Tilley, N. (1998b) Cook Book Methods and Disastrous Recipes: A Rejoinder to Farrington. *Evaluation*. 4: 2, 211–3.

Tashakkori, A. and Teddlie, C. (1998) *Mixed Methodology*. London: Sage.

Taylor, P. et al. (1999) *Demanding Physical Activity Programmes for Young Offenders Under Probation Supervision*. London: The Home Office.

Weiss, C. (1998) *Evaluation*. New Jersey: Prentice Hall.

Yin, R. (1994) *Case Study Research*. London: Sage.

5 A Model of the Process of Personal Development Through the Medium of Outdoor Adventure

Geoff Nichols

Abstract

This chapter presents a general model of the process of personal development, particularly of young people. It draws on several previous contributions to theory and research in outdoor education. It puts the use of adventurous outdoor activities in perspective; raising research questions about their value and use. Why might adventurous outdoor activities be a particularly effective medium for personal development with young people? Might they be ineffective with some? What is the nature of risk and how can it be managed to achieve the desired outcomes? How might we build on theory to design research which adds to it? A criticism of previous programme evaluations has been that they have failed to build on previous theory and research has revealed little about the process of adventure education (Barrett and Greenaway, 1995; Hattie, Marsh, Neill and Richards, 1997). Thus, if research is to start from theory, this model represents one starting point.

Introduction

Much of the material in the chapter originally appeared in the Australian Journal of Outdoor Education (Nichols, 2000a). It was qualified by the proviso that the model is concerned with adventure education which has an objective of personal growth. This is in contrast to programmes where the objective is inculcation of skills or attitudes which are required in the work place (as in outdoor management development) or the provision of a novel experience, which provides momentary satisfaction, but not personal development (as in some commercial activity holidays). Since then McDonald (1997), describing his work, mainly in one English local education authority outdoor pursuits centre between 1979 and 1991, has reminded me how important these qualifications are and how my perspective has been influenced by my own experience, especially that of working for Outward Bound in the UK between 1982 to 1987. Over the period described by McDonald the stated aims and objectives of outdoor education in the UK changed, while not necessarily taking all those who worked in it along with them. I believed that it was valuable to introduce young people to a sport which they might be inspired to take up for themselves and which I had gained so much from myself. Also that

the physical achievement, and the awareness of one's place in nature, were worthwhile objectives for their own sake. However, taking this further, I wondered what exactly it was I had gained from this type of experience, and how it could be replicated in the three week Outward Bound course (the traditional four week course had finished shortly before I joined.) I was very sympathetic to the more philosophical ideas underpinning Outward Bound which for me made it distinctive from any other similar organisation in the UK, although these ideas were articulated more in Outward Bound in the USA. Thus the model below is probably laced with my own value judgements but is built up, synthesising the contributions of Priest, Mortlock, Csikszentmihalyi, Hopkins and Putnam, and other writers on adventure education.

Priest's adventure experience paradigm

A model of the adventure experience paradigm was developed by Priest (1991) building on Mortlock's (1984) four stages of adventure (Figure 1).

This shows a subjective perception of the juxtaposition of risk and competence that is

Figure 1   The adventure experience paradigm (AEP) showing a realignment of perceived risk and competence (Priest, 1991)

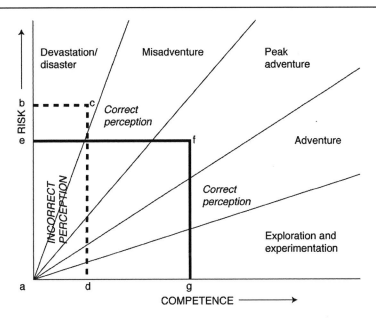

situation specific. For example; a novice canoeist on a grade five rapid might feel they were in the zone of disaster, but for an experienced canoeist the same rapid might merely represent an adventure. In contrast, if the novice canoeist happened to be an expert rock climber tackling a top grade of climb this might place them in the adventure zone. Thus the position of the 'correct perception' will vary between participants and situations.

Priest uses the AEP model to illustrate how facilitated experiences can help the participant more accurately relate risk to competence. A timid participant may have an incorrect perception of risk as too high and competence as too low, as in figure one (area a, b, c, d). By a 'facilitated adventure experience' (Priest, 1991: 159) they can be led through their own perceived misadventure zone, and possibly disaster zone, and shown that they can achieve more than they thought they could. Thus their perception of the balance of risk and competence moves towards the correct one; or at least the correct one as perceived by the facilitator (area a, e, f, g).

Thus for Priest the purpose of adventure education appears to be to help people move to a more correct perception of their own risk and competence balance. Presumably this could be

applied to the overconfident as well as the timid. For Priest the purpose of adventure education, as illustrated by the AEP, does not appear to be to help people grow, to expand their capabilities; rather to give them a more realistic view of what they are.

The theoretical contribution of Hopkins and Putnam

Mortlock and Priest's ideas were incorporated by Hopkins and Putnam (1993) into their understanding of the process of personal growth through adventure. As in Priest and Gass's (1997) work this understanding extended the range of risks to the emotional and the social (discussed by Ringer, 1995; 1997), but in contrast to Priest, the emphasis is on growth and development. Hopkins and Putnam's model incorporated the Kolb learning cycle of doing, reviewing and taking on the next challenge (Putnam, 1985). The experiential learning cycle might more realistically be regarded as an upward spiral as it involved increasing challenges and capabilities (Barnes, 1997). It should be noted that Kolb's concept was based on psychomotor learning of a rote skill and its validity in transferring learning to other domains, and Barnes's spiral, are conceptual tools rather than empirically tested processes (Loynes, 1998).

The words *learning cycle* may be misleading here. Rather, referring back to the outcomes of the process – strongly supported by previous research reviews (Ewert, 1983; Barrett and Greenaway, 1995; Hattie et al., 1997) – we can think of an individual increasing in self-esteem, cognitive competencies, locus of control, and possibly physical fitness all in parallel. For Hattie et al. (1997: 66–7) Outward Bound (by which he meant courses run by the Outward Bound organisation) 'stimulates the development of interpersonal competence', and 'in the self-concept domain has greatest effect on independence, confidence, self-efficacy, and self-understanding'. Barrett and Greenaway (1995: 50) conclude that 'improvements caused by some applications of outdoor adventure in dimensions of self-concept, locus of control and in socialisation with peers and adults are likely to contribute to the process of healthy adolescent development'. A link with criminology is that socialisation with peers, interpersonal competence, and self-understanding could all be regarded as part of the cognitive competencies observed by Ross and Fabiano (1985) in their studies of programmes for offenders and which have strongly influenced rehabilitation programmes in the UK (Rose, 2002).

Increases in capability, confidence, and an increase in the individual's ability to make judgements about experiences they can cope with all allow the individual to be presented with more demanding experiences, or after the adventure education programme, to choose to take on more difficult challenges. Thus the *learning cycle* is concerned with personal growth from new experiences, in the broadest sense.

An illustration of this process is taken from the author's evaluation of a sports counselling programme (Nichols and Taylor, 1996: 83). Prior to the programme the participant had been involved in the care system, and petty crime from age 14 to 17. At 16 he had left home and, partly due to extreme financial difficulties, had become involved in more serious crime, resulting in periods of probation. Following the twelve week long sports counselling programme, this participant had attended courses in nutrition, sports injuries and a Football Association Leaders' Award. These courses were also attended by the sports leader from the counselling programme, who offered guidance and support. The participant then, from his own initiative, started voluntary work in a nursing home for the elderly and then at a youth club. At the youth club the youth leader had encouraged him to take a course in youth work, which he was doing at the time of the research. One can see how self-esteem, confidence, cognitive competencies and locus of control have developed in parallel, allowing the participant to move through more demanding experiences and finally take charge of their own development. This process has had to be sensitively guided by initially the sports leader from the counselling programme, and later, encouraged by the youth worker.

This example, although from a case study of the use of sport in rehabilitation of offenders, is used because it illustrates the process of long-term personal growth, guided by mentors, through incremental stages. The same principles apply to a three week Outward Bound course in the UK. In this a group would be guided through a succession of more challenging experiences as their capabilities grew. Another UK provider, Fairbridge, is able to extend the period of support and development over as much as two years, through working in the participants' home environment. This may be useful with the disadvantaged and disaffected youth targeted by this organisation, although this is a research question.

Mortlock, Hopkins and Putnam (1993) believed personal growth required the facilitated progression through ever more demanding experiences and was not just incremental but transformed the individual's view of themselves and the world (Putnam, 1985). Putnam understood a strength of outdoor adventure to be its catalytic effect on personal growth. The main outcome of the process was a transformed self concept, reflected in this quote from a student. 'All through my life everything I do will somehow be related to these three weeks . . . we have so much in ourselves and yet we use so little' (Putnam, 1985: 6).

Hopkins and Putnam (1993) understood taking risks on the adventure education programme as a metaphor for the rest of life (Bacon, 1983), in the sense that taking apparent risks in the process of adventure education would inculcate an approach to risk taking that is part of accepting responsibility for one's own growth after the adventure education programme (Hunt, 1991; Nichols, 2000b). The extent to which a metaphorical transfer of approaches to learning in different situations occurs; or to which any of the experiences on a course provide a metaphor for the rest of life: is one of the research questions arising from this model. So is the role of risk.

The relevance of Csikszentmihalyi's concept of flow

Priest's model, and that of Hopkins and Putnam, can be related to Csikszentmihalyi's (1992; 1991; 1975) concept of flow illustrated below. This helps to show how Priest's AEP model can be adapted to take account of personal growth in the way described by Hopkins and Putnam, both during and after adventure education programmes.

The concept of flow was developed through a study of rock climbers, artists, chess players, surgeons and dancers (Csikszentmihalyi, 1975). Flow is a subjective state of mind in which 'The many ambiguities of everyday life are banished' (Csikszentmihalyi, 1991: 150) because goals and means are logically ordered. There is a merging of action and awareness, and the experience is intrinsically rewarding.

As Figure 2 illustrates, flow could occur at any level along a continuum, although at different degrees. Priest and Gass (1997: 44) relate this to the novice paddler on flat water (position A) or the expert in white water (position C). The flow model shows that for progress to be made up the flow continuum the individual may take on a new level of challenge that will stretch their capabilities. For example, an individual with a perceived capability at level A in the diagram might be presented with a challenge at level B. As a result of tackling that challenge successfully they realise that their capabilities are actually at level C. This may occur just because they did not realise their original potential; as in Priest's realignment of perceived and actual risk and competence or, as in the personal growth model, it may occur because they raise their skill level to cope with the new level of challenge. In whichever case they are temporarily in the zone of anxiety and perceived risk, which in Priest's model would be defined as

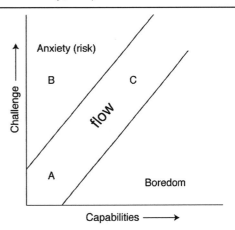

Figure 2 Csikszentmihalyi's concept of flow (Csikszentmihalyi, 1975)

misadventure. Progress up the flow continuum may occur through increased self-confidence, and increased skills. Such progress will involve an increasingly internalised locus of control. This will allow the participant to achieve flow at a higher level.

An interesting implication is that through symbolic restructuring of information it is theoretically possible for an individual to construct any situation in such a way that flow can be achieved. Csikszentmihalyi believed that learning to do this was important because in an ever more complex life, flow experiences could give people a sense of control. Again this raises the question of the extent to which experiences in adventure education or use of the outdoor environment can act as a metaphor: in this instance illustrating the value of a positive approach to perceived difficulties, seeing them as opportunities rather than problems.

A synthesis of theoretical approaches to adventure education

Priest's AEP model can be developed to incorporate a move up Csikszentmihalyi's flow continuum, representing personal growth (Figure 3).

By increasing competence, a participant could expand the range of risks that they perceived fell within their peak adventure zone. For example, a rock climber could develop skills, strength and mental application such that they could confidently attempt harder climbs and cope with

Figure 3   An extension of Priest's adventure experience paradigm

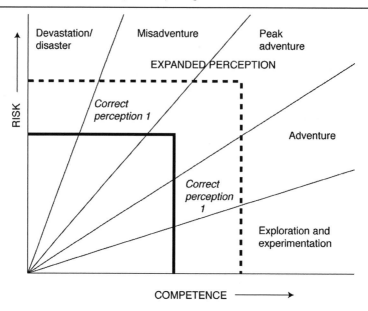

situations of greater objective danger. This is represented in Figure 3 by a shift from correct perception 1 to the expanded perception. This is consistent with Mortlock's (1984: 40) model of adventure education in which, through acquisition of skills and experience the participant can place oneself, 'on the edge of one's life, where all your experiences and abilities are being taxed to their utmost'. They are in flow at a higher level. In terms of Hopkins and Putnam's model, and assuming the metaphorical transfer of experience, an individual could 'grow' in many dimensions, not just physical skills. This would give them the confidence to take on a wide range of more difficult situations.

The importance of values in the process of personal growth

Flow theory has been criticised as failing to distinguish between good and bad states of flow (Mason, 1999). For example, it would fail to distinguish between people involved in violent crime, ecologically damaging activity, or voluntary work helping disabled children. Secondly, its attainment is confined to the satisfaction of needs. 'There is nothing in flow theory which enables one to articulate the ethical ideal of attention to values which are separate from, or transcend, the

satisfaction of needs' (Mason, 1999: 236). A crucial component of personal growth through adventure is the values that underpin it and give it direction. One of these is the value judgement that individuals should strive for personal growth. Growth itself is not value neutral (Nichols, 2000c). Values may vary between programmes and are not always made explicit. A similar criticism has been made of the goal of increasing self-esteem (Emler, 2001; Nichols, 2002). It might not necessarily result in the desired outcome.

The values of the programme staff, as role models and mentors, are influential in directing personal growth. This was apparent in the author's evaluation of a sports counselling programme (Nichols and Taylor, 1996) and in more recent research into programmes run by UK Probation Services (Taylor, et al. 1999: 42). Programme managers consistently reported that high quality staff was essential, and in assessing the quality of staff they put much more emphasis on the values they portrayed than technical skills. Again, these examples are not taken from programmes necessarily using outdoor activities as a medium, and are from programmes for particular types of participant. However, the principle of the importance of values is generally transferable to any programme with the objective of personal growth.

Conclusion on the process of adventure education

From the models above it can be concluded that adventure education is essentially an adventure into oneself; a redefinition of self-identity; in which the traditional 'adventure activities' or use of the outdoors, may, or may not, provide an effective catalyst and metaphor. Gains in self-esteem, a set of personal and social skills represented by cognitive competencies, and possibly physical fitness will enable an individual to achieve this. As a result, their perceived locus of control increases, meaning they are both willing and able to be more proactive. They are more prepared to take charge of their own lives. But the process of adventure education is not value neutral. The process is most relevant to young people as they are at the most formative stage of development of self-identity (Hendry, et al. 1993), but could be applicable to any age. The model implies that a set of 'success factors' will help a programme be successful. These include:

- A clear set of values associated with the activity leaders and the ethos of the programme. These values are pro-social.
- The ability to adapt a programme to individual participants' needs.
- The ability to offer long term-follow up (18 months to two years) and viable exit routes where the participant can become involved in activity and further opportunities for development and taking responsibility independent of the original programme.
- Sensitivity of staff in matching a progression of activities to participants' needs and development.
- The use of rewards of achievement, which will enhance self-esteem.
- A good relationship between participants and activity leaders; leaders taking a mentoring role.

The model above is concerned with personal development of young people in general. It has much in common with theory of youth work (Huskins, 1996; 1998) and criminological theory which has advocated countering 'risk factors' with 'protection factors' (Catalano and Hawkins, 1996). While it draws on contributions from adventure education using outdoor activities, these activities may not be a necessary component of the process.

Some research questions

The model above helps to formulate research questions; some of which are outlined below. These questions are all focussed on the use of outdoor activities. It would also be possible to construct a set of questions focussed specifically on young people at risk, or more generally, on development work with young people. The focus on outdoor activities is taken because the main purpose of the piece has been to draw together theory from this area; e.g. Mortlock, Priest, Hopkins and Putnam, etc. and provide a platform for further research.

The role of outdoor activities

What is the role of outdoor activities in the process of development of young people? Is it an effective catalyst to increasing self-esteem, social and personal skills? Dunbar's research (2000) involving an evaluation of the impact of five day courses run at Outward Bound Loch Eil as part of North Lanarkshire Council Education Department's initiative designed to encourage personal and social development in young people, examines this. Is it a catalyst for developing relations with mentors? Do outdoor activities provide effective metaphors for the rest of life (Bacon, 1983) and if so, are these developed consciously by activity leaders? In relation to risk, does the outdoors provide a particular metaphor for an approach to life that accepts risk as valuable for its own sake (Nichols, 2000b)?

Can outdoor activities be a greater catalyst than other experiences, such as sport in general (Nichols, 1997) or art, and therefore have greater potential to contribute to the transformed growth described by Hopkins and Putnam? Does the outdoor environment make a particular contribution to spirituality? Some, drawing on their own experiences (for example, Murray, 1982) or on the experiences of races in close touch with nature, (McLuhan, 1982) would claim this; or are such experiences equally accessible in all areas of life?

Does the outdoor environment make a particular contribution to other values, such as care for the environment? Or could this equally well be achieved in a city park, with less damage to the more open environments used by 'outdoor centres'?

Who benefits?

Is the outdoor environment better for some types of participants than others? Criminologists have suggested that a more active environment such as provided by outdoor activities is the best learning setting for many young people and that any programme must have sufficiently attractive activities to initially engage young people (Taylor, et al. 1999). On the other hand, as Huskins (1998) suggests, it may be less useful for young people who initially require a build up of trust and confidence. For those with low confidence in their physical abilities it may require great sensitivity to allow them to benefit from it (Nichols, 1999).

Is there an inherent gender bias in adventure education and how should this be overcome (Humberstone, 1994, 2000; Richards, 1999)? What is the potential for adventure education to dispel gender stereotypes? How can leaders be trained to do this (Woodward, 2000)? Could the potential for failure in outdoor activities be a threat to the masculinity of some young males (Nichols, 1999). Conversely, could success support their masculine self-image?

A progression of responsibility

How can outdoor activities best contribute to a progression of responsibility? This can be achieved by progressive training in outdoor pursuits, but is made more difficult in this medium because of the few opportunities for progressive experiences over a long period of time, increasing safety regulations, and society's increasing risk aversion where young people and outdoor activities are concerned. In relation to my experience working in UK Outward Bound in the 1980s, the three week courses allowed students to progress to planning and executing their own expeditions, but these could only be unaccompanied by staff in the Lake District and Wales, not in Scotland where the objective dangers were greater. To use an example from youth work (Huskins, 1998), it would be easier for a young person to demonstrate progression by organising catering services in their own youth club. It may well be possible for participants to gain more from a longer term progression of experiences in their home environment, such as that offered by the Fairbridge programme in the

UK. In this case, what is the best way of using an outdoor based course in this progression? Might it be more effective for some young people as one component of a long-term progression of experiences based in their home environment; as is the case in Fairbridge courses or some run by Brathay?

Benefits of physical activity

Are there any particular benefits of the physical activity involved in outdoor activities? Kurt Hahn, in the 1940's was reportedly obsessed with a set of social declines (Richards, 1991) which included a decline of fitness. There are health benefits of increasing physical fitness, and increased fitness has been related to increased self-esteem, but fitness levels have to be maintained by regular exercise. Unless the amount of exercise involved in most outdoor activities becomes a regular part of someone's life it will not confer these benefits. The question then is does 'one off' physical exertion during such activities detract from the potential learning or enhance it?

Differences between practitioners

How do different groups of practitioners themselves view the contribution of outdoor activities to their work with young people? Do the value judgements they hold determine the way they use these activities, and does this help or hinder their work?

Conclusion

The detailed model of the process of adventure education has provided a framework which can overcome the major criticism of research in this area – that it has failed to build on the understandings of previous work (Ewert, 1983; Barrett and Greenaway, 1995). Secondly, it allows many individual research projects to be linked in a complementary manner. However, it challenges some assumptions and helps frame questions. In particular it questions the assertion that all young people should have the opportunity to take part in adventurous outdoor activities – a recommendation of the Hunt (1989) report. If the main purpose is personal development, outdoor activities will be a wonderful medium for some young people and an effective catalyst, but may not be a general panacea. We need to know what works best for which type of young person (and older ones) in which circumstances. A better appreciation of the process will guide good practice.

References

Bacon, S. (1983) *The Conscious Use of Metaphor in Outward Bound*. Denver, CO: Outward Bound School.

Barnes, P. (1997) *Theory Into Practice, The Complete Practical Theory of Outdoor Education and Personal Development*. Glasgow: Faculty of Education, University of Strathclyde.

Barrett, J. and Greenaway, R. (1995) *Why Adventure?* Coventry: Foundation for Outdoor Adventure.

Catalano, R. and Hawkins, J.D. (1996) The Social Development Model: A Theory of Antisocial Behaviour, in Hawkins, J. D. (Ed.) *Delinquency and Crime*. Cambridge: Cambridge University Press.

Csikszentmihalyi, M. (1975) *Beyond Boredom and Anxiety*. San Francisco: Jessey-Bass.

Csikszentmihalyi, M. and Csikszentmihalyi, I. (1991) Adventure and the Flow Experience, in Miles, J. and Priest, S. (Eds.) *Adventure Education*. PA: Venture Publishing. State College.

Csikszentmihalyi, M. and Csikszentmihalyi, I. (1992) *Optimal Experience: Psychological Studies of Flow in Consciousness*. Cambridge: Cambridge University Press.

Dunbar, B. (2000) *Raising Achievement Through Outward Bound; A Study of The Effect of an Outdoor Education Programme on Pupil's Self Perception*. Unpublished Paper Presented at Sheffield University Research Forum, 29th October.

Emler, N. (2001) *Self-Esteem, The Costs and Causes of Low Self-Worth*. York: Joseph Rowntree Foundation.

Ewert, A. (1983) *Outdoor Adventure and Self-Concept: A Research Analysis*. Oregon: University of Oregon, Centre of Leisure Studies.

Hattie, J. et al. (1997) Adventure Education and Outward Bound: Out-Of-Class Experiences That Make A Lasting Difference. *Review of Educational Research*. 67: 1, 43–87.

Hendry, L.B. et al. (1993) *Young People's Leisure and Lifestyles*. London: Routledge.

Hopkins, D. and Putnam, R. (1993) *Personal Growth Through Adventure*. London: David Fulton.

Humberstone, B. (2000) Editor's Introduction, in Humberstone, B. (Ed.). *Her Outdoor: Risk, Challenge and Adventure in Gendered Open Spaces*. Eastbourne: Leisure Studies Association.

Humberstone, B. (1994) Equality of Access in the Outdoor World. *Journal of Adventure Education and Outdoor Leadership*. 11: 4, 26–7.

Hunt, J. (1989) *In Search of Adventure*. Guildford: Talbot Adair Press.

Hunt, J.S. (1991) Philosophy of Adventure Education, in Miles, J. and Priest, S. (Eds.) *Adventure Education*. PA: Venture Publishing. State College.

Huskins, J. (1996) *Quality Work With Young People*. London: Youth Clubs UK.

Huskins, J. (1998) *From Disaffection to Social Inclusion*. Kingsdown: Huskins.

Loynes, C. (1998) Personal Communication.

Mason, S. (1999) Feminist Ethics of Leisure. *Leisure Studies*. 18: 3, 233–48.

Mcdonald, P. (1997) *Climbing Lessons: Inside Outdoor Education*. Northland, New Zealand: Pete Mcdonald.

Mcluhan, T.C. (1982) *Touch The Earth*. London: Abacus.

Mortlock, C. (1984) *The Adventure Alternative*. Milnthorpe: Cicerone Press.

Murray, W.H. (1982) *Mountaineering in Scotland, Undiscovered Scotland*. Kings Lynn: Dent.

Nichols, G. (1997) A Consideration of Why Active Participation in Sport and Leisure Might Reduce Criminal Behaviour. *Sport Education and Society*. 2: 2, 181–90.

Nichols, G. (1999) Is Risk a Valuable Component of Outdoor Adventure Programmes for Young Offenders Undergoing Drug Rehabilitation? *The Journal of Youth Studies*. 2: 1, 101–16.

Nichols, G. (2000a) A Research Agenda for Adventure Education. *Australian Journal of Outdoor Education*. 4: 2, 22–31.

Nichols, G. (2000b) Risk and Adventure Education. *Journal of Risk Research*. 3: 2, 121–34.

Nichols, G. (2000c) What is Development Training?, in Barnes, P. (Ed.) *Values and Outdoor Learning*. Penrith: AFOL.

Nichols, G. (2002) Self-Esteem: What is it, Why is it Important, and Implications for Outdoor Education. *Horizons.* 17, Spring, 34–6.

Nichols, G. and Taylor, P. (1996) *West Yorkshire Sports Counselling, Final Evaluation Report.* Castleford: West Yorkshire Sports Counselling Association.

Putnam, R. (1985) *A Rationale for Outward Bound.* Rugby: Outward Bound Trust.

Priest, S. (1991) The Adventure Experience Paradigm, in Miles, J. and Priest, S. (Eds.) *Adventure Education.* PA: Venture Publishing. State College.

Priest, S. and Gass, M. (1997) *Effective Leadership in Adventure Programming.* New Hampshire: Human Kinetics.

Richards, A. (1991) Kurt Hahn, in Miles, J. and Priest, S. (Eds.) *Adventure Education.* PA: Venture Publishing, State College.

Richards, K. (1999) Learning Curve. *Horizons.* 3: 23–5.

Ringer, M. and Gillis, H.L. (1995) Managing Psychological Depth in Adventure Programming. *Journal of Experiential Education.* 18: 1, 41–51.

Ringer, M. and Spanoghe, F. (1997) Can't He See Me Crying Inside? Managing Psychological Risk in Adventure Programmes. *Zip Lines.* Summer, 41–5.

Rose, D. (2002). It's Official: Prison Does Work After All. *The Observer.* 5th May: 20–1.

Ross, R. and Fabiano, E. (1985) *Time to Think: A Cognitive Model of Delinquency Prevention and Offender Rehabilitation.* Ottawa: T3 Associates.

Taylor, P. et al. (1999) *Demanding Physical Activity Programmes for Young Offenders Under Probation Supervision.* London: Home Office.

Woodward, V. (2000) Gender Issues and Women's Windsurfing, in Humberstone, B. (Ed.) *Her Outdoors, Risk, Challenge and Adventure in Gendered Open Spaces.* Eastbourne: Leisure Studies Association.

Section 2:
The Users of Outdoor Education

6   Working with Young People

Steve Lenartowicz

Abstract

There is a very wide spectrum of work with young people in the outdoors. For example, the aims of a particular programme might be recreational, diversionary, educational, developmental or therapeutic. Activities range from problem solving activities to ropes courses, environmental arts, outdoor adventure sports and self-sufficient expeditions in remote areas. This paper focuses on some of the general issues of working in the outdoors with adolescents from a developmental perspective. It considers the key developmental tasks of adolescence and shows that outdoor education can make a powerful contribution to achieving them, using the concepts of empowerment and choice. Ultimately, it is argued that outdoor developmental youth work is well placed to play a central role in the type of educational system which we need in order to meet the needs of young people and society.

The challenges of adolescence

During the period of adolescence, as they undergo the transition from childhood to adulthood, young people face a number of challenges. Malekoff (1997) identifies four key 'developmental tasks' which young people need to fulfil in order to become healthy, functioning adults. Firstly, adolescents need to achieve emotional and practical independence from their family, parents and other adults in authority, and instead to build appropriate relationships with their peers. Secondly, they must adopt a healthy sexual identity, learning about and accepting their bodies and achieving a masculine or feminine social role. Thirdly, they have to develop a range of skills that will enable them to have successful relationships and a successful working and economic life. Fourthly, they must develop their own system of values that will enable them to live as socially responsible adults.

In simple terms, the challenge of adolescence can be seen as the need for young people to make the transition from dependence to independence. The key process involved is one of empowerment – helping young people to gain the values, attitudes and skills that will enable them to function as independent adults. However, individual empowerment is not sufficient. Growing up is also a process of becoming responsible members of a society. This requires young people to gain an understanding of their interdependence with other people and the natural and cultural world in which they live. True empowerment recognises this. We do young people no favours if we do not help them to recognise their social and environmental responsibilities as well as equipping them with the tools to be independent.

The outdoors and social skills development

Group work in the outdoors is a particularly powerful means of helping young people to make this transition. The immediacy and reality of outdoor situations mean that there are often real consequences to actions. Many young people relish the physical challenges inherent in certain activities and gain much in terms of self-esteem and self-confidence from the sense of achievement of a challenging task successfully completed. The idea of challenge, risk and adventure as central themes in outdoor education are discussed elsewhere in this book and have been analysed by authors such as Mortlock (1984) and Hopkins and Putnam (1993). Intense enjoyable experiences in the outdoors can help to develop a sense of connection with the natural world. However, in order for such activities to be truly effective in helping the process of empowerment, it is essential that there is a progression in terms of responsibility and social skills as well as activity skills.

Huskins (1996) presents a model which describes seven stages of participation in decision-making by young people, culminating in the adult leadership role where young people take full responsibility and control over their actions, having achieved independence. The youth worker initially builds a relationship with young people by essentially running activities for them. By facilitating a progressive participation in decision-making, the youth worker moves the young people through a series of stages. This begins with doing things with them and leads on to activities being run by them. Eventually this reaches the stage of full responsibility where young people are leading and are engaged in peer education, where the youth worker is no longer needed and activities happen through the young people. Huskins (1996: 18) links this progression to the development of a set of ten social skills:

- Self-awareness and self-esteem (how you feel about yourself).
- Communication skills (communicate effectively).
- Interpersonal skills (getting on with others).
- Explore and manage feelings (aware of, and open about, feelings).
- Understand and identify with others (feel as others do).
- Values development (what is right and wrong).
- Problem solving (solving problems).
- Negotiation skills (agreeing decisions with others).
- Action planning (planning ahead).
- Reviewing skills (learning from experience).

Such progression can be understood on a long-term scale over the whole period of adolescence, but it can also be a useful model for programme design on a small scale. For example, a week's outdoor course might build gradually towards an independent project where young people have the opportunity to put into practice the practical and social skills that they have developed during the week.

Experiential learning

For many young people, it can be very motivating and rewarding to learn the skills of an outdoor activity. The process of mastery of an activity can be a very effective way of gaining self-esteem, confidence, responsibility and other personal and social skills as well as possibly providing the beginning of a lifetime's interest (Higgins, 2002). However, much youth development work in the outdoors does not set out to introduce young

people to the skills of an activity. Rather, it uses a range of activities as a means of providing groups of young people with the opportunity of having stretching and engaging experiences which can be a source of learning and where the activity itself is secondary to the developmental aims. Whether or not the learning of activity skills is part of the focus, it is important for effective personal and social development that young people are encouraged to reflect upon their experiences in order to understand their feelings and actions, and those of others. Such an experiential approach (Kolb, 1984) often uses structured reviews and peer feedback as part of the learning process.

The facilitation of the process of empowerment is an important skill for outdoor leaders working with youth groups. Heron (1999) sees this as a political aspect of the leader's role. He describes three modes in which a leader can make decisions about working with a group – by making the decision alone; by making it in co-operation with the group; or by allowing the group to make the decision. In managing a learning activity, there are a number of elements and each of these can be managed in one of the three modes. Three important elements in a learning activity are the activity itself, the group process involved in undertaking the activity and the process of learning from the experience of the activity. For example, the activity might be a canoe journey on a lake. The group process might include the resolution of tensions caused by the range of physical abilities and motivation in the group. The process of learning from the experience might include a post-activity review during which the young people consider what they have achieved and what they could learn from what happened. Table 1 summarises the interaction of these elements with the three modes.

In the example given in Table 1, the leader negotiates with the group about what task they do, and together they decide to go canoeing. Responsibility for how the members of the group work together to achieve the task is given entirely to the group and the role of the leader is to shadow the group at a distance and only to intervene for safety purposes. However, the review of the experience in order to draw learning from it is directed by the leader. There are also higher levels of decision-making, for example, deciding which mode is used is a decision in itself, which

Table 1   Decision-making modes about elements of a learning event (after Heron)

	Decision-making mode		
Element of the learning event	**Hierarchy: Leader directs the group**	**Co-operation: Leader negotiates with the group**	**Autonomy: Leader delegates to the group**
Activity: What task will we do?		Leader and group together decide to go canoeing	
Group process: How will we work together?			Group is entirely responsible for how they work together during the trip
Learning process: How will we learn from this?	Leader directs the post-activity review and summarises the learning		

can be made using any one of the three modes. A programme designed to provide a progression towards empowerment will gradually move the locus of control from left to right in Table 1 in all three elements. A skilled leader will always be aware of what decision-making mode they are operating in and will be looking for opportunities to move from a hierarchical mode towards co-operation and group autonomy. Of course, there will be occasions when the demands of safety and other considerations mean that the leader will have to take back authority in certain circumstances.

Challenge, risk and choice

Because of public concerns about the risks involved in outdoor activities, outdoor leaders these days are generally well trained in the management of physical safety. It is also important that they are well versed in the management of emotional safety. Young people and leaders can be particularly vulnerable in the kind of situations they encounter in outdoor work. It is therefore vital that leaders are also well trained in the principles of child protection, and are aware of accepted standards of professional and ethical practice.

If the ultimate aim of our work is empowerment then coercion must be its antithesis. Choice is therefore a key issue when working with young people in the outdoors. Educational philosophers from Aristotle to Dewey and Rogers have argued that choice is a fundamental prerequisite for

learning and development. Others though, including Plato and Hahn, have made the case for impelling young people into experiences in order to provide them with opportunities for development (Lenartowicz, 2001). There is thus a tension in the outdoor education world between the two points of view – of 'challenge by choice' and of 'impelling into experience'. This can be resolved by emphasising and nurturing the trust and support in a group situation that enables young people to choose to accept challenges which they would have felt to be impossible without the trust in and support of their peers. Relationships are thus at the centre of outdoor work, and indeed of all youth work. In practice, the issue of choice is often not clear-cut. For example, in some cases young people may have been required to attend a course, perhaps by an employer or as part of a school programme, and so any choice offered by a leader may be within a context of compulsion. Peer pressure may strongly influence the ability to make free choice. It is also often difficult to distinguish between responsible encouragement of a young person who believes that they are not capable of a particular challenge, and irresponsible coercion of one who decides assertively not to accept the challenge. The choice of saying 'no' to a challenge, and being supported in that choice, can be a powerful positive experience for a young person who has experienced abuse. The facilitation of such situations, and the management of the emotional safety of the young people involved, is an essential skill for outdoor leaders.

Choice is not simply about the decision whether or not to participate in an activity. Young people can also be encouraged to make choices about the nature of participation and about the level of challenge or 'stretch' they feel willing or able to accept in an activity. Experience, review and feedback can help them to understand where they gain the most satisfaction and learning and to make judgements based on their growing awareness of and ability to express their feelings of, for example, trust and fear. In a similar way, outdoor activities give an ideal opportunity for young people to learn to assess and manage risk. There is some evidence that working with risk in this way can help young people to make positive decisions about risky behaviours such as drug-taking, though this is an area which requires highly skilled intervention (Nichols, 1999).

The central place of empowerment in youth work also requires that activities are selected in which young people can exercise control. This will often mean that activities requiring a relatively low level of technical competence and having a low level of real risk are most appropriate, rather than activities which require young people to be totally dependant on their leaders. Ideally, young people will have the opportunity to develop their skills so that they are able to take on more challenging activities.

Transitions and rites of passage

There are parallels between outdoor experiences designed to aid youth transitions, and traditional rites of passage and initiation. Maddern (1998) argues that many traditional societies evolved ways of helping young people to cope with the stresses and strains of reaching maturity and that these have been lost in the complexity of modern society. He identifies five components of such initiations: the symbolic journey; the challenge; the vision; responsibility; community participation – and suggests that the whole curriculum for 13 to 18 year olds could be based on this process. Interestingly, in recent years there has been a growing interest in educational policy in key transitions, such as from primary to secondary school, and at the end of compulsory education. The largest-ever government funded programme

in the UK involving the outdoors is a programme of summer activities for 16 year olds which targets those young people least likely to make a positive transition at this stage.

Outdoor education and the mainstream

In the UK, the government has identified three key issues which underlie its educational policy. These are social inclusion, citizenship and employability. It has become clear from a range of studies in all three of these areas that there is a common theme underlying them all. If young people are to grow up as responsible active citizens who feel a connection with society and who have the skills necessary to succeed, then they need to develop a range of personal attributes and social skills, similar to those defined above by Huskins. This has been recognised in recent policy documents which call for the development of 'Education with Character'. However, it is increasingly apparent that these needs cannot be effectively met in the classroom.

As Bentley (2001) points out, there are a number of paradoxes that affect our young people. The first paradox is that young people are now confronted with an unprecedented range of choices, riches and dangers and find it difficult to make them into a coherent and purposeful whole. The second paradox is that we want young people to be entrepreneurial and self-reliant, which involve considered risk-taking, but we continually attempt to protect them by eliminating risk from their lives. The third paradox is that the more resources we put into the education system the harder it appears to become to achieve the results we want; and the more young people appear to become disaffected. Bentley argues that the solution is to fundamentally re-think our education system so that it values and uses a much wider range of contexts for learning and removes the distinction between school as a place that learning occurs and the rest of life. The system needs to become more experiential, providing young people with a range of experiences and opportunities to reflect upon them and to use failure as an opportunity for learning. It needs to encourage creativity and innovation, and to make sure that it involves young people in making decisions. Clearly there is an opportunity here for outdoor education, based on a developmental perspective as outlined above, to make a significant contribution to addressing the concerns of society about young people.

Conclusion

The needs of young people in adolescence outlined above are normal and are common to all young people. Of course, many young people also have particular needs due to their personal circumstances or social environment. They may be unemployed or homeless, they may be carers of siblings or parents, they may be travellers or from minority ethnic groups, they may be disaffected or offenders, they may be affected by drugs, abuse, crime, mental health problems, physical disabilities or learning difficulties. Outdoor youth work is often used to address the needs of such young people, and indeed many funding streams are available for working with this kind of group. While such work, in the hands of sensitive and experienced leaders, can often be extraordinarily effective, it must not be forgotten that developmental outdoor youth work is a very powerful means of helping all young people to achieve their potential as adult human beings.

References

Bentley, T. (2001) Learning Beyond the Classroom, in *Transitions: Experiential Learning and the Process of Change* (Conference Report). Ambleside: Brathay Hall Trust.

Heron, J. (1999) *The Complete Facilitator's Handbook*. London: Kogan Page.

Higgins, P. (2002) *Learning As Adventure: Theory for Practice: The Summer Activities for 16 Year-Olds Scheme*. Edinburgh: University of Edinburgh.

Hopkins, D. and Putnam, R. (1993) *Personal Growth Through Adventure*. London: David Fulton.

Huskins, J. (1996) *Quality Work With Young People.* Bristol: Youth Clubs UK.

Kolb, D. (1984) *Experiential Learning*. New Jersey: Prentice Hall.

Lenartowicz, S. (2001) *The Philosophy of Development Training.* Ambleside: Brathay Hall Trust.

Maddern, E (1998) *A Vision for a New Education.* Gwynedd: Cae Mabon.

Malekoff, A. (1997) *Group Work With Adolescents.* New York: The Guildford Press.

Mortlock, C. (1984) *The Adventure Alternative*. Milnthorpe: Cicerone Press.

Nichols, G. (1999) Is Risk a Valuable Component of Outdoor Adventure Programmes for Young Offenders Undergoing Drug Rehabilitation? *Journal of Youth Studies*. 2: 1, 101–15.

7 Towards a Philosophy and Understanding of Working with Special Needs Students

Phil Woodyer and Peter Barnes

Abstract

Like so much in the outdoors any discussion regarding working with students with special needs falls neatly into two parts; the philosophical and the practical. This is reflected in the structure of this chapter, which first examines a philosophy and investigates our understanding of the benefits of outdoor education for groups with special needs. The second part of the chapter gives some examples of the contrasting demands made on the instructor who chooses to work with special needs students.

Introduction

How does outdoor education benefit those with disabilities and/or special needs? Does it have value for them? Do we assume that there is some intrinsic worth that carries through into all areas of outdoor education? Do the leaders and the carers take responsibility for informing us that it is worthwhile? Do we take their world as the experts? Have they thought it through? If we are not the carers can we, as outdoor leaders, interpret the reactions of those with limited communication abilities? Sally, for example, had no use of her limbs and her head was floppy; to do an abseil she had to have complete support. Although she found it difficult to communicate, she had a big smile and when she had done the abseil once, she smiled at the suggestion that she should do it again. She smiled when she came the following year and did the abseil again. But was she reacting to the experience or just to the instructor, or was it to both? In the first instance there was a look of apprehension on her face and it was only when she was about half way down that the smile appeared. In her case she was well aware of what she was doing and her trust in her carers and in the instructor had enabled her to achieve something. It is not easy to answer questions such as these. Whilst it may be easy to justify much of our work with groups with disabilities and special needs on purely emotional grounds, there are areas that perhaps need further thought. Not all the answers will be found within this chapter; indeed much of the following discussion is anecdotal and it may be that it is not even possible to measure such things; even if we wanted to.

Many of us have had occasion to ask ourselves; 'What worth has this activity for someone with no demonstrable response who cannot make their own decision about whether or not they want to be doing this thing?' What can be the justification for taking this person – down an abseil, into a cave, onto the water? There is a definite surge of energy and emotion coming from the instructor or carer transmitted towards the person with the disability when an activity/exercise is achieved; the hope is that this is somehow passed to that person. Even if the instructor sees no change in the participant, the carer will often say, 'She enjoyed that,' or, 'He really got a lot out of that.' Suppose this reaction is purely subjective and it made no difference to the person with the disability whether or not they did the activity, does it still have value? Sometimes the effect of doing something with a person with a severe disability is not immediate and cannot be judged there and then in isolation. It may be part of a series of developments, which together improve their lifestyle. It's like the person being physically helped up a rock face by someone moving their feet; are they showing a determination to succeed? It is a matter of degrees; they may be showing great determination if they are pulling as hard as they can with their hands and arms. If they cannot do this, they are still choosing to do the activity and if they can communicate a desire to do the activity again, they have made a choice based on experience and have learned to like something that they had never done before. Going up or down a vertical wall is a different experience and it may be that the person having this experience is helping themselves as much as they can because they want to get to the top or get to the bottom. Even if they are not helping themselves at all, they are experiencing the outdoors, rock face, ropes, harness and the encouragement; things that the person without a disability or special need would also experience. To what extent they are experiencing or to what extent it may positively enrich their lives we may never know, but we may never know this about any of the people we encourage into the outdoors.

Benefits

So what are the benefits or positive outcomes that we might expect from working in the outdoors with special needs groups? Do they exist? What are they and do they have worth? What are the opportunities for personal development and confidence building? Are there building blocks that will lead to further developments, to more independent living? Are there opportunities to stimulate changes of behaviour or changes of attitudes? In a lot of circumstances in their everyday lives, people with special needs or physical disabilities are not encouraged to do things. Indeed, in some cases they may be actively discouraged. The reasons for this are many and varied, mainly because it is physically more difficult to accommodate a physical disability or it takes more time to explain to someone with an educational special need. It takes longer, needs more patience, may need special equipment and cannot be achieved in the normal run of things. This means that some of these people are missing out on many opportunities for personal and social development. In the setting of a course of outdoor education there is more time to spend with people and their needs. Instructors in this field tend to have more patience and be more laid back in their approach to life. To be fair, they do not have the constraints of a rigid timetable or a demanding curriculum and they are often not even too bothered about specific times for meals. This unhurried, but concentrated approach can bring out the best in those with special needs and physical disabilities.

During a residential course people can be encouraged to do more for themselves; wash up, set tables, choose the correct clothing for the activity. Even going to the local village pub and ordering a drink is something which is not so daunting in a small, friendly rural setting with plenty of positive support. One boy in his late teens when asked what he had learned that was of most benefit from his course said that he had learnt to shave himself. Formerly, his father had always shaved him but away on a residential the leaders and carers had too much to do for others and encouraged him to shave himself. This he did and could now go home a little more independent than when he arrived. This may have even changed his attitude to his father and his father's attitude to him and helped him towards more independent living.

Because outdoor education can be intense and the challenges so different from the routine of ordinary everyday life, changes can sometimes be instant and dramatic. Two good examples of this concern two elective mutes. These are people who are physically capable of speech and have spoken but for some reason have now chosen not to speak. In the first instance, about two thirds of the way through her course it was noticed that a particular student was missing from a briefing. Questions were asked, where is she? To the astonishment of all concerned she was found on the telephone talking to her mother excitedly about the course. Her mother was also shocked because normally the girl did not speak to anyone, including her. The heightened stimulus and excitement of an outdoor course had made her want to communicate again. The second instance involved a student, again an elective mute, at a climbing session in a local quarry. She had been kitted up with harness and helmet and was at the bottom of a climb belayed on a bottom belay. She was stood with her head down seemingly ignoring all the encouragement from the laid back, sympathetic instructor to coax her to climb up the rock face. After about two minutes of this coaxing she turned to the instructor and muttered her first immortal words, 'Why don't you F . . . Off?' The power of speech returned. This time it was a negative reaction but the intensity of what she was being asked to do, provoked her to speak. We do not know if this speech continued after the girl returned home but we do know that what she was doing made her speak again. Whilst some of the changes such as these brought about by an outdoor education course are dramatic, others are evolutionary and present building blocks for further development. What confidence must it give someone who may have been excluded from PE and games lessons at school to be able to abseil down a sheer rock face or to journey through a cave, a seemingly hostile environment?

A lot of participants may gain or regain the pleasure of a physical experience. None of us like to continue trying things that we conceive we are no good at or at which we always fail. Because these courses always go for a positive outcome and are about what you can do, not what you can't do, there is a lot of positive encouragement about what is achieved, no matter how little this may seem to others. Some achieve great things. Look at those who through some accident have become paraplegic and now do physical things they did not attempt when they were able-bodied. When a person's possibilities are curtailed, it can make them more positive and determined about what they can achieve. The value of sharing, helping others, being part of a group both on the activities and within the residential setting are also all part of a valuable learning experience. Could this be done elsewhere? Probably; but it would be more difficult in a more everyday, routine setting where it would be easier to discourage rather than encourage and the strictures of time would make it easier to do things for people rather than to encourage them to do things for themselves or for others.

Practical matters

Much of what is involved in outdoor leadership is generic and applies to all activities and differing groups. When working with groups who have special needs or disabilities, particular skills are required and particular knowledge of groups and individuals needed. Given that the variety of people with special needs is as great as any other group of students, a detailed discussion of practical skills is outside of the scope of this chapter. What are presented here are some examples that may serve to highlight the issues faced when working with special needs groups. Activity briefings, for example, may be meaningless to some special needs groups without special interpretation from the groups' leaders or carers. So, although the briefing may be to the whole group, it may only be understood by some group members or may be mainly for the benefit of the leaders. Groups with sight

impairment can vary from those with no vision to those who can see shadows or those with a limited range of vision. For these groups, the main input is through the other senses. Thus, for example, when describing equipment it is important to let the group members feel the items of equipment they may be using. Verbal instructions will be understood, but examples cannot be illustrated by looking at things. There is a tremendous amount of trust put in a leader by people who can't see, so it is important to talk in a calm and reassuring way. It is also beneficial for leaders to try activities such as abseiling, whilst wearing a blindfold so they can appreciate the amount of trust this person is putting in the leader.

Again, there may be a range of hearing loss within a group and some may be able to hear and understand a group briefing only if wearing hearing aids. It is important when talking to groups with hearing impairments for a leader to face the group so that all the individuals can see their mouth and read their lips. If the group uses sign language a signer may be next to the leader for the group briefing but it is important for a leader to communicate with group members not to the signer. It is always appreciated if the leader has some knowledge of sign language even if it is only to be able to say hello and who they are. Whenever giving instructions connected with safety it is important to emphasise points so they are fully understood and to make use of visual interpretation. This applies to any group, but it is particularly important for those with hearing impairments. It is important to set limits to areas of safe operation for these groups because they cannot be called back if they go too far. And it may be too late to run after them to stop them going into a dangerous area. It is always important to keep groups with hearing impairments in sight of the instructor or the group's leaders and carers.

Groups with learning difficulties may not always react in ways that seem logical. They may have the normal fears associated with activities like fear of heights, fear of enclosed spaces and fear of water but, in addition, they may also be afraid of the equipment or afraid of the leader. It is therefore important to be aware, sympathetic and build up the trust necessary for doing the activities together. Some students with learning difficulties may have no concept of fear. They need to be observed closely or they may do something dangerous before they have been fitted with the correct safety equipment or been given the correct briefing.

Group members with ambulant problems are well aware of all the restrictions on what they can do; this is something they do not need reminding of. What they need is encouragement and help to do as much as they can. Briefings should be positive, not negative. It may be better to sit down and discuss things with the group rather than stand over them emphasising their disability. When discussing how to do things it is important to talk or communicate with the person with the disability rather than talking over them always to the group leader.

Often, the first problem with students who have behavioural problems is the building of trust. They can be less likely to have faith in what the leader is saying. It is important to be calm and clear when giving instructions but not too authoritarian. The group members may be very unpredictable in all situations so it is important to have a high ratio of leaders or carers to individuals and to keep a close eye on group members at all times. They may put themselves in dangerous situations for illogical reasons. It is important that group leaders are in close contact with group members who are most likely to be a problem and also to try to anticipate what might be problem areas and neutralise these before they occur. It is also important to keep an eye on safety equipment that may be tampered with.

There are many other special needs that require individual special attention such as those with limbs missing, hydrocephalus, brittle bones or cystic fibrosis. In most cases, group leaders will be able to enlighten leaders on any special information required when working with these individuals. With groups or individuals that have diabetes, the session should not be too long or tiring without the opportunity to rest and eat. Only some of the individuals concerned will be able to monitor their own condition and be aware of any danger signals. Those who are prone to epilepsy will normally be controlled with drugs but leaders should be aware of any situations that could trigger a fit. This could be fatigue or stress and the leader should always be able to reach a person who is prone to epilepsy and to be able to make them safe and comfortable if they are having a fit.

There is an increasing amount of equipment that has been specially made for those with special needs. If any of this specialised equipment is being used it is important to be completely familiar with the methods for use before working with students. Sometimes specialist equipment may be inappropriate. For example, if an individual has their own specially fitting shoes it is usually better to let them wear these than to try to squeeze them into a standard boot or wellington. Apart from specialised equipment, people working with special needs groups have produced much modified and adapted equipment. For example, extra pieces of tape can be used for modifying sports equipment and outdoor gear; clothing and buoyancy aids can be used for padding and support for people sitting in boats. It is also important to make sure when fitting clothing or equipment that it is securely fastened and not uncomfortable or likely to rub and cause sores.

The shared experience

Whilst we often talk about working with groups with disabilities or special needs or with 'able-bodied' groups; rarely do we talk about working with mixed groups. This is actually far more likely in a situation such as running a youth group or for a multi-activity instructor. It is worth considering that many people will be embarrassed not so much by disabled people as by their own reactions to them. They will be reluctant to make the first step because they feel out of their depth or unsure about how to act. It is a responsibility of the instructor to show them that they can act towards a disabled person in the same way as they would act towards anyone else; perhaps just with a little bit more consideration. There are also many positive aspects to a mainstream school group and a group from a special school being in a centre together; living together, sharing the building and facilities, sharing the activities. The mainstream pupils learn about disability or relating to someone with special needs. The special need's group learn to relate with mainstream students in a small, friendly setting which they are more able to deal with.

There has to be thought and care in the matching of groups to share. Some groups who need their own space in order to develop confidence may be better on their own without the added burden of having to form relationships with strangers; sharing may reduce the value for them. Others such as those with emotional/ behavioural difficulties may have enough problems relating to each other and thereby create a heady cocktail that would be difficult to contain when sharing. These groups may benefit from another mainstream set of individuals to distract them from the complexities of their own group dynamics but sometimes this mixture may be to the detriment of the mainstream group.

The need for research

Rather than try to devise a system of measuring any long-term benefits or changes of outdoor education with special needs groups, experienced practitioners, including the authors of this chapter, would rather cite another few hundred examples to illustrate the benefits of what they do. It may be, however, that there is an opportunity for others to do this long-term work and the results could help to maximise the experience for the benefit of others. One issue is that once the participants have finished a course and left, this is often the last we ever see or hear of them. Some of the changes that took place and were stimulated by the course are never followed up to see what the possible long-term effects are. The long-term benefits of outdoor education for those with disabilities and special needs maybe one area where there is a need for objective research to be done. One question that could be asked is, does being in the outdoors and the countryside bring a love of and respect for this environment? One might expect that a positive, pleasurable experience in the environment should encourage a positive attitude towards it. Perhaps it is for others to devise ways to measure this attitude with clients who have varying degrees of difficulty with communicating. The questions are there to be asked but the answers may be harder to derive.

Conclusion

A mystique has unfortunately grown up around working with people with disabilities or special needs. Many of us are torn between being frightened of working with disabled or special needs people and being full of admiration for those that do. In essence, this goes to the heart of working with disabled people. They are just the same as everyone else, but they have special needs to be accommodated. Indeed, people with disabilities or special needs nearly always have the same physical, social and emotional needs as any other person; and all the same problems and confusions. It is important when working with people with special needs or disabilities that they are given the same rights and respect as any other person. Practical things such as talking directly to them instead of to their carers, or allowing them the same personal space and dignity as any other person are all important. They should also be given the same expectations, opportunities and boundaries as their 'able-bodied' peers and allowed to make mistakes in the same way.

Unfortunately a lot of the conflict in working with people with disabilities and special needs has been brought about by 'experts' themselves who have developed a language and culture that can be seen to intimidate those not in the know. For example, a politically correct organisation may insist on the term 'with disabilities'. But a disabled person may have no problem with being called disabled and indeed may see it as the most apt description. Obviously, words such as spastic, invalid, mental and Mongol have now all rightly been consigned to history and it is important that derogatory terms such as these are avoided. More importantly, however, it is essential that, whilst not denying the special needs of people with disabilities, we recognise them as individuals without being frightened of occasionally doing or saying something wrong. As with all groups, what is required is sensitivity to the individual's needs and a vast amount of patience. In no circumstances should the difficulties of working with special needs groups or groups with disabilities be used as an excuse for inaction. There are additional issues involved, but as long as these are treated with intelligence and sensitivity, working with special needs students can be a rewarding and life-enhancing experience for all involved.

8 Outdoor Management Development: Issues Relating to Systematic Evaluation

Adrian Ibbetson[1]

Abstract

Much has been written about the use of the outdoor environment and activities employed within it as a vehicle for learning with corporate populations. Providers of such forms of management development programmes proclaim many potential benefits (Krouwel and Goodwill, 1994; Yeadon, 1995) however, due to a lack of systematic evaluation they remain largely unsubstantiated (Badger, Sadler-Smith and Michie, 1997; McEvoy and Buller, 1997). Therefore the discussion as to the effectiveness of this type of development activity has tended to be polarised between believers and sceptics. It is fair to say that much of the previous literature has been written from a descriptive perspective but that there is a growing body of evidence that reflects more rigorous enquiry. This in part reflects the relative infancy of this field of investigation but also reflects the difficulty of performing systematic evaluation where programmes and styles of provision are inherently diverse. The aim of this chapter is to discuss the factors that influence and impact upon systematic evaluation.

Terminology

There are many terms used in the literature to refer to the use of the outdoors for the purpose of management development (cf. Broderick and Pearce, 2001; Ibbetson, 1998). If they were used in a systematic way that discriminated between different types of provision then they would be helpful, but they do not. Instead, they represent a confusing proliferation essentially referring to the same product market. For the purpose of this chapter the generally accepted British term 'outdoor management development' (OMD) will be used (Badger et al., 1997; Burke and Collins, 1998; Hamilton and Cooper, 2001; Ibbetson and Newell, 1998, 1999, 2002). It must be recognised that there are problems surrounding the use of such a global term because not all experiences on such programmes are contingent upon the outdoors (Symons, 1994). Some programmes deal with corporate clients other than managers (cf. Badger et al., 1997; Industrial Relations Services (IRS), 1992) and some providers use the descriptor 'training' rather than 'development' (see Endres and Kleiner, 1990). For the purpose of this chapter OMD will be defined as:

A process of development which allows the work-related competencies of the participants to be improved, in order that they become more effective and efficient in their work role. Typically the recipients are in positions of influence within the sponsoring organisation. The activities employed are conducted, at least in part, in the outdoors and, in general, they are seen as a means to an end and are therefore, to a varying degree, connected to the reality of the workplace.

The historical roots of OMD

The term 'Development Training' was formalised by the creation of the Development Training Advisory Group (DTAG) in 1977. This term prevails in the psyche of those associated with some of the founding member organisations such as Outward Bound and Brathay Hall. However, the development training work of such organisations tends to encompass, but distinguish between, working with youth and working with corporate groups (Figure 1).

Further, historical information is provided by Bank (1994), Everard (1993), Hopkins and Putnam (1993), Ibbetson (1998), Krouwel and Goodwill (1994) and Tuson (1994). The term OMD has therefore been deliberately chosen in order to avoid confusion because the focus of this chapter

---

[1] The author is indebted to Prof. Sue Newell for her help with the development of many ideas included in this chapter.

Figure 1   A schematic representation of the roots of outdoor management development from a British perspective

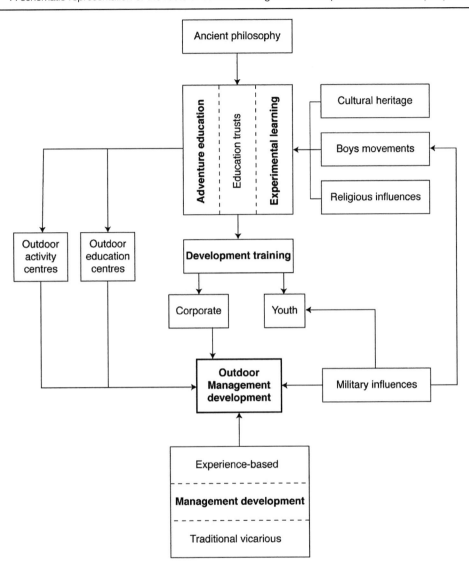

is on working with corporate clients in order to improve work-related competencies.

From Figure 1 it can be seen that the roots of OMD are eclectic. Providers come from a variety of backgrounds. At the risk of over-simplification, practitioners tend to come from one of three predominant backgrounds: a general 'education' background, which not only encompasses such educational trusts mentioned above but also includes mainstream outdoor education and commercial outdoor activity centres; a 'training and development' background; and an

'ex-military' background (for further information see Ibbetson, 1998; Krouwel and Goodwill, 1994). Individuals bring varying sets of skills and philosophies to the provision of OMD programmes dependent upon their backgrounds. This influences the degree to which activities are seen as a means to an end and the degree to which programmes actually are connected to the realities of the workplace.

The growth and diversity of OMD

Although Hopkins and Putnam (1993) state that the lead was taken by institutions such as Brathay in 1971 and Outward Bound and the Leadership Trust in 1975, the 1980s has previously been cited as the main period of growth and establishment of OMD in Britain. Maxted and Field (1991) provide evidence that approximately 80 per cent of the 113 providers listed in the 1991 OMD Directory and Yearbook were established during this period. However, since then the number of UK operators listed in 'The Outdoor Source Book' as providing OMD programmes has risen from 170 in 1993/94 (Adventure Education, 1993) to 412 in 2002/03 (Outdoor Learning Services, 2002). In 1993/4, 45 per cent of the 170 providers of OMD were also listed as providers of outdoor activities. The classification system within the Outdoor Source Book has become more sophisticated and direct comparison is problematic but in 2002/03 the percentage of outdoor learning providers that were listed as offering corporate training (OMD) as well as working with school groups was 85 per cent.

The growth that has occurred in the provision of OMD programmes has not been regulated (Symons, 1994) and therefore the 'industry' is characterised by diversity. One of the problems of using a generic, 'catch-all' term is that OMD is not a unitary concept 'with universally agreed and accepted concepts, processes and outcomes' (Jones and Oswick, 1993: 11). This diversity not only creates potential 'confusion about the product and the providers in the minds of potential users' (Symons, 1994: 7) it also makes evaluation difficult. This is because it makes the comparison of like with like and the contrasting of difference problematic. A classification system that enables consumers to distinguish between different types of provision and also provides a framework with which to contextualise previous research and upon which to base future research has been put forward by Ibbetson and Newell (2002) (see Figure 2).

It builds upon previous work (Dainty and Lucas, 1992; Holman, 1993; Krouwel and Goodwill, 1994; Mazany, Francis and Sumich, 1997; Peckham, 1993) to provide a typology of OMD that accounts for varying physicality, different types of activities, different philosophies of provision, varying amounts of theoretical input and review and different degrees of integration between programmes and the workplace. The physicality dimension encompasses the fact that some providers use the concept of comfort zone and believe that participants need to explore its edges (Tuson, 1994). Providers with this belief tend to utilise high adventure, outdoor pursuit-type activities to achieve this aim and as such providers tend to associate with an underlying philosophy of peak experience (Mortlock, 1984). Providers that align more strongly with experiential learning tend to use more isomorphic, metaphoric activities (Gass and Priest, 1993), especially those who do not merely pay lip-service to the idea of connecting with the reality of the workplace. This differing use of activities links with Dainty and Lucas's (1992) concepts of 'tight' and 'loose' activities (see Figure 3).

Arguably the more 'loose' an activity then the more control can be taken by the participants themselves and the greater the variety of aspects to review. The amount and nature of review depends upon the underlying philosophy. It can be contested that those providers attempting to make metaphoric connections to the workplace utilising a deliberately facilitated experiential style will potentially review in a more anagogic rather than pedagogic manner (Tuson, 1994). The final dimension draws upon Kirk's (1986) ideas regarding theoretical reality. Some providers are able to provide a better theoretical bridge between the programme and the workplace. Some programmes occur as one-off inoculations to particular organisational ills, whereas other programmes conceive OMD as one form of action learning. As such, they are more integrated with the workplace often having a more iterative process of repeat interventions that 'build on the learning from each stage over a period of time' (Yeadon, 1994: 28) and thus potentially better support development and change.

Three main types of OMD provision are identified by the typology: management development outdoors (MDO); adventure-based management development (ABMD); and macho management development (MMD) (Figure 2). The different types tend to align with the historical roots of OMD. MDO provision tends to be high on the dimensions of review and theoretical input but

Figure 2   A typology of OMD provision

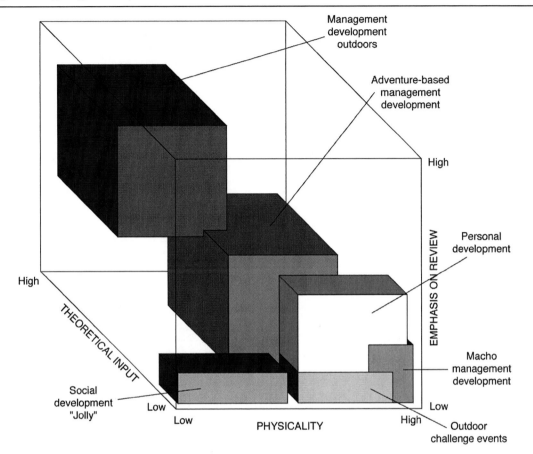

low on physicality because underpinning philosophies of experiential and action learning do not necessitate peak experience built on high adventure. Indeed not all the learning experiences might be outdoors, as Kelly (1996: 12) suggests, the outdoors can be used 'to augment classroom activities' rather than being 'an unpleasant challenge to the courage of the participants'. The starting position of much ABMD provision tends to be 'what activities fit the bill?' because it is often associated with an extension of existing activity-based education or commercial provision. This tends to produce programmes that are in the mid ranges of the dimensions. MMD tends to be high on physicality and low on review and theoretical input as the main premise is to push the limits of the comfort zone to explore the hidden potential of individuals and teams. The types, or terms, themselves may not be as

important as recognising that the style of provision can vary along the specified dimensions of diversity.

It is suggested that three further types of provision can be identified that may be confused with OMD but that their connections to it may be inappropriate. Outdoor challenge events are often company-wide motivational events that are not focused on 'management development' per se. Personal development which is the 'youth' side of development training that is often lumped in with analyses of corporate provision. Social development programmes which have a 'jolly' element that act as motivational and reward tools within organisations but that are without 'management development' objectives. This typology attempts to be comprehensive within the realms of being comprehensible and therefore as with any simplification of reality it may be accused

Figure 3   Dimensions of diversity

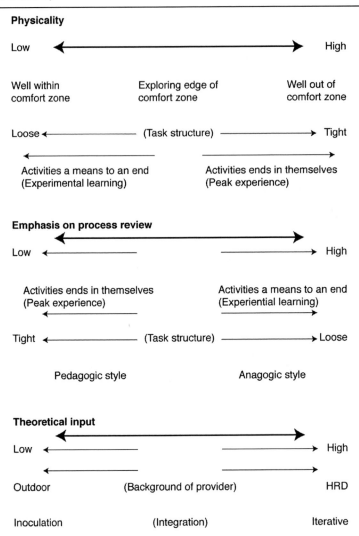

Physicality

Low ←——————————————————————→ High

Well within   Exploring edge of   Well out of
comfort zone   comfort zone   comfort zone

Loose ←———————— (Task structure) ————————→ Tight

←—————————————   ———————————————→
Activities a means to an end   Activities ends in themselves
(Experimental learning)   (Peak experience)

Emphasis on process review

Low ←—————————————   ———————————————→ High

Activities ends in themselves   Activities a means to an end
(Peak experience)   (Experiential learning)
←—————————————   ———————————————→

Tight ←———————— (Task structure) ————————→ Loose

Pedagogic style   Anagogic style

Theoretical input

Low ←—————————————   ———————————————→ High

←—————————————   ———————————————→
Outdoor   (Background of provider)   HRD

Inoculation   (Integration)   Iterative

of being over-simplistic (for further explanation see Ibbetson and Newell, 2002).

Espoused benefits

Many benefits of management development programmes utilising the 'great outdoors' as the learning medium have been 'described' in the literature. Although the following list is not exhaustive, such 'benefits' include:

- The immediacy of consequences due to the fact that 'outdoor' activities involve real situations, requiring real behaviour and real solutions (Krouwel and Goodwill, 1994).

- The unfamiliarity, or novelty, of the tasks used in 'outdoor' scenarios (Tuson, 1994) as this leaves delegates with only their raw abilities to solve problems laying the underlying management processes bare (Creswick and Williams, 1979).
- Enabling the experimentation with different modes of behaviour in a psychologically safe environment (McEvoy and Buller, 1997).
- The emotional intensity can leave a lasting impression and can lead to the development of trust and strong emotional bonds between the delegates (Yeadon, 1994).
- The flexibility that allows the challenge can be tailored to match the level of abilities within the

group (Dainty and Lucas, 1992) – although this is not exclusive to this particular form of training and development.

However, in large part, although many of these claims may make intuitive sense, they have not been rigorously tested. In fact, Irvine and Wilson (1994) suggest that aspects of novelty, flexibility and the fact that participants take psychological risks rather than actual risks are not unique to OMD programmes, as opposed to other forms of management development; the reputation upon which OMD relies is an illusionary mystique. Indeed, it is claimed that the urban outdoors can provide the same aspects of novelty and unfamiliarity and that indoor environments can be used to produce adventurous management development programmes (Broderick and Pearce, 2001).

The need for systematic evaluation

There are many espoused benefits of OMD but not all provision is the same and therefore it is reasonable to speculate that different types of provision will produce non-uniform outcomes. For instance, two providers could theoretically be contracted by the same client to address the same programme issues but the way they choose and use activities, the amount of actual connection to the workplace and the way transfer of learning is approached could vary enormously. Furthermore, two different clients could express very similar development needs and could end up undertaking very similar programmes with the same provider and the outcomes could be very different due to varying organisational factors. What is needed is a systematic approach attempting to tease out factors that influence the success of OMD programmes. Figure 4 attempts to produce a process model of OMD in order to help identify and systemise the factors that affect outcomes.

The model suggests that a variety of programme characteristics need to be taken into account. An often cited starting point for evaluation is the objectives of the programme (Badger et al., 1997). Research suggests that individual and group/team outcomes can be differentiated and, in some instances, positively evidenced against stated objectives (Bronson, Gibson, Kichar and Priest, 1992; Ibbetson and

Newell, 1996, 1998 and 1999; Lucas, 1992; Mazany et al., 1997; Wagner and Roland, 1992). It has been previously discussed that the way in which the programme is delivered and formatted is likely to determine whether it achieves its aims and objectives. For instance, findings suggest that competitive and non-competitive formats can affect outcomes and that the element of competition needs to be used with care (cf. Ibbetson and Newell, 1996 and 1999; Smith and Vaughan, 1997).

OMD is sometimes seen as a panacea, suiting the needs of all individuals, teams and organisations. However, individuals and teams have antecedent factors that can affect outcomes perhaps even predisposing them to benefit, or not to benefit, from this type of development activity. For example, previous research has investigated preferred learning style and preferred team role (Ibbetson and Newell, 1996), although the results were inconclusive. Other research has investigated team climate and occupational motivation and pressure management (Hamilton and Cooper, 2001) and these results showed that outcomes related to the OMD programme were mediated by the amount of pressure individuals were under within the organisation. Furthermore, McSherry and Taylor (1994) found that individual differences effected transfer of learning from an OMD event. More research is necessary to increase understanding of factors that potentially mediate outcomes so that they can be addressed and potentially managed in order to maximise the experience for the participants and client organisations.

If OMD is effective then the learning should be able to be demonstrably linked to increased effectiveness back in the workplace. The model encompasses Kirkpatrick's (1967) seminal taxonomy which suggests that outcomes from training and development events can be evaluated on four levels: reactions, learning, behaviour and results. Reactions and initial perceptions of learning can be immediately captured upon completion of a course. However, learning can also occur after a period of reflection which may manifest itself in changes in work-related behaviour and therefore more longitudinal approaches to evaluation are necessary if such distal outcomes are to be captured. The ultimate level of outcome, in relation to the 'bottom-line'

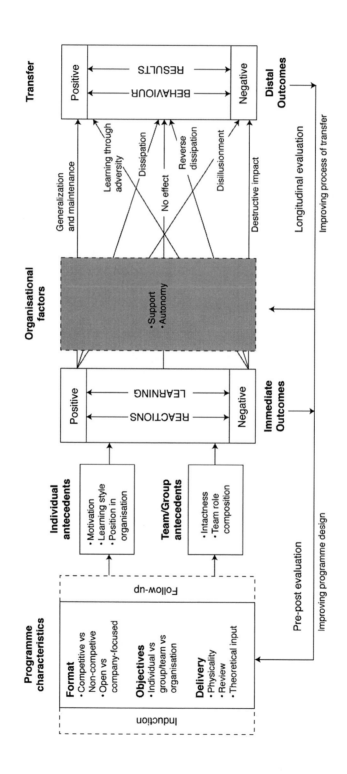

Figure 4 A process model of OMD

and return on investment is measurable changes in performance-related results. The paradox is that reactions are very easy to capture but are of low relative value in comparison to aspects of change relating to behaviour and results that are of higher value but are more difficult to measure (Badger et al., 1997).

Previous research relating to the effectiveness of OMD has been lacking in rigour. An Industrial Relations Service (1992) survey of 62 companies using OMD reported that 81 per cent consistently used only post-test 'happiness sheets' to evaluate outcomes from the procured programmes – thus only evaluating reactions. Only 3 per cent of clients consistently used test-retest comparisons. Moreover, Jones and Oswick (1993) found that out of 45 studies reported in the UK literature which supposedly investigated outcomes of OMD, only 16 per cent of studies had attempted to evaluate outcomes on anything like a systematic basis. Even later work has either relied solely on post-course questionnaires (Bank, 1994) or on anecdotal testimony (Kelly 1996). Therefore, much of the research relating to the effectiveness of OMD has failed to measure even immediate outcomes with a reasonable degree of methodological rigour let alone attempting to evaluate more longitudinal work-based outcomes.

The model encompasses Alliger and Janak's (1994) criticisms of the hierarchical, causal and 'positive' nature of Kirkpatrick's (1967) original model. For example, a participant might have negative reactions to a programme but after a period of time they might reflect that they have learnt things from that experience (e.g. learning through adversity). Figure 4 also incorporates criticisms that can be levelled at other models of transfer of learning (i.e. Baldwin and Ford, 1994) that only refer to positive aspects of transfer, i.e. generalisation and maintenance. Indeed, there is some evidence for positive programme outcomes to be positively transferred to the workplace (Ibbetson and Newell, 1998; McSherry and Taylor, 1994) but this is not the only outcome. For example, participants that had positive initial perceptions regarding a particular OMD programme might not have the support or inclination to implement the initial learning back in the workplace and thus these initial positive perceptions dissipate once back in the work environment (which is evidenced in one case study in Ibbetson and Newell, 1998). Moreover, Lowe (1991) reports an example of disillusionment, whereby the team building encouraged on an OMD programme was turned into a destructive-positive as the 'united' line managers reportedly conspired against their unsupportive bosses. Thus negative workplace behaviours resulted from positive programme outcomes.

The benefits of evaluation

There are several reasons why training and development programmes might be evaluated. Easterby-Smith (1986) offers a simple trichotomy: proving, improving and learning. Many of the articles emanating from the training and development press cited within this chapter have attempted to confirm the effectiveness of OMD. Unfortunately, many previous claims of positive outcomes have been made without the necessary rigour to substantiate them. The two main stakeholders that benefit from such proof are the providers selling courses and the training managers procuring them. There is a recognisable conflict of interest if these parties undertake evaluation of their own programmes for the purpose of 'proof' which has previously lead Jones and Oswick (1993) to warn of the dangers of systematic bias. Therefore independent evaluation, or at least verification, is necessary if credible, external 'proof' is to be accepted. However it should be encouraged that providers and clients regularly attempt to 'internally' evaluate their practice in order to improve their programme designs and the process of transfer to the workplace (Figure 4), so that the subsequent effectiveness of programmes can be increased (Nichols, 1994). Finally, greater academic enquiry is necessary to learn more about OMD programmes in order to examine programme characteristics that influence programme design, to explore antecedent variables that influence experiences and to investigate factors that influence the transfer of learning to the workplace. This needs to done in a rigorous manner that accounts for the diversity in provision in order that generalisation might allow practice to be reviewed and improved.

Conclusion

Many benefits of OMD have been previously espoused in the literature by its advocates. However, these claims have been largely unsubstantiated which has led sceptics to suggest that such benefits are based upon faith rather than evidence. The irony is that the burden of proof lies with those who provide and procure OMD courses but that evaluation undertaken by these parties is open to suspicion of bias. More independent research is needed in future but this cannot be done without the consent of providers and training managers as a certain amount of risk is inherent in the process. However, in the spirit of 'walking the talk' and reviewing practice in order to apply what is learnt, then providers should be willing to evaluate their practice in order that they can continuously improve their product. Moreover, from a learning perspective, the diversity inherent in the provision of OMD means that it is impossible to elicit uniform outcomes. Therefore more research is necessary to learn what works and what does not in which situations, in order that knowledge of good practice can be established and disseminated. Future research might concentrate upon programme characteristics and antecedent variables that influence the experience and, therefore, immediate outcomes and also upon the process of transfer of learning to the workplace and organisational factors that facilitate or hinder this process. Finally, if technical practice is not to outpace an understanding of the process then evaluation needs to be allowed to explore the edges of the comfort zone.

References

Alliger, G.M. and Janak, E.A. (1994) Kirkpatrick's Levels of Training Criteria: Thirty Years Later, in Schneier, C.E. et al. (Eds.) *The Training and Development Sourcebook*. 2nd edn. Amherst: Human Resource Development Press.

Baldwin, T.T. and Ford, J.K. (1994) Transfer of Training: A Review and Directions for Future Research, in Schneier, C. E. et al. (Eds.) *The Training and Development Sourcebook*. 2nd edn. Amherst: Human Resource Development Press.

Badger, B., Sadler-Smith, E. and Michie, E. (1997) Outdoor Management Development: Use and Evaluation. *Journal of European Industrial Training*. 21: 9, 318–25.

Bank, J. (1994) *Outdoor Development for Managers*. 2nd edn. Aldershot: Gower.

Broderick, A. and Pearce, G. (2001) Indoor Adventure Training: A Dramaturgical Approach to Management Development. *Journal of Organisational Change*. 14: 239–52.

Bronson, J. et al. (1992) Evaluation of Team Development in a Corporate Adventure Training Program. *The Journal of Experiential Education*. 15: 50–4.

Burke, V. and Collins, D. (1998) The Great Outdoors and Management Development: A Framework for Analysing the Learning and Transfer of Management Skills. *Managing Leisure*. 3: 136–48.

Creswick, C. and Williams, R. (1979) *Using the Outdoors for Management Development and Team Building*. Unpublished Paper for The Food, Drink and Tobacco Industry Training Board.

Dainty, P. and Lucas, D. (1992) Clarifying the Confusion: A Practical Framework for Evaluating Outdoor Development Programmes for Managers. *Management Education and Development*. 23: 106–22.

Easterby-Smith, M. (1986) *Evaluation of Management Education, Training and Development*. Aldershot: Gower.

Endres, G.J. and Kleiner, B.H. (1990) How to Measure Management Training and Development Effectiveness. *Journal of European Industrial Training*. 14: 9, 3–7.

Everard, B. (1993) *The History of Development Training*. Cumbria: Adventure Education.

Gass, M. and Priest, S. (1993) Using Metaphors and Isomorphs to Transfer Learning in Adventure Education. *Journal of Adventure Education and Outdoor Leadership*. 10: 18–23.

Hamilton, T. and Cooper, C. (2001) The Impact of Outdoor Management Development (OMD) Programmes. *Leadership and Organisation Development Journal*. 22: 7, 330–40.

Holman, S. (1993) Outdoor Challenge. *Training Officer*. 29: 88–9.

Hopkins, D. and Putnam, R. (1993) *Personal Growth Through Adventure*. London: David Fulton Publishers.

Ibbetson, A.B. (1998) *Understanding Outdoor Management Development: The Role of Evaluation*.

Unpublished PhD Thesis, University of Birmingham, England.

Ibbetson, A.B. and Newell, S. (1996) Winner Takes All: an Evaluation of Adventure-Based Experiential Training. *Journal of Management Learning*, 27: 163–185.

Ibbetson, A.B. and Newell, S. (1998) Outdoor Management Development: The Mediating Effect of The Client Organisation. *International Journal of Training and Development*. 2: 4, 239–58.

Ibbetson, A.B. and Newell, S. (1999) A Comparison of a Competitive and Non-Competitive Outdoor Management Development Programme: The Role of Evaluation. *Personnel Review*. 28: 58–76.

Ibbetson, A.B. and Newell, S. (2002) *Outdoor Management Development: Towards a Typology*. Paper Presented at The International Conference, Whose Journeys, Where and Why? (Outdoor and Adventure Education), Buckinghamshire Chilterns University College.

Industrial Relations Services (1992) The Role of Outdoor-Based Development: A Survey of 120 Employers. Employee Development Bulletin 34, *Industrial Relations Review and Report*. 522: 2–17.

Irvine, D. and Wilson, J. P. (1994) Outdoor Management Development: Reality or Illusion? *Journal of Management Development*. 13: 25–37.

Jones, P.J. and Oswick, C. (1993) Outcomes of Outdoor Management Development: Articles of Faith? *Journal of European Industrial Training*. 17: 10–8.

Kelly, J. (1996) Case Study: Using the Outdoor for Team-Building. *Management Development Review*. 9: 2 11–4.

Kirk, P. (1986) Outdoor Management Development: Cellulose or Celluloid? *Management Education and Development*. 17: 85–93.

Kirkpatrick, D.L. (1967) Evaluation of Training, in Craig, R.L. and Bitten, L.R. (Eds.) *Training and Development Handbook*. New York: Mcgraw-Hill.

Krouwel, W. and Goodwill, S. (1994) *Management Development Outdoors: A Practical Guide to Getting The Best Results*. London: Kogan Page.

Lowe, J. (1991) Teambuilding Via Outdoor Training: Experiences From a UK Automotive Plant. *Human Resource Management Journal*. 2: 42–59.

Lucas, D.M. (1992) *The Outcomes of Personal Development Within Manager Development as Exemplified by the Use of the Outdoors*. Unpublished Doctoral Dissertation, Cranfield University.

Mazany, P., Francis, S. and Sumich, P. (1997) Evaluating The Effectiveness of an Outdoor Workshop for Team Building in an MBA Programme. *Team Performance Management*. 3: 97–115.

Maxted, P. and Field, R. (Eds.) (1991) *The Outdoor Management Development Directory and Yearbook 1991*. Falmouth: Addico Publishing.

McEvoy, G. and Buller, P. (1997) The Power of Outdoor Management Development. *Journal of Management Development*. 16: 208–17.

McSherry, M. and Taylor, P. (1994) Supervisory Support for the Transfer of Team-Building Training. *The International Journal of Human Resource Management*. 5: 1, 107–19.

Mortlock, C. (1984). *The Adventure Alternative*. Cumbria: Cicerone Press.

Nichols, G. (1994) Major Issues in the Evaluation of the Impact of Outdoor Based Experiences. *Journal of Adventure Education and Outdoor Leadership*. 11: 11–4.

Peckham, M. (1993) Management Development and The 'Outdoors': Exploring The Myth. *Training and Development (UK)*. May: 17–8.

Smith, D. and Vaughan, S. (1997) The Outdoors as an Environment for Learning and Change Management. *Industrial and Commercial Training*. 29: 2, 26–30.

Symons, J. (1994) Understanding and Analysing Outdoor (Management) Development Programs. *Journal of Adventure Education and Outdoor Leadership*. 11: 6–12.

Adventure Education (1993) *The Outdoor Source Book (1993/94)*. Penrith: Adventure Education.

Outdoor Learning Services (2002) *The Outdoor Source Book (2002/03)*. Penrith: Outdoor Learning Services.

Tuson, M. (1994) *Outdoor Training for Employee Effectiveness*. London: IPM.

Wagner, R.J. and Roland, C.C. (1992) How Effective is Outdoor Training? *Training and Development Journal (US)*. 46: 7, 61–6.

Yeadon, W. (1994) Why Use the Outdoors? *Management Development Review*. 7: 27–9.

9 Outdoor Education and the Voluntary Sector

Janet Shepherd

Abstract

An introduction to the outdoors is something we all experience to varying degrees. The opportunities may start as play in the back garden or local park, and for many there will be ever increasing opportunities to engage with the outdoor environment. For others there may be little more than the briefest of encounters. Education of young people takes many forms and the value of the outdoors as a learning environment is increasingly seen as offering unique and quite special circumstances.

Voluntary youth organisations such as the Scout Association and Girls Brigade, the RSPB and National Trust have always recognised the value of outdoor education. They recognise and value the personal skills that are developed by young people through a progressive informal programme; those of self-reliance, leadership skills, teamwork, other transferable skills and raising self-esteem. This chapter looks at some of the issues around volunteering and the voluntary sector. Volunteers come from all walks of life. The value of this sector is unrivalled in terms of best value and the challenge ahead is how to support this ever-growing sector.

Introduction

When the question – 'What first got you interested in the outdoors?' – was recently put to a number of outdoor enthusiasts, the response was quite intriguing. Many replied that they had been introduced to the outdoors through a youth organisation such as being a Guide with Girl guiding UK or a Cadet with the Army Cadet Force Association. Others had been involved in a hill walking club run by a teacher in their spare time or in a Duke of Edinburgh's Award (D of E) group. A small number indicated that their family had been keen on the outdoors and they had been involved throughout their childhood. This was by no means a scientific or qualitative survey but the results were none the less very interesting. Almost all of these people had been introduced to the outdoors, when they were young by adults voluntarily operating in this field.

What is the 'voluntary sector'? It can mean different things to different people but this chapter includes everyone who could be regarded as working voluntarily in the outdoors and in particular with young people. It includes all the national voluntary youth organisations and many smaller more local organisations. It includes teachers and outdoor instructors who are employed in the statutory sector but who work in an outdoor environment in a voluntary capacity over and above their normal work. It includes youth workers, social workers and others who work beyond their normal workload to provide young people with greater opportunities. It includes organisations that are not membership organisations but who, nevertheless, encourage work in the outdoors as programme providers. It includes the voluntary, independent youth groups who target specific groups – often disadvantaged young people – and activity clubs that operate in a voluntary capacity. There are a large number of other organisations that are regarded as voluntary organisations, including Brathay, Outward Bound and the Abernethy Trust. These often have charitable status and operate under trust deed but, for the purposes of this chapter, are not specifically included here as they often operate with paid staff. However, one important aspect of their work is the training of young, keen outdoor enthusiasts on an 'on the job' basis and often in a voluntary capacity.

The exact nature of outdoor education has been explored fully in other chapters although it is not a term usually used by the voluntary sector for their work with young people in the outdoors. It is a term more usually associated with college/university courses and centres specifically set up by education authorities and charities. The term does not always refer to outdoor adventure and outdoor learning undertaken by young people in other settings. The results of the simple question mentioned before however, show how important is an introduction to the outdoors in these more informal settings and groupings. Often, such introductions have a long-term affect. Why is this and what are the implications?

History

Informal education in the outdoors (adventure education) has been in existence for many years and has a long tradition of voluntary leadership. Sir William Smith founded the Boys Brigade in 1883. The Scout Movement began with an experimental camp in 1907. Kurt Hahn introduced the Moray Scheme, the forerunner of The Duke of Edinburgh's Award in 1934. All of these organisations used the outdoors extensively in their programmes and continue to do so today. Some of these national voluntary organisations also have their own residential outdoor centres using a mixture of paid and volunteer staff. All of these organisations have similar stated aims and benefits for young people. Unsurprisingly, these are almost identical to the aims and benefits of the statutory sector. These include, amongst others, opportunities to develop self-confidence, teamwork, practical skills, self-awareness, personal adaptability, communication skills, social awareness, environmental awareness, self-esteem, empathy with others, independence and problem-solving skills. Two elements that have recently become even more important are experiencing the natural elements and becoming more self-reliant.

We live in a very protective and comfortable society in Britain. For example, central heating, cars parked at the front door and indoor entertainment at the press of a button all discourage people from venturing outside into the elements. This is so for all people not just the young. However, young people have even less opportunity to take part in activities that encourage them to travel outside in spite of the increasing number of opportunities open to them. Young children are discouraged from playing outside and less sport is played, especially out of doors, with leisure and sports centres providing excellent indoor facilities. Even outdoor centres have been affected. Very few now include

camping in their basic programmes. Young people are less able to cope, to look after and entertain themselves when their everyday comfort zone is unavailable to them. Many 'cook' using a microwave, have entertainment at the press of a button and cannot imagine life without two showers a day! If they are then asked to make their way using public transport to an unknown location – an expedition takes on a whole new meaning!

Adventure, such as an unaccompanied two-day expedition for a Bronze D of E Award, (following appropriate training) provides challenges to which young people rise and usually thoroughly enjoy. They often comment that the enjoyment is largely because they are 'allowed' to undertake the activity by themselves. Whilst the requirements are the same, the challenges are far greater than perhaps for young people 20 years ago. Society should not deny young people these kinds of experiences, opportunities to make real decisions and to cope with the consequences in a fairly controlled situation. Otherwise, real opportunities for young people to develop skills and to learn to take responsibility for themselves and others are lost. We cannot expect them to suddenly develop these at 18 years of age with no training, experience or support. If proof were needed, take the example of the 15 year old boy who sailed cross the Atlantic single-handed in January 2003. It is likely he was able to do this only because he had both learned the appropriate skills and been given the opportunities to make decisions and take increasing responsibility for his actions from an early age.

Volunteer leaders

Volunteers come from all walks of life. They have often become volunteer leaders as a direct result of being a participant within an organisation. They may have worked their way up through the leadership and development programme offered within that organisation (e.g. The Scout Association). Others may find that their own children wish to join a local group that needs new leaders. Some recognise a need within their local community for the sort of skills and interests that they have and are keen to share (e.g. environmental projects such as the John Muir Award). Others have an interest in an activity and recognise that the future may depend on attracting new blood and in particular young members (e.g. a canoe club).

Volunteers come from various backgrounds. They may be structural engineers, accountants, postmen, retired bank managers, country park rangers, doctors, health and safety officers, teachers, outdoor instructors, prison officers, computer experts, shop assistants, unemployed, managers and manual workers alike. In fact, in just one youth programme there are examples of all of these as volunteers. The one thing that they all have in common is commitment. They are all committed to the organisation, to young people and to the personal and social development of young people. They also have an interest in the welfare of and an empathy with young people. The enthusiasm and commitment of volunteers is what makes this sector different and special. That is not to say the statutory sector is any less enthusiastic. Having worked in local education authority outdoor centres for many years, I know of the many hours, months and years of enthusiasm from paid staff in terms of their job. But I also see on a daily basis the voluntary commitment where people give so much of their own time over and above their normal work. In spite of family and other financial commitments, evenings, weekends and holidays are spent taking groups away to experience adventure in the outdoors. A price cannot be put on this work and volunteers should not be forgotten or taken for granted especially in terms of resources, training and support (financial and otherwise), as outdoor adventure is once again seen as something that all young people should experience.

Programme progression

The programmes followed by young people in the different voluntary organisations are often developed over a long period of time. This allows for a progressive approach to the development and acquisition of skills, with plenty of time to review and reinforce before moving forward to the next stage. For example, with many voluntary youth organisations, young people from the age of five may begin to learn to find their way in the outdoors using a simple plan or sketch. With more instruction at a basic level, they may go on to take part in a simple orienteering course or a nature quest. They can work away, reinforcing their

knowledge, enjoying the outdoors at an appropriate level using the skills in context, and enjoying overnight camps and weekend residentials. If they remain with the organisation they may go on to undertake the Bronze and Silver levels of The D of E Award from the age of 14. By the time they have achieved these they might plan to take part in a three-week international gathering, undertaking expeditions with young people from other countries. If they chose to become a leader in the organisation they can work towards their Gold Award and undertake a Basic Expedition Leader Award or local accreditation and then on to the Mountain Leader Summer Award in order to lead others. All of these steps could be undertaken with the same voluntary organisation under the leadership, very often, of the same volunteer adults.

Sustainability

Sustainability is something voluntary organisations need to take quite seriously. The voluntary sector is, by its very nature, about long-term commitment. Young people are introduced and enthused about an activity or organisation and expect to stay as long as that interest remains. They may enjoy the short introduction, but it then leaves them dissatisfied if there are no opportunities to continue. They need to have some means of continuing even if they decide not to take it. The choice should be theirs. Time is a crucial component and is most difficult in today's hectic life style with a fairly mobile workforce. The days when organisations can survive on the goodwill and support of one committed individual may be changing. A team approach by leaders, each taking on different parts of the workload, seems to work best and recognises that people have other commitments. This has implications for organisations that have benefited and relied on lifelong 'one-man-band' leaders. It is not unusual to find volunteers who have been with organisations for several decades! The challenge for voluntary organisations is to attract new leaders including the development and training of some of their older participants to ensure the success and continuation of their organisations.

In people's increasingly busy lifestyles an offer of help is not made lightly and organisations need to be ready to respond quickly with induction and training opportunities and a system of support. Why does a teacher choose to run a hill walking or canoe club as an extra-curricular activity? It is certainly not because of financial reward or the chance of promotion. Firstly, they are very interested in the activity and have a wish to share their interest with others. Teachers also find that the relationships they build with the pupils in an informal setting have a significant impact on relationships in the classroom. Pupils are interested, have chosen to take part, and they see the teachers in a different and more positive light. Relationships are very important and for young people to remain in the group for more than a couple of years, strong relationships will have developed between leaders and participants and between participants. More and more responsibility can be given to the participants with a truly individual and progressive approach to their individual programme and their personal development. These relationships are built on trust and respect and are two-way. From the outset the intention is to help young people to achieve their potential and for young people to take responsibility for and within their own lives. This includes developing an awareness of risk, being able to assess it and to know how to minimise it.

Training

Support and training is as crucial in this sector as with the statutory and commercial sectors. The safety and well being of participants is paramount. Many organisations endorse National Governing Body awards whilst others have their own system of training and accreditation. This allows people to operate at an appropriate level and to progress at their own pace with a definite development pathway mapped out. It does not always depend on NGB awards, as very often the areas that people use are area or site specific. The NGB awards only go some way to providing what leaders need. Systems, similar to the local authority local accreditation schemes, have been developed over a number of years. For example, Girl guiding UK has a clearly defined Walking Safely scheme which operates at a number of levels and encourages and endorses people's competence to work at their own level. It also encourages people with appropriate experience to enter the BELA and ML schemes.

This training may be offered in house, although some NGB awards can be very expensive for the volunteer, both in time and financially. For example a volunteer already giving up their own time will have to give another week of their holiday to undertake an ML training course. Whilst good value for money it is also a huge commitment financially. This is an area that needs to be addressed in terms of support to volunteers. It is encouraging to see some businesses backing the lead in offering time to meet some of the voluntary commitments of their employees.

Other training that is equally important is training in child protection issues, health and safety issues and risk management. Voluntary organisations, excluding their outdoor residential centres, are usually out of scope of the AALA licence requirements. Nevertheless, they will be judged against the same standards and requirements if an incident occurs. Organisations need to be fully aware of, and to meet current good practice and legal requirements. This is becoming increasingly more difficult as it requires systems that rely on a great deal of administration. This puts even greater pressures on voluntary organisations that typically have a small headquarters' staff.

Future challenges

There has been, and still exists in some quarters, tensions between the voluntary and the statutory sectors. This was highlighted in an Outdoor Activities Survey carried out in 1989 (Hunt, 1989):

A distrust of volunteers occurs amongst the professional ranks, and in its strongest form was expressed as 'unpaid volunteers prevent proper rewards for professionals; this outweighs all the advantages of volunteers.'

Hopefully, efforts on both sides and the formation of good working partnerships have ensured that these feelings are inappropriate. By working together, recognising the strengths of each party, outdoor adventure can continue to grow to give even more young people the experiences to which they are entitled. Joint training has helped to break down these barriers and there is a realisation that many people operating in the statutory sector also volunteer in their own time.

Increasing legislation and the increasingly litigious society in which we live are having an adverse effect on the morale of existing leaders and on the ability to enthuse and recruit new ones. The culture of blame is having a negative effect with many volunteers feeling particularly vulnerable. In today's society there appears little room for accidents. When an accident occurs there is an increasing appetite to find someone to blame. This appears, unfortunately, more to do with compensation and with organisations opting out of taking responsibility rather than for increasing the safety of participants or improving standards. Support to, and the training of volunteers becomes increasingly important and the voluntary sector is only too aware of this. Commonsense does not always seem to prevail, although recent court cases have gone some way to address these concerns. Ways must be found to deal with these issues, which are much wider than outdoor education. The system operating in New Zealand where a form of national insurance policy against accidents exists is an interesting alternative.

So why do people volunteer? They recognise a need and know they have something to offer. In order to make the most of this organisations must try to minimise the problems, red tape and paperwork. This will ensure that what people have volunteered for is supported, is of a high quality and actually answers the need. Volunteers must feel valued. Finally, it is important to note that in spite of everything, more and more people are volunteering.

Reference

Hunt, J. (1989) *In search of adventure*. Guildford: Talbot Adair Press.

Further information can be obtained by visiting the website for The Duke of Edinburgh's Award (www.theaward.org/scotland)

10 Outdoor Education and Participation from Ethnic Communities

Judy Ling Wong and Peter Barnes

Abstract

This chapter discusses the participation in outdoor activities and outdoor education by people from ethnic communities. Cognisance is made of society's role in the image of ethnic communities and outdoor activities as well as specific issues relating to the outdoors itself. Suggested reasons for a lack of participation by ethnic community groups are discussed along with societal, organisational and individual strategies for overcoming these barriers.

Introduction

Of all the groups identified as having their own needs, people from ethnic communities are probably one of the most diverse and yet, ironically, the most likely to be 'lumped together'. Young people from ethnic 'minority' groups could be from a number of diverse cultures, religions and backgrounds. They could be from first, second or third (or more) generations new to this country. English may or may not be their first language and depending on where they live, they may be in the minority or the majority in their local community. And all this is on top of differences such as gender, class, education. However it is almost certainly true that (Williams, cited in Webb, 2001: 9):

The simple matter of the colour of one's skin so profoundly affects the way one is treated, so radically shapes what one is to think and feel about this society, that the decision to generalise from such a division is valid.

But, why should outdoor organisations feel they should reach out to involve ethnic communities? What is the context that makes people committed to take action to enable ethnic participation in British Society? Nowadays, everyone uses the term multi-cultural society. Too often it seems simply to mean that we are trapped on these islands with people whose origins stem from different cultures. It is a matter of coping with these 'alien' intrusions. It is a situation which says ethnic persons do not belong here.

The presence of settled ethnic communities in Britain is viewed as a consequence of past history. Rather, it is a fact of an inextricable relationship of mutual engagement that extends into the present and the future. Unless this is recognised then there is no need to think about ethnic communities. Working with 'them' is seen as doing 'them' a favour, rather than making amends for the consequences of long term neglect and putting into place rights which have been denied for too long. Furthermore, we are told that British people need to be tolerant to ethnic groups. Tolerance is neither adequate nor appropriate for settled ethnic communities. To arrive at equality, members of ethnic communities need to be seen as full-time, legitimate members of British society. Only then will action to enable ethnic persons to fully participate in the future of Britain be seen as an overdue central social theme. What then does this mean to the outdoor education field?

Implications for outdoor education

There is a concern that through the simple process of 'targeting' a group such as young people from ethnic communities they are automatically marginalised with the differences between 'them' and 'us' emphasised, rather than the diversity that exists in society as a whole. It is also true that young people from ethnic communities are still likely to face discrimination in their dealing with authority in their public and professional lives. They are also far more likely to be amongst the more deprived or underachieving members of our society. The outdoor educator working with young people from ethnic communities therefore has a difficult balancing act to fulfil. They will need to recognise and celebrate diversity whilst at the same time recognising that some of those same groups will be marginalised by virtue of that very diversity. This balancing act can take the form of appreciating the ways you work with people from different ethnic and cultural backgrounds. Simple practical things such as referring to 'first' names rather than 'Christian' names or not making assumptions about religion or 'countries of origin' are significant.

It is important that outdoor educators feel able to ask: 'I do not feel that I know enough about this, but I feel that it is important. Would you help me to know a little bit more?' To be able to ask such a question with interest and care is an indication of a high level of confidence and skill in relating successfully to young people from different ethnic communities. It is essential to establish meaningful contact and to be open to the specific information a person can give, against an awareness of the different settings against which difference is played out. Programmes of activity need to be designed to reflect the needs and concerns of the many social and cultural backgrounds of the people concerned. Anyone working with people from ethnic communities needs training to gain the awareness and skills to effectively nurture and bring forward their unique individual contribution as who they are. Notably, many people belonging to the immigrant generation have specific needs around loss, culture clash, language difficulties and social isolation. It is particularly important to include elements of their culture of origin so that the inevitable introduction to what is new takes place against some anchors of familiarity. An effort should be made to ensure that any family members understand and approve of the programmes of activity offered. Conversely, people from ethnic communities who are born here are bi-cultural if not multi-cultural. They are British with a special cultural relationship to their country of origin. There is a need to attend to both elements of identity. As Britons they should lay claim to all that this country offers, but this is constantly undermined by the reality of racism. The pressure this puts on the already enormous task of negotiating identity against multiple cultural backgrounds means that support is much needed. Research (e.g., Roberts and Drogin, 1993; Ashley, 1990) has shown that issues which may affect people from ethnic communities include:

- Access to leisure and sports opportunities.
- Various areas of activity perceived as the preserve of particular social groups and not open to everyone.
- Lack of gender-specific activities and events in particular for young people where religion is an important factor.
- Language is an obstacle for some but in particular for refugee communities.
- Disillusionment with authoritative institutions such as the local authority, the police and the national government.
- Decisions being made about local matters without consultation of young people, who have significant knowledge of their locality.
- Community safety, crime and being victims of crime.
- Unemployment.
- Access to educational and training opportunities.
- Racism and other prejudice from other members of the local community.
- Lack of ability to be independent from family.
- Lack of public transport and other affordable transport in relation to the provision of programmes of activities.
- Lack of equipment such as basic outdoor or sports kit.
- Lack of role models.
- Legacy of exclusion resulting in the lack of participation by young people in many areas of activity and a sense of powerlessness to affect change.

Barriers to involvement

Most fundamentally, when discussing participation in outdoor activities and education it is evident that:

> . . . participation in outdoor adventures has traditionally been primarily stereotyped as a white, male activity. Although difficult to ascertain, the socialisation of [people from ethnic communities] has been exclusive of opportunities for outdoor adventure experience.
> (Roberts, 1996: 227)

The media and many outdoor brochures rarely include a single picture of anyone who contradicts the white, middle class stereotype. As Roberts (1996; 228) asks, 'if there are no women like me in these pictures of outdoor activities, why should I participate?' Ashley (1990) identifies four main areas which cause a lack of participation in outdoor activities; no interest or desire to participate, lack of funds, lack of knowledge or understanding, strong feelings or distrust for others. Crucially, he maintains, there is:

> . . . a need for more minority leaders in experiential education and also a need for providing experiential education for minority youths. Inability of non-minority leaders to communicate with the minorities [is] another factor. The fact that some minorities may not be able to relate to an experiential education experience, and that such experience is simply not a priority, are two other rationales for low minority participation.
>
> (Ashley, 1990: 370)

Ashley says that perceived stereotypes need to be challenged from the viewpoint of the traditional white, majority, and just as importantly, from the perspective of those belonging to ethnic minority groups. Both the perception of outdoor activity and the perception of participation for certain groups in outdoor activity need to be re-visited.

Strategies for action

At the present time, human rights, equal opportunities, access and social inclusion are on everyone's tongue. Funders structure their schemes to resource initiatives focused on such themes. In an increasingly multi-cultural society within a globalised world, young people from ethnic communities have a special contribution to make if they are provided with the support that they need. Although too many young people from ethnic communities have more than their fair share of the burden of growing up, when the right conditions are provided their energies, once directed, can be a powerhouse for action. Frameworks to enable full participation by young people from ethnic communities should meet a number of criteria. Firstly, organisational development should be underpinned by senior level commitment to equal opportunities. Secondly, the development of a strategy to enable full participation by young people from ethnic communities should include:

- Outreach to organisations working with young people from ethnic communities, including ethnic community groups.

- Consultation with young people from ethnic communities.
- Focused initiatives, in partnership with organisations working with young people from ethnic communities, including ethnic community groups.
- Use of positive images in communication and resource materials.
- Development of socially and culturally relevant range of activities.
- Allocation of staff time and resources.
- Structured staff training and development.
- Evaluation using measures which recognise that 'Equal opportunities means equal outcomes'.

In organisational terms this implies a commitment to equal opportunities at a senior level; adequate resources; organisational cultural change; personnel development and a framework for action. In particular, outdoor organisations need to ensure that:

> . . . a culturally competent and responsive program is one that demonstrates sensitivity to, and understanding of, cultural differences in programme design, implementation and evaluation.
>
> (Washington and Roberts, 1999; 360)

Within the environmental, outdoor activity and outdoor education sectors there are huge networks providing a comprehensive range of activities, developmental opportunities, training, social and leisure opportunities. These can significantly enhance the quality of life of disadvantaged and vulnerable groups, including ethnic groups. It is also a positive setting for the engagement of mainstream groups with ethnic groups. It is worth noting that outdoor activity and education can contribute through the following:

- The opportunity to enter a supportive framework.
- Exposure to a widened range of roles and values which assist self-determination.
- Exposure to a widened range of stimulation.
- Opportunities to participate in activities which enhance the quality of life.
- The widened availability of guidance.
- Opportunities to engage in activities which give direct control over aspects of one's life and immediate surroundings, thereby nurturing a sense of personal power.

Opening out opportunities for participation in a wide variety of activities affects vulnerable persons at the core of their being. Gradually they are enabled to arrive at something which all of us take for granted in our everyday life – the ability to work towards the fulfilment of ordinary life goals and therefore 'dream for real'. In order for a person to feel motivated, to feel that they can make choices, to shape and direct their lives it is essential they possess a sense of personal potential, sense of personal power, resources and access to resources. All too often these simple needs are denied to those from ethnic communities and particularly so in the outdoor activity and education field which is widely seen as an alien and alienating environment. Access to engagement with the outdoors is not only about physical access (e.g. provision of transport) but also about intellectual access. The generation of activities, heritage resources and site-interpretation which reflect and draw from diverse cultures are also critical. Multi-cultural interpretation takes place within a framework which recognises that all cultures are multi-cultural and that culture is in evolution. We are all recipients of culture as well as creators of culture. Of course, it is of the utmost importance that local, national and international culture is presented, but we must acknowledge that the values which frame its presentation are our own. All of us need to work consciously at positioning ourselves socially and culturally and be aware of our personal impact on the people we work with. Nowhere is this more important and more apparent than when acting as agents for social change. As Draguns (1989: 15) explains:

> . . . our legitimate role as agents of social change is limited by our level of knowledge on the one hand, and by the imperative of imposing one's convictions and beliefs upon a client on the other.

Those of us who run programmes of activities with the remit to serve all sections of society need to examine how we make our special contribution through the expertise of our field of work. At the same time we must engage those we serve in a relevant way. A crucial development is to jump to connect and enjoy engagement with a part of society that is also part of us. A lot of work needs to be done around facilitating the enjoyment and

valuing the excitement of a multi-cultural society. Much of this will touch on revelatory experience, discovery and personal transformation – a shift of vision about what being in a multi-cultural society means. Outdoor education in its broadest sense can have a significant role to play in this.

References

Ashley, F. B. (1990) Ethnic Minorities' Involvement with Outdoor Experiential Education, in Miles, J. and S. Priest (Ed.) *Adventure Education.* State College, Penn: Venture Publishing Inc.

Draguns, J. (1989) Dilemmas and Choices in Cross-Cultural Counselling: The Universal versus the Culturally Distinctive, in Pederson., P. et al. (Eds) *Counselling Across Cultures.* Honolulu: University of Hawaii Press.

Roberts, N. (1996) Women of Colour in Experiential Education: Crossing Cultural Boundaries, in Warren, K. (Ed.) *Women's Voices in Experiential Education.* Dubuque, IA: Kendall/Hunt Publishing.

Washington, S. J. and Roberts, N. S. (1999) Adventure Education for Teaching Cross-Cultural Perspectives, in Miles, J. C. and Priest, S. (Eds.) *Adventure Programming.* State College, Penn: Venture Publishing Inc.

Webb, M. (2001) Black Young People, in Factor, F., Chauhan, V. and Pitts, J. (Eds.) *The RHP Companion to Working With Young People.* Lyme Regis: Russell House Publishing.

11 Overseas Youth Expeditions: Learning and Leadership Considerations

Nina Saunders

Abstract

In this chapter, the expedition experience will be explored. It will offer ideas from the writer's experience working on many types of expeditions in a variety of contexts and over a number of years. It focuses on the concept of overseas expeditions for young people from the United Kingdom from leadership, group management and personal development aspects. The youth expedition has historically formed a key element of many outdoor learning programs, for example, Duke of Edinburgh and Outward Bound. It is the most common type of expedition experience that the outdoor educator is likely to become involved in. The concept of an expedition is of a diverse nature, which can prove challenging for both leader and participant alike. But what is it that makes the expedition so important? The aim of this chapter is to stimulate some discussion and critical thought, but not necessarily through an exhaustive examination of all the relative concepts.

History

> *Something hidden. Go and find it*
> *Go and look behind the Ranges*
> *Something lost behind the Ranges.*
> *Lost and waiting for you. Go!*
> Kipling (The Explorer, 1898)

When many of us hear the word 'expedition,' it conjures up images of early popular explorers such as Shackleton and his crew fighting for survival in the Antarctic or perhaps the later pioneers of Himalayan mountaineering such as Hillary on Everest. These are famous images that cover only a small part of the meaning of an expedition.

The first expeditions were quests for acclaim and recognition. Later, the pursuit became one for wealth as typified by Marco Polo and Drake. Then came the mission for knowledge and the scientific explorers such as Cook, Mungo Park, and Scott. It might be suggested that science was the excuse for these adventurers and as they filled the last 'blank on the map' they became the first modern day explorers. Today, the search, particularly for participants of youth expeditions, can be less for scientific or external knowledge and more a search to discover about oneself. As Mortlock (1984: 5) suggests, 'Your success is determined by your efforts and not by results, and you may come to realise that the most important journey is the journey inwards.'

Meaning

In the Oxford English Dictionary (1989), an expedition is defined as, 'A journey, voyage or excursion made for some definite purpose.' However, this is extremely vague and covers a wide variety of contexts. The expedition has more specifically been described as:

> *The setting forth for definite purpose. It involves leaving the status quo of one's personal, cultural island and launching forth into uncertainty and change. By its very nature it involves risk – the risk of the unknown and the challenge of new experience.*
> (March and Wattchow 1991: 4)

By nature, the expedition is usually an extended experience; it can take place in many mediums, using many forms of transport that allow us to undertake 'the journey.' This concept of 'setting forth' is central to the expedition. An expedition could therefore be anything from a three-day canoe trip for a group of teenagers to acquire new paddling skills on Loch Lomond to an exploratory scientific journey to the Amazon, or even first ascents at high altitude in remote mountain ranges.

It must have aims or objectives, or at very least 'a purpose,' and it will have responsibilities. Edwards (2000) suggests these responsibilities are not only to the expedition members themselves, but also to others who have an interest in the team's objectives. These could include sponsors, educational institutions and individuals who support the expedition's proposals. The expedition itself will also have responsibilities to the host country being visited, both on a community and environmental level. Before embarking on such a trip, the leaders and team members have to consider very carefully as to whether they can commit to these responsibilities and join in its vision.

There are many reasons why people may undertake an expedition, whether solo or as a team. These range from the claim to becoming 'the first to make a journey,' to the advancement of science, community aid or development, to education and fundraising. Therefore, expeditions are a vehicle for some process of change that we believe is important, whether or not the goal is attained. The experience cannot be predestined and the process extends beyond that of a physical journey.

Types of expeditions

With much of the world having been significantly explored and mapped today, there are now less of the so-called 'ground breaking' expeditions. However, new frontiers are continually being broken down. For the purposes of this chapter, three types of expeditions; personal, commercial and youth expeditions will be defined and described. It will then concentrate on the benefits to participants and the responsibilities and expectations of a leader.

Personal expeditions

These are expeditions, which are organised as a private trip amongst friends or colleagues. At the very least, each team member will have a responsibility to the other members to share the planning, organisation and fulfilment of the expedition's goals. An expedition such as this could be anything from a week in North Wales with a group of friends wanting to increase their rock climbing experience to a team of colleagues heading to Chile to spend three weeks sea kayaking around a remote area of Patagonia.

Most of these types of expeditions are self-funded. They may receive some sort of financial support from organisations such as the

Mount Everest Foundation (MEF) or the Scottish Mountaineering Trust (SMT); if the expedition fulfils the sponsors' requirements. For example, the 'Heart of Asia Expedition 2002' to Mongolia received some monetary aid from these organisations, approximating one fifth of the expedition's expenditure. Leaders or team members may not be involved in outdoor education. Furthermore, they may not, and need not, hold any formal leader qualifications.

Commercial expeditions

These are trips organised by private companies, many of which are based in the United Kingdom. The guided trip has the clearest norms for the leader and follower, and ones that are fairly public knowledge. Expedition members, or clients, will pay a set amount of money to the company to be formally 'led' by a guide on a predetermined trek or climb. The guide makes virtually all decisions; client involvement is a matter of the guides' discretion.

Such trips are a fairly modern phenomenon and the vast majority involve adventure tourism and/or trekking elements, but they are still commonly referred to as 'expeditions.' However, the term 'expedition' is currently more suitably applied to trips of an advanced nature, such as those organised to climb the Himalayan giants in Nepal and Pakistan. No personal development goals may be stated. However, clients may experience personal development and emotional satisfaction from taking part in this type of expedition.

Commercial trips have received much criticism as clients may have very little experience. There have been incidents in which clients have lost their lives, such as the Everest disaster of 1996 (Krakauer 1997; Gammelgaard 1999). Since then, the IGO 8000, an International Association whose members represent professionally organised expeditions to the 8000 metre peaks, has been established to ensure that high standards of professional conduct, client care and environmental responsibility are adhered to (IGO 8000, 2002).

Qualifications held by leaders working for UK based expedition companies may range from none at all, to International Mountain Guide. Many companies place as much emphasis on leader's personal experience of overseas activities and general travel as well as formal outdoor qualifications.

Youth expeditions

Youth expeditions typically involve persons aged between 16 and 25. There will normally be extensive fundraising prior to the actual expedition. Furthermore, it is not uncommon for such expeditions to 'use the overseas environment as a classroom for both skills and self-learning' (Powter, 1998: 40). There will normally be formal elements of personal development for all participants and other aspects, such as science or community related elements.

The Young Explorers Trust (YET) is the umbrella organisation for all UK based youth expedition companies. It includes a number of charities and private companies offering opportunities to young people including; World Challenge Expeditions, BSES Expeditions, Raleigh International and Quest Overseas. They all have their own history and philosophies. Group sizes range between 10 and 70 and trips may run from between four weeks to four months. Leaders normally have some formal outdoor qualifications as well as outdoor or travel experience, depending on their leader status and type of expedition.

With the 'gap year' becoming an increasingly popular British phenomenon (Simpson, 2002) the subsequent demand on youth expedition companies is high and places on these trips are becoming extremely competitive. Recently, even Prince William took part on a youth expedition in his gap year between school and university (Hardman, 2000).

Expedition phases

A youth expedition comprises of different phases, most of which will involve the leader. The following phases are typical:

- **Build-up phase:** this occurs prior to the expedition; it may include the leader, group members, legal guardians and the school. Everyone is briefed, an itinerary detailed and aims or objectives finalised. There may be team building, fundraising events, fitness and skills training, e.g. mini camping trips. The leader must ensure that their team is aware of all aspects of the expedition.

- **Expedition phase:** the expedition itself is an incredibly intense period for both the students and especially the leader, who can sometimes feel very isolated, especially if they have a small group and there are no other leaders in the local area. The actual expedition may be broken down into different phases, depending on the expedition's main objectives. Some may take place independent of each other, whilst other expeditions may use a more integrated approach.

- **Adventure phase:** the team may embark on a multi-day trek or canoe trip with suitable objectives and there may be some specialist training. This should be progressive, (throwing people in at the deep end can sometimes do more harm than good) and it should be challenging but fun. The leader may be selected for their qualifications and experience in specific activity to correspond with the adventure phase objectives. Within the adventure phase, there may be smaller but significant phases, such as the independent team trip or a solo element.

- **Community phase:** the team could be responsible for helping out in a local community on a formal or informal level, perhaps teaching English, painting a school, digging wells etc.

- **Scientific phase:** the team may carry out scientific studies suitably matched to the experience of the leader and team. The time available, location, expertise, and local knowledge must all contribute to the project that should be worthwhile and enjoyable.

- **Post-expedition phase:** a review of the expedition and its phases is necessary to enable the participants and leader to learn from the experience. Reports should be written and reunions or slide show evenings may be organised. Team members should also be prepared for the often difficult readjustment to regular life upon return, referred to as 'post residential syndrome' (Allison, 2000: 75).

Leadership on youth expeditions

Leadership is the capacity to move others toward goals shared with you, with a focus and competency they would not achieve on their own.

(Graham 1997: 12)

The issue of expedition leadership is a complex matter. An expedition leader is typically experienced, qualified and a positive role model to the students. They may not be paid for their time and talents; they may even pay to go, depending on the companies' guidelines and philosophy. They should be selected for their personal qualities, technical knowledge and skills, interpersonal group work skills, and active experience (Putnam, 1994b: 3).

Early research into leadership suggested that a certain group of personality characteristics were fundamental to being a good leader. However, the attempt to generalise successful personality traits of a 'charismatic' leader is now outdated. Many other theories of leadership have been explored (Yukl, 1994; Adair, 1989). Although charisma may help, most theorists now accept the notion that leadership is 'emergent' and successful leadership 'is more likely to be determined by environmental and intra-group factors than by any predetermined characteristics of the leader himself, such as charisma' (Toft, 1998: 38).

However, some would argue that charisma is an important quality for those leading expeditions over a prolonged and intense period. A leader can often motivate the team, combat low morale and generally set the tone of the whole expedition. The personal qualities of the leader can hold the expeditions components together. It is not easy to explain or identify these qualities but Putnam (1994a: 17) suggests they 'include self-awareness; sensitivity to people, the environment and changing situations; a sense of values; the ability to inspire; common sense; and sound judgement.'

There are many leadership theories, styles and qualities, which are discussed elsewhere in this book. The expedition leader should be aware of these and use them appropriately.

Responsibilities

When working on an overseas youth expedition, there will be additional issues to those that the leader encounters in the UK. The responsibilities of the leader revolve around three main relationships, as discussed by Mortlock (1984: 19), the relationship to one's self, to others and the environment. The blend of these three elements will constantly change.

Whose expedition is it anyway?

By accepting responsibility for the expedition and its members, the leader should continually remind themselves that it is the students' expedition. So whilst the team may be making errors, this is their experience to learn from, (unless safety is compromised). There may be a fantastic looking unclimbed route on a nearby peak; however, the leader will have to save these personal ambitions, as their responsibilities are to the group being led. Further, it is important that the leader is mature enough and prepared for the responsibility of taking students overseas.

Qualifications versus experience

In the UK, technical skills and qualifications are considered essential if an outdoor educator wishes to lead groups on outdoor activities. However, for overseas expedition leadership, there are no hard and fast rules, and recently the issue of leader's qualifications has attracted a lot of attention. With the introduction of the Adventure Activities Licensing Authority, some youth expedition companies have responded to the standards and recommendations for UK based adventure and applied them to their overseas operations, setting their own standards, codes of practice and guidelines.

The leader must assess any added risks such as the effect of altitude, the wilderness setting and glacial travel. They may hold the company's standard qualification for leading in winter conditions in the UK, but are they ready for the added responsibility in an overseas setting?

It is not sufficient to have just the so-called 'technical skills' of outdoor leadership; the leader must be competent in many other areas. Many companies employ leaders on the basis of their experience; including general travel, foreign language skills, knowledge of specific areas and personal contacts. Being able to deal with the different environment, culture and the so-called 'soft and meta' skills of leadership are just as important for those working on expeditions. They are all part of the leaders 'judgement' which is fundamental in an expedition environment.

Environmental responsibilities

Typically, an expedition may take place in a fragile environment. In the expedition context 'environmental responsibilities' are also associated with cultural and sociological issues. Environmental responsibilities extend to the impact of the group on the land. The expedition and its members must adopt a minimum impact approach, for example, burning toilet paper and avoiding using wood for cooking. The cultural background, traditions and customs of the local people may not encompass knowledge and use of modern environmental ethics or responsible behaviour, and if the team intends to educate them, they must do so with sensitivity. However, if the expedition team can improve the local environment, this sets an example to the local people, even if they don't follow suit. Consider this example from Mongolia:

> There are few Mongolians who actually follow the western ethics and environmental ideals that many of us have grown up with. They will hunt in a protected area and dispose of rubbish randomly. I suppose to some extent this is their way of life, and have lived like this for thousands of years. However, they will throw all rubbish out of the car window (we tended to have a little stash of rubbish in the back of the jeeps when travelling, but if our driver found it, she would curse us and try to throw it out). If at all possible, take any rubbish from your campsites back to the local town, for a half decent disposal, rather than just being thrown into the countryside. Mongolia has the potential to become the worlds greatest rubbish dump, particularly along the roadsides.
>
> (Saunders, 2003: 26)

Other issues may be fundamentally embedded in the society or the local community that the expedition may be entering. Concerns such as the team's impact on the local people, the community and the country itself have to be considered. Will the local people start begging if sweets are handed out to local children? Whilst in itself this is not a harmful gesture; it may encourage unacceptable behaviour. Will the community become reliant on tourism and forget their traditional ways of life? If local people are employed, it is important to negotiate fair wages and consider their welfare. Foster good relations with the local people by researching cultural traditions; how to act, what to wear, taking photographs etc. Be politically aware; is the presence of the team perceived in a positive light? Team members should behave and act as ambassadors from their home country.

Safety, risks and hazards

The expedition will include elements of adventure, danger and risk. Risk can be perceived or real, and it is the leader's responsibility to strike an appropriate balance between the two. The uncertainty of the outcome of risks and challenges faced on the expedition can provide the crux for development. The leader should ensure that safe practices and company procedures are followed. Putnam (1994b: 2) suggests leaders should take into account the age of participants, level of experience, capabilities, group numbers and any unique hazards or risks when on the expedition. A leader working on a youth expedition has a 'duty of care' and if the expedition members are under the age of 18, then the leader is also in a position of *in loco parentis* ('in place of a parent'). The leader is responsible for the care, conduct and custody of all members of the expedition and this extends to any local people employed, such as porters or cooks (Deegan, 2003: 35).

It is generally accepted that a risk assessment will have been completed and the team informed of hazards, risks, and safety procedures before the expedition takes place. If anything untoward happens, the leader must take complete control if the safety of the group is under threat. It should be recognised that young students are just embarking on their adult lives and their experience, technical competence and judgement is far less advanced than that of the designated leader. Many situations and incidents are unanticipated, and the leader must use their judgement to assess them and retain a flexible leadership style to suit their team's choice of level of involvement. An overseas expedition may encounter different kinds of risks and hazards to those found in the UK (Table 1).

Personal development

What I hear – I forget
What I see – I remember
What I do – I learn
(Chinese proverb)

Table 1   The kinds of hazards which can occur on overseas expeditions

Environmental hazards	Health hazards	Activity related	Travel	Communications	Accidents and emergencies
Different terrain (e.g. glaciers, high passes)	Increased risk to general health	Swimming (e.g. rip tides)	Use and standard of local transport (e.g. buses, taxis)	Language difficulties	Infrastructure/ availability of rescue services
Naturally occurring incidents (e.g. landslides, flooding, rock fall, avalanche)	Presence of different diseases (e.g. cholera, typhoid)	Trekking (e.g. steeper terrain)	Standard of local infrastructure (e.g. dirt tracks, mountain passes)	Misunderstandings between team and local people	Inaccessible location (e.g. walking in remote/wilderness areas)
Water features (e.g. deep, cold, fast flowing, steep banks)	Impure water sources	Camping (e.g. cooking)	Employees (e.g. qualifications, sobriety of drivers)	Negotiations and bargaining (e.g. purchase of goods)	Lack of medical facilities (e.g. equipment and medical expertise)
Weather/climatic extremes (e.g. heat, cold, humidity)	Unhygienic food preparation	Rafting (e.g. river rapids)	Flying to overseas destination	Internal group communications	Political unrest or terrorism
Flora and fauna (e.g. poisonous plants and dangerous animals such as bears, snakes, spiders)	Effects of higher altitude (e.g. altitude sickness, dehydration)	Inadequate equipment			Natural disasters (e.g. earthquake, volcanic eruption)
Food and water (e.g. unusual and limited/variable sources)	Psychological and physiological stress				
	Medication and use of different drugs (e.g. Diamox, anti-malarials and other non-prescription drugs)				
	Sexual activity				
	Human behavioural				
	Violence, robbery, kidnap, theft, rape (by locals or team members)				
	Abnormal group behaviour (psychological and physiological) due to cultural factors, stress and the environment (e.g. bullying)				
	Culture shock				

It is assumed that the leader has relevant experience, knowledge and understanding of the outdoor experience and the application of theories in practice. Personal development is often one of the major goals on a youth expedition, and this cannot be achieved if the leader controls the team in an authoritarian manner for the duration of the expedition. Throughout the expedition, the leader must give the team and its members the opportunity to display, use and develop their skills. Mistakes may be made, but this is part of the learning process. Therefore, the term 'leader' in the expedition context may not be the most appropriate, in this context, the term, 'facilitator' is more suitable. An expedition leader must remain flexible and be someone who can liberate 'people to do what is needed in the best possible way' (Graham 1997: 9). They should promote the idea of expedition ownership and the expedition as a, 'community or a shared venture with each member as a stake holder' (Putnam 1994a: 5).

Ownership

The expedition is about leaving the known, discovering new skills in a new environment with different people or unfamiliar combinations of these factors creating new situations. Today's expeditions are for the most part about the exploration of these new situations rather than a new country or mountain range. It is important to realise that every task, team, individual and environment mix will be unique; this leads to a great 'social unknown' as teams explore issues internally and externally. Consider this example from the author's experience as a leader on a six week expedition to Alaska in 1999:

The first week was really hard work, helping the students put up their tents, showing them how to use the stoves etc. But as they became used to living in the wilderness, I began to take a step back. The team began to coordinate themselves and proved they were responsible. One of the culminating points of the expedition was for them as a team to head off on a three-day trip independent of the leaders. When I visited their campsite, I was astounded at how organised, safe and creative they had all been. That night together sleeping under the stars, we were treated to an amazing display of the Northern Lights and I felt proud of the

individuals and the team that were with me, knowing that they had learnt and achieved so much in so little time.

The students were gradually enabled to take on more responsibility for themselves as the leader took small steps back. At the beginning of the expedition, the leader had all the knowledge; a 'full glass' of information, skills and experience, whereas each student had an empty glass; no knowledge. Gradually, the leader imparted their knowledge, filling the students' glass with information, skills and relevant expertise. Their skills increased in the form of fitness, human, technical and environmental skills which Mortlock (1984: 27) considers to be central to the adventurous journey. The team's glass was eventually overflowing, as they were receiving information not just from the leader, but also from each other, their own newfound skills, experiences, independence, and the environment which all contributed to their ingenuity. The leader, whilst still occupying a position of overall responsibility gradually became redundant. The mix of factors was suitably balanced and whilst the developmental experience may not have been perfect, the team's progression led to an unanticipated but distinct synergy.

The concept of challenge is inextricably linked to the unknown and it has been documented that there is a need to remove learners from their comfort zones or 'cocoon' in order to develop and learn. This concept is relevant in the context of an overseas expedition. Simply being in a different country removes the participants from the familiarity of their normal life. The cocoon then refers to a group's new 'in country' experiences and defines its parameters. As a team gains experience, there is a substantial widening of their cocoon and the parameters are continually redefined; unless the team proves to be highly incompetent. At the start of the expedition, individual team members have a limited degree of knowledge and skills; their cocoon is fairly small and restricted. Making mistakes is central to the process of the cocoon's expansion, and the leader should be able to give members increasing responsibility as the expedition progresses, leading to an increasing synergy and fewer mistakes.

Budgets, resources, safety, common sense and even the objectives of the programme often limit options, but the onus is on the leader to provide some level of ownership for participants. The process of meeting challenges and subsequential ownership of the expedition provides the learner with the material for reflection that can create developmental opportunities. Therefore the expedition is a particularly powerful learning vehicle.

Let the mountains speak for themselves

The extended process of reflection or reviewing often falls into phases that allow the team to review their experiences (actions and inactions) on a regular basis. These cycles of 'plan, do, review, learn, and apply' can then be utilised in its following phases, therefore allowing continuity and growth. There is also the idea that 'the mountains speak for themselves,' and this concept also has its place within the expedition experience. However, for transference to occur there is a need for some level of reflection.

Women, culture and leadership

Women make just as good leaders as men, but they don't lead the same way as men and they shouldn't try.

(Graham, 1997: 40)

It is necessary to say something regarding women and leadership on overseas youth expeditions. The basic principles for leadership are the same. However, women can experience a lack of acceptance by some group members, which can make their job difficult. The female leader should be ready for this type of prejudice, which in the first instance can be ignored. Graham (1997: 41) suggests that female expedition leaders have often found they have had to 'prove themselves' to men in particular. However, a female leader should not adjust their behaviour to gain respect. He advises that if unacceptable behaviour continues, they should confront the offender firstly alone and then, if further action is required, in front of the other team members. The leader must assert overall control.

Culturally, leaders and group members may also come across constraints associated with travelling in overseas countries, such as different dress codes in Muslim countries and differences in

the way local men view women in leadership positions. Knowledge of cultural differences should be discussed as a team, so as not to cause offence to local people. Finally, there may be added feminine medical concerns and hygiene requirements that will have to be dealt with by both males and females in the group; these should be addressed before the expedition departs.

Conclusion

So why might the expedition be a suitable vehicle for learning? Expeditions are complex and unique and Mortlock (1984) suggests that, for these reasons an expedition can bring together everything that is central to outdoor and adventure education. An expedition can represent the pinnacle of all outdoor experiences, bringing together elements of discovery through new experiences, including camping, community, experience of new cultures and independence from the familiarity of home and family. For some young people, expeditions constitute giant steps in their experience. Through their reactions to these situations, they can form relationships through their new experiences and develop the 'self' as well as their practical skills.

The accepted view in outdoor education is that a good expedition leader facilitates ownership of the expedition for the team. When this happens, group members gain most in terms of personal development. The review process is also important in enriching member's experiences. It should be an ongoing process, from conception to the conclusion of the expedition. Evidence suggests that the more a participant is involved in the expedition, then the more participants benefit.

Therefore, experiential education and democratic empowerment (Powter, 1998) is the focus for developing participants, and the expedition leader should be familiar with these concepts and their application in the expedition environment. Every expedition is different; there are no hard and fast rules to predict successful outcomes. Potential leaders should, however, be aware of key principles before embarking on a youth expedition. This chapter had identified many of those principles including some features of good leadership. The key function of a leader as a positive role model should be to inspire, enthuse and be sensitive to the needs of the young people for whom they have responsibility.

References

Adair, J. (1989) *Effective Leadership: A Self-Development Manual.* Aldershot: Gower.

Allison, P. (2000) *Research from the Ground up: Post-Expedition Adjustment.* Cumbria: Brathay Hall.

Deegan, P. (2003) Welfare State. *Summit.* 29: 34–7.

Edwards, D. (2000) *Exploring New Frontiers.* Glasgow: Royal Scottish Geographical Society.

Gammelgaard, L. (1999) *Climbing High: A Woman's Account of Surviving the Everest Tragedy.* London: Seal Press.

Graham, J. (1997) *Outdoor Leadership: Techniques, Common Sense and Self-Confidence.* Seattle: The Mountaineers.

Hardman, R. (2000) Prince Has a Mountain to Climb in Patagonia. *The Telegraph.* 30th September.

International Guiding Operators (2002). Retrieved April 19th, *www.igo8000.com/statement.htm*

Krakauer, J. (1997) *Into Thin Air.* London: Macmillan Publishers.

March, B. and Wattchow, B. (1991) The Importance of the Expedition in Adventure Education. *Journal of Adventure Education.* 8: 2, 1–5.

Mortlock, C. (1984) *The Adventure Alternative.* Cumbria. Cicerone Press.

Powter, G. (1998) *Group Dynamics from a Leadership Perspective*, in Toft, M. (Ed.) *Playing it Safe.* Alberta: The Alpine Club of Canada.

Putnam, R. (1994a) *Safe and Responsible Youth Expeditions.* London: Young Explorers Trust.

Putnam, R. (1994b) *Code of Practice for Youth Expeditions.* London: Young Explorers Trust.

Saunders, N. (2003) *British Heart of Asia Expedition Report.* Unpublished report compiled for the Mount Everest Foundation. (Reference 02/35).

Simpson, K. (2002) *Power, Knowledge and the World: Youth Travellers Constructing Global Communities.* Paper presented at the International Conference on Global Youth, Plymouth University, 3–5th September, 2001.

The Oxford English Dictionary (1989) *The Oxford English Dictionary.* Oxford: Clarendon Press.

Toft, M. (1998) *The Trip Leaders Responsibilities.* in Toft, M. (Ed.) *Playing it Safe.* Alberta: The Alpine Club of Canada.

Yukl, G. (1994) *Leadership in Organisations.* New Jersey: Prentice Hall.

Section 3:
The Practice of Outdoor Education

12 Outdoor Leadership: Art or Science?

Peter Barnes

Abstract

This chapter presents an overview of the skills and attributes needed by effective leaders in general and outdoor leaders in particular. It provides a synthesis of some of the most commonly used theories and models of leadership and relates this to outdoor situations. It also discusses whether leadership is a skill to be learnt or an innate art. As of necessity, it presents only a small snapshot into a large and fascinating subject.

Introduction

Outdoor leadership represents one of the most complex and demanding areas of leadership; it remains one of the very few places where a potential outcome of bad leadership can be physical or psychological injury or even death. Likewise, it continues to be an area where a good leader can make a real and significant impact on the people they are responsible for. Outdoor leadership encompasses a great number of attributes, many of which are covered in detail elsewhere in this book. There are also a number of ongoing issues and discussions, notably about professionalism and the assessment and training of outdoor leaders; in particular, the skills that can be formally assessed. This chapter aims to take a step back from issues such as the technical/interpersonal skills debate and look instead at what makes a good outdoor leader. For truly effective leadership there are few definitive or prescriptive guidelines; the approach and style both depend on the people and circumstances involved. Graham (1997: 11–2) suggests that:

Leadership is not a science to be picked up in one book or course, but an art to be learned over time. It's not simply a set of rules to be followed, but an ability to build relationships. It's not merely skills and techniques, but a subjective blend of personality and style. Leadership involves not only the body and the mind, but the spirit and character as well: good leaders have the intuition, compassion, common sense and courage it takes to stand and lead.

Whilst this may seem a lot to ask of any one person it is important to emphasise that some of the dimensions of leadership that Graham highlights could be considered innate whilst others might be learnt. Indeed, Graham is emphatic in his assertion that leadership is an art rather than a science. This topic is returned to later.

In one of the most significant books written on outdoor leadership, Priest and Gass (1997) identify a number of what they consider to be the key attributes of a leader. To do this they use the analogy of a wall:

- **Bricks (hard skills)**: technical skills, safety skills, environmental skills.
- **Bricks (soft skills)**: instructional skills, organisational skills, facilitational skills.
- **Mortar (meta skills)**: effective communication, flexible leadership style, professional ethics, problem solving, decision making, experience-based judgement.
- **Foundation (underpinning)**: social psychology, history and philosophy.

The Priest and Gass list can be adapted to give the following attributes:

- vision and motivation
- judgement and responsibility
- leadership styles
- leadership orientation
- caring leadership
- being true to yourself

The various skills; technical skills, communication, and instructional skills and so on are all essential and specific components of good leaderships. But the six attributes listed above can be maintained as the very heart of being a good leader – these help define the spirit and character of a leader.

Vision and self-motivation

It has been said that leadership without vision is leadership for its own sake. Sharon Wood, the first

American woman to reach the top of Everest (cited in Graham, 1997: 16) wrote that:

> The most important aspect of leadership is having a reason for leading beyond investing in your own ego . . . always check your intention. Ask yourself why you lead.

In nearly every occasion the reason for leadership will come down to having some sort of vision of what it is that a person hopes to achieve as a leader. This vision might be something that is kept private and serves as a motivating force or it might be something that is shared; in the nature of visionary leadership. Vision is not only about the work of a leader; it is also about a leader's ability to be honest with themselves. As Sharon Wood said, a leader must question their reason for wanting to lead. The answer, if honest, will influence not only how a person works and leads, but also the sort of work they choose to do. However, like all simple questions, the answer can lead to more complex debates. For example: 'What can I bring to my work in the outdoors?' and, even more difficult, 'What are my beliefs with regard to working in the outdoors?' Finally, and even more difficult yet, is the question 'Is my vision and motivation relevant to the needs, wants and possible vision of the people that I work with?'

Working in the outdoors, particularly with young people may often require a leader to take a middle road between idealist and realist and this is something that leaders must learn to deal with in their own way. A significant difficulty with young people is that they often have no overt vision of their own. This is not to say that all young people are aimless drifters. This is clearly not the case. However, the teenage and young adult years are all about exploration, discovery and often frustration; the vision tends to come later. The important consideration is to temper idealism with realism. Warren (2001: 48) illustrates this compromise beautifully:

> When I was a newly qualified teacher I was seriously expecting a glamorous life, filled with moments of learning breakthroughs and touching pastoral Dead Poet's Society hugs and personal revelations. It took me about three months to realise that this was total garbage, and if I wanted my working life to mean anything it would be because Darren actually remembered his homework diary after two weeks of persuasion.

Judgement and responsibility

One attribute that is at the heart of all leadership decisions and often only acquired through making mistakes and learning from them is the ability to exercise judgement. This is usually taken as the ability to make decisions based on experience, knowledge, qualification, personal skill and 'gut instinct'. More than anything else it is this aspect of leadership that requires experience and maturity. Judgement is, in many ways, the hardest aspect of leadership to master precisely because of its intangible nature. Essentially, judgement could be considered as taking all the facts at the leader's disposal, using their experience to have a good guess at the facts they don't know and then deciding whether the intended action is prudent and reasonable rather than negligent.

Obviously, but often missed, the biggest unknown when working in the outdoors may be the possible action of the people in the group. You might think you have all the angles covered and then the people in your care do something completely unexpected. This is where experience and 'expecting the unexpected' come into play. It is important, however, to always recognise the legal implications and responsibility of your judgement. All inexperienced people in the outdoors can sometimes act irrationally and children cannot, in the eyes of the law, be expected to act reasonably at all. This means that even if, in your judgement, you could trust the people involved to act in a certain way and they do something else that results in them being harmed it is usually you who is at fault and not them.

Leadership styles

To a large extent the essence of good leadership lies in the style and orientation of the leadership adopted. Two of the most effective models for demonstrating this are the leadership continuum of Tannerbaum and Schimdt (1973) and the situational leadership matrix of Hershey and Blanchard (1982). The leadership continuum consists of a sliding scale with the leader telling, selling, testing, consulting, joining and delegating. These actions or roles can be split into three

Figure 1 Situational leadership (cited in Ogilvie, 1993: p54)

Relationship (Low → High) / Task (Low → High)	Low task	High task
High	High relationship **Participatory** Low task	High relationship **Adaptive/flexible** High task
Low	Low relationship **Delagatory** Low task	Low relationship **Authoritarian** High task

pairings which give an indication of the broad leadership style: autocratic (telling and selling), democratic (test and consulting) and abdicratic (joining and delegating). At the left of the continuum, telling, the leader enjoys total autocratic leadership. This is usually a very safe style of leadership but can be stifling for those the leader is working with. At the other extreme the leader has abdicated leadership authority, but not responsibility and the group is allowed to make its own mistakes. There is a time and a place for this style of leadership as much as for autocratic leadership. However, it can quickly lead to unsafe or out-of-control situations. It may seem as if the ideal position is somewhere between these two extremes but the truth is that the style of leadership a good leader displays can be swinging back and forwards on an almost constant basis.

The situational leadership matrix combines the leadership style with the group's inter-relationship level mapped against the level of task difficulty. It presents four leadership styles:

- **Authoritarian**: high task/low relationship.
- **Adaptive/flexible**: high task/high relationship.
- **Participatory**: low task/high relationship.
- **Delegatory**: low task/low relationship.

Authoritarian

The leader is making all the decisions, although these decisions may be 'sold' to the group. This style of leadership is very effective for task-oriented activities where there is no room or time for flexibility or discussion. This style of leadership does not, however, allow any room for personal growth, (although morale and motivation may be boosted by success) because it stifles initiative and creativity. This style would also be adopted where a group is just getting used to each other and there is uncertainty regarding the abilities and skills held by individuals within the group. The other circumstance in which this situation might come about is where there is an emergency that takes priority over any group development or interaction.

Adaptive/flexible

This represents a stage further in engaging the group with the decision-making process. The power of the final decision rests partly with the group, but mainly with the leader. Personal growth is therefore enhanced by the group being given the chance of contributing to the discussion; even if, ultimately, they have a limited ability to determine the final decision. The essence of the leadership style in this instance is that it needs to be able to respond to circumstances. The leader needs to be able to stand back and allow the considerable learning and development that is going on to take place but be ready to step in if the circumstances require outside facilitation or direction.

Participatory

This is a consensual decision-making process with the leader presenting the scenario and any information plus possible decisions and then engaging in a genuine exchange of ideas. Decisions in this style are joint decisions made with the group and leader on equal terms. Personal growth is therefore fostered to a large extent with the leader playing a facilitating role as much as a leadership role. The leader will now be

Figure 2   The leadership continuum

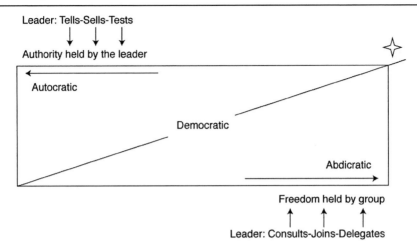

Leader: Tells-Sells-Tests

Authority held by the leader

Autocratic

Democratic

Abdicratic

Freedom held by group

Leader: Consults-Joins-Delegates

able to allow the task dimension to resolve itself whilst remaining involved with the group to ensure that individual and group learning within the group is maximised.

Delegatory

Here because the task dimension is low, either because it is simple or the consequences are not important, the leader is able to take on a role that will directly foster group and individual development. To this end the leader will be delegating the task and allowing the group and individuals within the group to carry out the task unsupervised. Therefore, the learning involved is less about the successful completion of a delegated task and more about how the task was undertaken.

Total abdication

There is a final style of leadership to the right (star) of the leadership style continuum. This is total abdication where the leader delegates all authority and responsibility. This can arise through a deliberate policy of delegation or through a leader losing control. In either case it is never a suitable style of leadership when working in the outdoors. Even when the group is out of the direct control of the leader, they should still be able to monitor the progress of the group and be in a position to assume responsibility for its actions.

Leadership orientation

Another fundamental feature of leadership in the outdoors is the idea of leadership orientation. One of the most popular ways of looking at what leadership involves and what it needs to take into account is through the Action Centred Leadership model of John Adair (1988). In essence, this model shows that there are three aspects to effective leadership that must interact, these are: achieving the task; developing each individual within the team; and building and reinforcing the team spirit and teamwork. The reason for these three aspects can be seen as the chained need or aim, to achieve a task through the use of a team of people who are all individuals. The effective leader needs to address each aspect, usually simultaneously. If one aspect takes priority then the other two still need to be maintained. As each aspect overlaps both of its neighbours, it can be seen how lack of attention to any one aspect could be to the detriment of the other two. Action centred leadership, although primarily a managerial leadership model, is a useful generic model that can be applied to many leadership situations. It demonstrates that leadership is not complete unless all three aspects are at least considered. For example, if the leader's job is to instruct a team but they spend the whole session working with one member who has problems with a particular skill, the team will not only fall apart but they won't learn the skill that was the object of the session. If however, the leader concentrates exclusively on practising the skill very little team spirit will be developed and the troubled individual will be left even more isolated. Finally, the leader could spend the entire session running team bonding activities that neglect the task, the skill, and the individuals within the team. To be effective in this situation, the leader needs to be able to get the team working together, build up individual skills, make every member of the team feel valued and complete the task.

Caring leadership

Caring leadership is one very important way of maintaining a working balance that allows a leader to address a variety of needs and adopt the range of leadership styles but without losing sight of individuals within their care. It is more than simply focusing on the needs of individual people. It is about being able to relate to them as people and being able to empathise with their problems and feelings. Evans (cited in Graham, 1997: 70) suggests that the first step towards being able to do this is:

> . . . you have to be vulnerable. You can't put yourself on a pedestal. You must be accessible to the people around you, making them understand that you're human too.

This kind of leadership dictates that leaders regard people as individuals in their own right. Wheal (1998: 82–3) says:

> Caring about someone arises from respect for them as a person and, if we get to know them as a person, usually develops into valuing them as people . . . Giving responsibilities and setting expectations which enhance a . . . person's sense of self-worth are likely to reassure a . . . person that they are cared about.

Caring leadership requires that the leader demonstrates a higher than usual level of attributes such as sensitivity, time, energy and commitment. It means that they cannot be the sort of leader who regards outdoor leadership as simply a job; it must have an extra, personal, dimension that lifts it above that. The notion of caring leadership essentially means that the leader puts the needs of the individual person at the forefront of their priorities. This may well require a delicate balancing act with the needs of the individual being balanced against the needs of the group. However, one advantage of this way of working is that it will, in time, become a two-way process. Once people realise that a leader genuinely cares about them, a bond of trust will be formed which will permeate throughout the work they are engaged in. This should mean that if a group activity is stopped to allow a less able person to catch up, the group will respond in a positive manner because they can appreciate the reasons behind the action. It is often only when caring leadership is present that groups of people can genuinely work together and act to resolve conflict amongst themselves. Greenaway (1996: 21) suggests that good reviewing is a feature of caring leadership:

> By reviewing activities we show that we care about what . . . people experience; that we value what they have to say; and that we are interested in the progress of each individual's learning and development. But it should not just be the reviewer who demonstrates these attitudes: ideally the whole group should reflect them – especially if it is an influential peer group.

Being sensitive to people's needs, listening to their problems without being judgmental and acting on issues and problems which are bought forward are all symbolic of a healthy leadership relationship. Clearly, caring leadership, if seen through to its natural fulfilment, will make the work of a leader easier and allow them to spot any potential problems that might have remained hidden if a bond of trust did not allow people to be open. It will also help the progress of the ideal of an outdoor leader; that their groups should start to take responsibility for their own learning and welfare, looking after each other rather than always looking to the leader to help out.

Being true to yourself

Although good leadership comes from knowing when to use appropriate styles and techniques, with which individuals and groups and in which situations, a person's leadership grows from their personality. Any good leader will have their own unique way of working which is over and above the styles and relationships identified so far in this chapter. It may be that one person leads everything in a very precise and ordered manner whilst another person prefers a more chaotic, spur of the moment style. Likewise, one leader may find that it very easy to be friendly with people whilst another may prefer to be a little more detached. Leadership, as mentioned at the start of this chapter, is not about following a list of rules or structures; rather it is about a combination of heart and head. People skills, as opposed to technical skills, are often more about 'gut reactions' and feelings than they are about following the 'correct' pattern of working.

A leader should never try to conceal their own personality and character because not only would such a façade be impossible to maintain, but also people would quickly judge such a leader to be false. A good leader will recognise the strengths and weaknesses of the way they work and act on them in a positive manner, working always to their strengths whilst accommodating their weaknesses. As Paul Petzoldt, the founder of the National Outdoor Leadership School in America (cited in Graham, 1997: 18) says: 'Leadership is not just passed on from the more experienced to the less experienced'. There are many ways that a leader will learn, from others, from experience, from books and courses; and from making mistakes. Ultimately, all of these routes will need to be incorporated into one whole that has at its foundation the personality and character of the person involved.

The role of a leader

The role of a leader is far from clear-cut, although Graham (1997: 12) gives a good starting point for the discussion when he writes that:

> Good leaders sometimes tell people what to do, but leadership is not just giving directions – it's liberating people to do what's needed in the best possible way . . . Leadership is the capacity to move others towards goals . . . with a focus and competency they would not achieve on their own.

Some people are uncomfortable with the idea of being termed leaders. As a result, a variety of terms, such as tutors, facilitators and instructors, are used in outdoor education. How then does leadership differ from 'simply' working with people? In essence, it is both similar and yet more. When we use the term 'working with' it usually, if not always, implies some element of leadership. It may not be the overt 'follow me' type of leadership. It could just as easily be a facilitative or encouraging type of leadership; but it is leadership

all the same. We reserve the right to be leaders working with the people in our care usually because we feel that we have experienced something or know something or believe in something that we wish to share. Often it is because we want to help people towards the goals that Graham mentions above. We want to lead others, in this instance people in the outdoors, into sharing that certain something or into moving in a certain direction. It may simply be the knowledge that they don't need us as leaders and there would be nothing wrong with that. Leadership in the context of outdoor education is more than 'working with' people. It is about inspiring or encouraging people to have the ability to lead themselves to the best of their ability and to meet their full potential.

Let us return to the question posed at the start of the chapter. Is leadership an art or a science? Undoubtedly many of the attributes of being a good leader such as empathy, care, judgement, self-confidence and so on are predominantly innate and could suggest that leadership is an art. However, if that was totally the case there would be no need to write books or run courses on leadership; people would either make good leaders or they wouldn't. Whilst not everyone can be taught to be great leaders, the great majority of people can be taught to be competent or even good leaders. Skills such as communication, group control, ethical procedures, etc. can all be taught. More importantly, the innate skills or 'art' side of leadership can be improved through teaching, evaluation, experience and peer-review. There are a very few people who are great leaders based purely on their own innate skills. For the rest of us it is part art, part science and, most importantly, part learning from our mistakes.

References

Adair, J. (1988) *The Action-Centred Leader*. London: The Industrial Society.

Graham, J. (1997) *Outdoor Leadership*. Seattle: The Mountaineers.

Greenaway, R. (1996) *Reviewing Adventures, Why and How*. Sheffield: NAOE Publications.

Hersey, P. and Blanchard, K. (1982) *Management of Organizational Behaviour: Utilizing Human Resources*. 4th edn. Englewood Cliffs, New Jersey: Prentice-Hall.

Priest, S. and Gass, M. (1997) *Effective Leadership in Adventure Programming*. Leeds: Human Kinetics.

Tannerbum, R and Schimdt, W, H. (1973) How to Choose a Leadership Pattern. *Harvard Business Review*. 51: 3, 162–80.

Warren, G. (2001) A Bit of Road Rage is a Wonderful Thing. *The Times Education Supplement*. 3rd August; 48.

Wheal, A. (1998) *Adolescence: Positive Approaches for Working with Young People*. Lyme Regis: Russell House Publishing.

Further reading

Barnes, P. (2002) *Leadership with Young People*. Lyme Regis: Russell House Publishing.

Priest, S. and Gass, M. (1997) *Effective Leadership in Adventure Programming*. Leeds: Human Kinetics.

13 Risk in Outdoor Education

Bob Sharp

Abstract

Very few activities in life are risk free; driving to work, eating out in a restaurant, walking in the mountains are all accompanied by risks of varying kinds and severity. Risk has both positive and negative dimensions. It also has a subjective quality; it reflects the nature of environment hazards as well as the way people perceive those hazards. People actively seek risk through adventurous activities. Risk is thought to aid self-development and help people realise their potentials, limitations and interests. On the downside, high risk can have negative consequences resulting in injury and loss of life. Risk plays both roles in outdoor education. The key factor is balance. Challenging activities need to be selected, managed and delivered in a way which fulfils, differentiates and stimulates people to learn about themselves and the environment, but with due regard to the potential negative consequences. There is growing evidence that outdoor education and society at large is changing in a way that is shifting the optimal balance point; challenges are being diluted and potentials reduced by an excessive concern to eliminate risk. The need to redress the balance is a major challenge for the outdoor education profession.

Risky business!

Adventure education is a profession of risk taking, but of risk taking with a purpose. The exposure to a variety of risks in an outdoor context produces an uncertainty of outcome which is central to the adventure experience.

(Brown, 1999)

Risk plays a central part in the lives of everyone. Risk is omnipresent; taking a train journey, cooking a meal, walking in the hills, painting a house all present risks. Risk is associated with challenge, uncertainty, danger and decision-making and has the potential to influence attitudes, personal growth, self-esteem, team cohesion, and confidence, and commitment, psychological and physical health. Risk has both quantitative and qualitative dimensions; sometimes the extent of a risk depends on how risk is perceived. Society places great importance on risk; more so in recent times. Often, minor incidents are blown out of proportion and distorted by the media (Furedi, 2002; Hobbs, 2000; Lindon, 1999). Fatal accidents sometimes receive massive national publicity for extended lengths of time. Accidents are increasingly seen to be 'caused' by someone. There is a rising 'culture of fear' and a tendency to protect people, particularly the young, from situations previously considered to be innocent and risk free. An increasing body of opinion advocates this trend stifles initiative, creativity and adventure in a way that compromises the normal development of youngsters. These are the kinds of issues addressed by this chapter.

What is risk?

Hazards (sometimes called perils or dangers) are the kinds of things that cause or have the potential to cause some of kind of difficulty, injury or accident (Wharton, 1995). A hazardous environment can be one where assistance is difficult to obtain. In the context of outdoor activities, examples are fast moving rivers, steep boulder strewn mountain slopes and bad weather. Hazards may be known or unknown. For example, an experienced mountaineer will know and understand the weather/terrain conditions that predispose a slope to avalanche. In contrast, a summer rambler may be unaware of avalanche difficulties or the special navigation problems of winter. A hazard which is unknown, unforeseen or not recognised presents a greater risk than one which is known because of the greater uncertainty it presents.

Whilst hazards are defined in absolute terms (e.g., cliff faces, fast moving water, strong winds, snow fences) they generate different levels of risk depending on their context and the experience of the individual confronting the hazard. Risk is the likelihood that danger or harm will result from a hazard (Health and Safety Executive, 1999a). The extent of risk depends in part on how competent a person is in dealing with the hazard; it is a function of how a person 'sees' or 'feels' a situation and combines both environmental and human factors. In kayaking for example, environmental factors would include rocks, low water, bends, and fallen trees. Human factors would include experience of the paddler, level of leadership, size of party, and so on. Thus, risk may be different for each individual even though the measured risks may be identical in size.

Various procedures are used to quantify risk. One uses Fatal Accident Rates (FARs) per million hours spent on an activity. Using this approach, Turner (1994) showed that smoking is more dangerous than climbing which in turn is more dangerous than skiing. The Health and Safety Executive has proposed a maximum tolerable FAR of 0.48 for workers in all occupations, below which no action is required by the employer to reduce risks further (Loynes, 1995a). Another procedure uses injuries (as opposed to fatalities). Using this approach, it has been shown that skiing is more risky than climbing. This is not a contradiction to Turner's findings, rather, it reveals differences in the profile of injuries sustained in different outdoor activities. Other methods of quantification involve looking at probability, frequency and severity of risk (Barnes, 1997).

Safety, of course, is another key concept. Safety is the antithesis of risk; one is positive and the other is negative. The Concise Oxford Dictionary defines safety as ' . . . freedom from danger or risks . . . being sure or likely to bring no danger.' Baillie (1996) suggests safety is a multi-faceted subject; safe practice involves a consideration of factors such as equipment and clothing, leader and individual responsibility, legislation, leadership, attitudes and technical competence.

The subjective nature of risk

As mentioned before, risk depends on the individual. In this sense, it can have physical, psychological or social connotations. Physical risk is perceived when there is risk of physical danger

to the individual, e.g., falling off a rock face, being swept away by an avalanche. Psychological risk is related to fear; the feelings experienced when paddling towards a serious rapid or when lost in white-out conditions. Social risk occurs when the individual feels they are acting outside their assigned or normal social role such as when a shy person is asked to adopt a leadership role. Risk is most commonly connected with physical harm, but practitioners should be mindful of its multi-dimensional nature.

There is an important distinction between real and perceived risk. The perception of risk sometimes bears no relation to the real risk; people respond to hazards as they see them and this depends on factors like experience, personality and skill level. Loynes (1995b) distinguishes between three kinds of risk. Perceived risk is something that seems risky but in actual fact is fully controlled (e.g., top rope climbing). It is a measure of how the person feels about the risks and may have little bearing on the actual risks. Subjective risk is something that is risky but can be controlled with equipment; skill and judgement (e.g., lead climbing). Objective risk (e.g., rockfall, avalanche, fast moving water) cannot be controlled. It can, of course, be avoided. A major concern for practitioners is how to structure outdoor activities to yield risk levels that do not cause harm, but which still generate challenge, interest and learning. The quandary is to create a sense of perceived risk which is meaningful (often to a group of varying individuals), but which does not detract from the nature of the activity. This can present enormous practical difficulties for those leading groups of people. The challenge is one of matching the individual to the situation so that everyone operates within their 'challenge zone' and none flounder in their 'comfort' or 'panic zones'.

Why take risks?

It is widely accepted that the element of danger which is inherent in adventure activities is a significant attraction for many participants (e.g., Csikszentmilhalyi, 1990). Mortlock (1984) argues that all members of the human race have a ' . . . yearning for excitement, risk and challenge'. He suggests that risk is as important to adventure as competition is to sport. Further, it is fundamental to helping young people grow to their full potential.

Risk taking behaviour has been subject to numerous investigations over the years and various models have been proposed to explain why some people seek thrills and novel experiences where others avoid situations that make them anxious or fearful. A number of authors have tried to establish why risk is important in outdoor education (e.g., Priest and Gass, 1997; Nichols, 2000). A common position is that risk serves two essential purposes. The first has an educational basis. Liddle (1998) purports that risk plays a pivotal role in developing personal characteristics such as self-esteem and confidence and is critical to the learning process. The logic here is that risk helps people gain a better understanding of their capabilities, weaknesses and emotions. Many authors have discussed this matter. Mortlock (1984) talks about 'peak experience' and the importance of 'frontier adventure'. Here, the individual fears harm or stress but can, with considerable effort, overcome the situation without accident. Csikszentmihalyi and Csikszentmihalyi (1990) refer to 'flow'; a state of mind in which action merges with awareness and complete concentration. Flow is achieved when risk and competence are matched in situations of increasing complexity. Within this framework, personal growth occurs when the balance between risk and action tests the person within the bounds of personal safety. With experience, they are able to take on greater challenges which, in turn, engender further awareness and learning of the 'whole' person. On this basis, a key task of the outdoor educator is to devise situations were the balance between risk and competence allows maximum opportunities for development. Further, the balance must account for individual differences and also recognise the difference between real and perceived risks. Priest and Gass (1997) argue that leaders need to be particularly sensitive to match activities to the individual's perceived balance of risk and actual competence. This is especially vital when situations are developed to include mental and social risks.

The second point about risk is less utilitarian. Nichols (2000) argues that the development of an adventurous approach to life is a valuable outcome in its own right. He and others (e.g. Mortlock, 1984) propose that the presence of risk in adventure education can lead to the development of risk taking skills at higher levels which in turn transfer to other facets of life. As with many other aspects of outdoor education, there is little evidence to support such a stance.

The management of risk

If the balance between risk and safety is central to outdoor education, then risks cannot be ignored or left uncontrolled. In short, risk has to be managed. Brown (1999) defines risk management as the:

> . . . systematic application of management policies, standards and procedures to the tasks of identifying, analysing, assessing, treating and monitoring of risk. The prime objective . . . is to minimise the potential for physical, social, emotional or financial loss arising from participation in an unusual activity in an unfamiliar environment with unknown outcomes.

A number of principles and procedures are central to this process. The need to maintain an accurate accident database is one. Accident analysis allows lessons to be learned, helps to generate casualty profiles and also inform strategies to minimise re-occurrences (Sharp, 2001; Health and Safety Executive, 1999b). Objective information also serves to highlight the real risks involved in outdoor education. There is a continuing need to quell the 'media-driven panic' that distorts the true risks of outdoor activities (Lindon, 1999). It is only by stating the facts and by making comparisons with other areas of everyday life (e.g., youth suicides, slips in the home) that the safe nature of outdoor activities will sink in. Baillie discusses this matter at length in Chapter 20. Risk management also requires a systematic, step by step approach which includes attention to the identification of risks, evaluation of their magnitude, procedures for controlling, reducing or eliminating risks, monitoring procedures, documentation and evaluation. Two key aspects of risk management are risk assessment and risk control.

Risk assessment

Risk assessment is concerned essentially with evaluating the risks associated with hazards and deciding whether enough precautions have been taken to prevent harm. A key aim is to ensure that particular hazards have not been overlooked. To give a broad example, a risk assessment of say a group of retired people playing bowls would probably yield few hazards and little risk to life and limb. In contrast, a risk assessment of a large group of novices involved in a charity abseiling event might yield more hazards and a greater degree of risk to participants (and perhaps onlookers). Risk assessment is not always straightforward; quantification of risk is often uncertain, decisions have to be made about the acceptability of reducing risk and there are invariably financial implications. The Health and Safety Executive (1999b) suggest five steps to risk assessment; a model which is almost universally accepted in outdoor education. The steps are:

- To identify the hazards which are present.
- To list those individuals who might be harmed and how.
- To evaluate the degree of risk associated with each hazard and make decisions about what must be done to reduce risks to acceptable levels.
- To record the hazards and what has been done to reduce risks, and to make this public to all those who may be affected.
- To carry out periodical reviews and revisions of all assessments.

Risk assessment must be carried out by all employers including the self-employed as a requirement of the Health and Safety at Work Act, 1974. Course providers (those who provide adventure activities to young people under the age of 18 in return for payment) are required to operate within the law as defined by the Adventure Activities Licensing Authority (The Activity Centres – Young Persons Safety Act, 1995). They assess risk within the context of the environment in which they work and focus on those hazards which if not managed or avoided, could foreseeably result in death or disabling injury. The law does not apply to outdoor clubs (e.g., mountaineering clubs) or groups involved in outdoor activities for pleasure. However, many governing bodies recommend that because clubs are concerned with safety of their members, they should consider some aspects of the regulations, particularly the provision of information for club members useful to developing knowledge of key hazards, i.e., they must show duty of care. At the time of writing, the Department for Education and Skills is undertaking a tri-ennial review of licensing. Various alternatives are suggested including a voluntary scheme that includes all providers and activities (Department for Education and Skills, 2001).

It should be noted that risk assessment procedures are not universally accepted. Many are highly sceptical of the paperwork and administration chores involved. McDonald (1997) questions whether risk assessment is a good product of exemplary professional practice, or is '. . . woolly and generalist, conveyor belt safety, the product of an academic view of a complex human process with the practical usefulness of Esperanto.' It has been suggested that the current emphasis on risk assessment has contributed to the negative way risks are viewed. Brown (2000b) indicates that over-attention to hazards results in individuals playing only a passive role. She argues that 'people factors' (e.g. leader confidence, or the desired outcomes for the group) should be considered before an evaluation is made of the environment or activity. She says further that risk assessment implies 'perfect' answers can be found (a false assumption) and helps to generate a 'mindset' that risk should be contained or eliminated. Baillie, elsewhere in this book, urges that risk assessment should take full account of the 'benefits' of adventurous activities.

Risk control

In some cases, risks have to be controlled. What procedures exist? Haddock (1993) identifies four strategies, viz., retention, reduction, avoidance and transference. Risk retention (taking no action) applies in cases of extreme low probability and low consequences of loss. Risk transfer (where outcomes could be catastrophic) involves using highly competent instructors or giving participants information to make a choice and take responsibility themselves. The other two approaches are more commonly adopted in outdoor education. Risk avoidance involves removing a hazard or avoiding it by changing the activity. For example, a two-day expedition could be reduced to one day. Or if it were judged that to cross a steep snow slope presented too high a risk of avalanche danger, a change of route to climb an adjacent ridge would eliminate that risk. Risk reduction involves retaining the hazard but reducing the risk using particular strategies, e.g., employing trained staff, using appropriate clothing or equipment, supervising the activity more closely or modifying the design of the activity.

Above all, any system of risk management should ensure participants are fully aware of the hazards and risks. It is argued this should not be a one way process, but one that facilitates an understanding of risk and empowers individuals to make their own decisions about what is and what is not risky (Everard, 2000a). This is consistent with the self-reliance philosophy expressed by some governing bodies of outdoor activities (e.g., Mountaineering Council of Scotland, 2003).

The culture of fear

Risk assessment has assumed a higher profile in recent years partly through a change in society that is more inclined to place blame on people when accidents happen. This is paralleled by an increasing tendency for people to take out litigation, especially if they feel they can gain financially. Many argue that society is rapidly moving to a situation where there is no such thing as an accident if a person is hurt; someone somewhere must be responsible. This is summarised very clearly in the words of Everard (2000b):

Many outdoor practitioners are concerned about the creeping sanitisation of adventure, as societal influences seem to be increasing public aversion to risk, and to be intensifying the pursuit of someone to blame when things go wrong. The idea of ill luck and bad fortune has gone out of the window, and an accident in the sense of an unforeseen contingency is taken to imply incompetence on the part of someone who has failed to read the future correctly.

The 'fear factor' has heightened significantly since the Lyme Bay tragedy of 1993 (Harris, 1999) and other well-publicised incidents such as the fatal accident to a scout on Snowdon (Cousins, 2001). It is suggested further that enforcement of the Adventure Activities Licensing Regulations has highlighted concerns over accidents and injury to those taking part in outdoor activities.

What are the consequences of this trend? Putnam (2000) argues that the concern to protect people stifles enterprise and creativity and is leading to an increasingly restrictive approach to life where hazards must be avoided and risk taking is unacceptable. Furedi (2002) and others (e.g., Lindon, 1999) have researched this matter in

some detail and have shown that simple experiences in everyday life such as a child walking to the shop are becoming or are in danger of becoming rare events. Within the world of adventurous activities there is already evidence that providers have been forced to avoid some outdoor activities (McAvoy and Dustin, 1990). Nichols (2000) expresses the problem very succinctly when he says:

. . . society has become increasingly averse to the risks associated with adventure education. Risks are associated entirely with negative consequences rather than also with the potential to achieve something positive. This combined with an increasing professionalism of adventure education, and increasing concern with legal liability and the concentration of media attention on negative outcomes is likely to diminish the potential of adventure education to use risk constructively.

There are a number of expressions about how the 'culture of fear' should be addressed. Purves (2000) suggests there needs to be greater acceptance of the presence of risks and less emphasis on apportioning blame every time something goes wrong. Barton (2000) suggests we should re-think the over-dependence on paper management that accompanies risk assessment. Critically, he believes there should be a change of focus so that children (and others) should be provided with the tools of risk management rather than have the outcomes of risk management imposed on them. A recent conference devoted to this topic, *A Question of Balance*, (see Reed, 2001) concluded there is a need to quell society's focus on risk and remind the public that the risks in outdoor activities are minimal compared to those taken in daily life. An initiative designed to fulfil these objectives has been coined the *Campaign for Adventure* (Putnam, 2000); a national initiative (www.campaignforadventure.org) that has arisen from the current over-concern to protect people from harm. One of its aims is to promote the message that unnecessary pessimism, over-caution and an unadventurous approach to life leads to low expectations, lack of creativity and under-achievement. It remains to be seen how effective this will be and how society's current fear of risk and challenge will develop. Current signs are not encouraging.

References

Baillie, M. (1996) Risk Assessments, Safety Statements and All That Guff. *Journal of Adventure Education and Outdoor Leadership*. 1: 3, 6–7.

Barnes, P. (1997) *Theory Into Practice: The Complete Practical Theory of Outdoor Education and Personal Development*. Glasgow: University of Strathclyde.

Barton, B. (2000) *New Routes to China: Risk Management as Opportunity*. Paper Presented at The Conference on Risk and Adventure in Society (Association for Outdoor Learning). November, Royal Geographical Society, London.

Brown, H. (2000a) Working With Risk in the Outdoors: An Empowering Approach. *Newsletter of The Association for Outdoor Learning*. 37: 8.

Brown, H. (2000b) Working With Risk in The Outdoors. *Horizons*. 11: 4.

Brown, T. J. (1999) Adventure Risk Management, in Miles, J. C. and Priest, S. (Eds.) *Adventure Programming*. State College, PA: Venture Publishing Inc.

Cousins, J. (2001) *Finlay V Crown*. Manchester: UK Mountain Leader Training Board.

Csikszentmihalyi, M. (1990) *Beyond Boredom and Anxiety*. San Francisco: Jossey-Bass.

Csikszentmihalyi, M. and Csikszentmihalyi, I. S. (1990) Adventure and The Flow Experience, in Miles, J. C. and Priest, S. (Eds.) *Adventure Education*. State College, PA: Venture Publishing.

DfES (2001) *Health and Safety of Pupils on Educational Visits*. Sudbury: DfES Publications.

Everard, B. (2000a) New General Teaching Requirement for Health and Safety. *Horizons*. 10: 16.

Everard, B. (2000b) Danger and Risks. Balancing Risks and Benefits. *Horizons*. 9: 13–14.

Furedi, F. (2000) *Culture of Fear: Risk-Taking and Morality of Low Expectation*. 2nd edn. London: Continuum.

Haddock, C. (1993) *Managing Risks in Outdoor Activities*. Wellington, NZ: New Zealand Mountain Safety Council Inc.

Harris, I. (1999) Outdoor Education in Secondary Schools: What Future? *Horizons*. 4: 5–8.

Health and Safety Executive. (1999a) *Reducing Risks, Protecting People*. London: The Health and Safety Executive.

Health and Safety Executive. (1999b) *Five Steps to Risk Assessment*. London: The Heath and Safety Executive.

Hobbs, M. (2000) *Mind The Gap*. Paper Presented at The Conference on Risk and Adventure in Society (Association for Outdoor Learning). November, London.

Liddle, J. (1998) Risk Management: Walking The Tightrope. *Journal of Experiential Education*. 21: 2, 61–2.

Lindon. J. (1999) *Too Safe for Their Own Good?* London: The National Early Years Network.

Loynes, C. (1995a) The Public Perception of Risk. *NAOE Newsletter*. 15: 1.

Loynes, C. (1995b) Focus on Risk and Safety. *Journal of Adventure Education and Outdoor Leadership*. 12: 4, 4.

Mcavoy, L. H. and Dustin, D. L. (1990) The Danger in Safe Recreation. *Journal of Physical Education, Recreation and Dance*. 61: 4, 57–9.

Mcdonald, P. (1997) Ease of Long Practice. *Horizons*. 3: 22–4.

Mortlock, C. (1984) *The Adventure Alternative*. Milnthorpe: Cicerone Press.

Mountaineering Council of Scotland. (2003) Qualifications or Experience. Retrieved on 1st May, 2003 Http://Www.Mountaineering-Scotland.Org.Uk/Leaflets/Qualif.Html

Nichols, G. (2000) Risk and Adventure Education. *Journal of Risk Research*. 3: 2, 121–34.

Priest, S. and Gass, M. A. (1997) *Effective Leadership in Adventure Programming*. Champaign, IL: Human Kinetics.

Purves, L. (2000) *The Reputation of Adventure*. Paper Presented at The Conference on Risk and Adventure in Society (Association for Outdoor Learning). November, Royal Geographical Society, London.

Putnam, R. (2000) *Proposal for A 'Campaign for Adventure'*. Penrith: Association for Outdoor Learning.

Reed, C. (2001) The Pot Was Well and Truly Stirred. A Question of Balance-Responses. *Horizons*. 13: 16–8.

Sharp, R. H. (2001) The Quick Way Off The Mountain. *The Scottish Mountaineer*. 9: 9–10.

Wharton, N. (1995) Heath and Safety in Outdoor Activity Centres. *Journal of Adventure Education and Outdoor Leadership*. 12: 4, 8–9.

14 Creative Ways of Working

Alan Smith

Abstract

This chapter explores some less traditional learning styles in outdoor work and offers alternative ways forward based on involvement and experience. Problem solving, simulating, modifying and simplifying are all used as starting points for developing challenging activities. Emphasis is given to spontaneous ideas, outdoor games and the importance of weather as a focus for learning. Some ideas on group organisation, ways of motivating and working with minimum resources are briefly outlined. Several well tested suggestions for creative preparation work and follow-up exercises are given as a conclusion.

Introduction

Why work creatively? This question can be answered by looking at both ends of the scale. At one extreme, students are allowed no creativity. For example, in a 'follow the leader' situation, the group merely walk behind their instructor. In this case participants can gain relatively little from their experience, other than some physical exercise. At the opposite extreme, students are allowed maximum creativity. For example, in a situation where teams work on a complex problem solving exercise in unfamiliar outdoor environments within extended boundaries. These examples are generalised, but aim to illustrate two diverse ways of working. With thorough planning and organisation the latter example can offer numerous opportunities and educational benefits. It is not possible to be fully creative in our planned activities as there will always be limitations and restrictions based upon ability levels or maturity of the participants and on safety considerations.

By working creatively in outdoor education we can make maximum use of the positive benefits to be gained by interacting socially in teamwork situations, responding to challenging and unusual problems, applying skills, developing ideas, making mistakes, correcting, improving and finally, achieving. The sense of achievement and the special feeling of success can be shared by students who are given opportunities for working in this way. My approach to outdoor work has three main fundamentals. These are to ensure that the participants have fun in their work, to allow all individuals to be actively involved within their capabilities and to provide activities that are carefully planned and run to ensure proper safety standards.

Creative outdoor education or traditional outdoor sport oriented education?

My particular style of creative outdoor education as taught in secondary schools has very much been a personal approach.

The methods outlined in *Creative Outdoor Work with Young People* (Smith, 1994) have evolved over a period of 20 years and reflect a need to make the most of valuable opportunities in the outdoor environment. The growing importance of a residential outdoor experience for young people in the 1980s helped to focus thought on the thorough planning of ventures. At times, new activities (particularly problem solving tasks) developed as a matter of necessity when outdoor work off site was restricted for various reasons, and groups had to work with limited resources around an urban base.

Young people can pursue a variety of traditional 'outdoor sports', for example canoeing, orienteering and climbing for the development of skills and for challenge and competition. These healthy pursuits often lead to local and national awards through a progressive training programme of courses.

Creative outdoor education also aims to develop these skills and challenges but not always with the same emphasis or priority on sporting achievement. Creative outdoor education seeks to make full use of outdoor situations to maximise educational and social benefits, and to encourage individual participation and enjoyment.

This integrated approach requires a balanced perspective towards outdoor work so that time can be allocated for games, for learning situations and for individual needs, as well as the pursuit of traditional outdoor sports. Environmental education is seen as an integral part of this work.

Problem solving

Probably more than any other aspect of outdoor education, problem solving stands out as a way of offering creative challenges both for the young people involved and for the adult workers who set the tasks. The benefits to be gained by involvement in problem solving are infinite and in recognition of this fact, the development of this style of outdoor work has become widespread. Organisations from schools, colleges, youth groups and universities to businesses and industries have seen the desirable potential.

Problem solving tasks

These are also known as decision-making exercises or team initiative tasks and can be used at various levels as suggested in the following range of examples. One basic task is called 'shaduf'. Here, teams of students devise a method of raising and collecting water using poles, lashing cord and containers. This involves co-operation and perseverance. A more technical task such as sign post involves teams of students constructing a sign post which should point accurately to about ten places, giving place names, directions and distances. This involves map and compass skills and delegated responsibilities. There are more demanding multi-problem tasks such as all night problems. Here, teams of students are expected to navigate at night, solve problems along the route and improvise a shelter to sleep in at the end of their journey. This is intended for more experienced participants with navigation skills and requires planning, training and organisation.

With thorough planning, preparation and vigilance, problem solving tasks such as these can be very rewarding for all concerned.

Simulating

By designing suitable simulation exercises, imitating real life outdoor situations and utilising role-play methods, participants are faced with some unusual problems they are unlikely to encounter in conventional training environments. This work involves initiative, leadership, problem solving skills and decision-making opportunities. Simulation exercises are also widely used for training purposes by industries, the armed forces and examination boards. They can be used to focus on particular skills by confronting selected problems. Individuals are required to absorb and understand essential new information and apply this knowledge in order to successfully complete the task. Various outdoor first aid or safety related simulation exercises could provide valuable experiences for young people including multi-problem tasks such as hypothermia, stretchers and search and rescue. This work can be great fun as well as exciting and absorbing. Some planned time is advisable for reflections and conclusions when team members can talk about their adventures.

Working with minimum resources

The safety of participants depends largely on the generous provision of appropriate protective clothing and equipment to suit the nature of the activities and the outdoor conditions. Having made this important statement, the main point of this section is to emphasise the wide range of stimulating outdoor work that can be tackled with minimum resources in the local area (lowland countryside).

Studying the environment

Basic fieldwork techniques for studying aspects of the environment require little more than clipboards and prepared resource sheets, with measuring equipment if needed. Urban surveys, farmland surveys and wildlife studies require mainly observation and recording skills. Improvised measuring equipment made by the students, for example poles or canes marked off in centimetres and metres can easily provide a less costly alternative.

Navigation and orienteering

Local parklands often provide excellent training areas for map and compass skills without the need for restrictive transport costs. Public transport may be convenient for these ventures. Depending on the objectives, the main expense is likely to be in the provision of maps and compasses. Although Ordnance Survey maps are essential for many navigation exercises, using alternative maps such as special park maps, often available from the park shop or tourist information office, can make economies.

Problem solving and camp activities

Many problem solving activities can be completed with basic items such as canes, poles, twine, polythene sheets and lengths of lashing rope. The equipment can be re-used for other exercises. Some activities can be devised with no equipment necessary such as the mini assault course.

Organising into groups

Due to the inherent safety requirements of most outdoor work with young people, small groups are to be recommended with an appropriate ratio of experienced adult workers. Within this fundamental framework many interesting ways of working in even smaller groups can be arranged so that all individuals can potentially gain maximum benefit from their experience. Each method of group organisation will have its advantages, disadvantages and restrictions, but a basic principle worth noting is that an individual in a large group situation will generally show less initiative and rely more on other participants than in a small group situation where everyone must be fully involved for the successful outcome of the exercise. A few examples follow: a group of ten young people accompanied by one or more adult workers are following the same route on a navigation walk. If the adult or one volunteer take on all the responsibility for map and compass work, then other members of the group will gain little from the navigation experience. If, however, the group is told at the beginning of the walk that each pair in turn will be given responsibility for navigating a leg of the route, and that all participants should therefore follow the route on their map at all times, then individual involvement will be considerably increased (see leading in turn). A variation on this scenario would be that at a pre-planned point during the walk, the group stops to deal with a simulated first aid situation, such as a case of hypothermia or a suspected fractured ankle. For this initiative task the group is sub-divided into two or three smaller groups, thus concentrating responsibilities and decisions onto particular individuals. Another example is a larger group or class divided into teams of three members at the outset. With clear instructions and guidelines including a strict time limit, they are sent out into the local environment to complete a specific survey (eg, a neighbourhood plan or village survey). This method has obvious implications for safety and responsibility, but with careful planning this teamwork approach can be very rewarding.

Finally, after whole group introductory work, a beginner's orienteering class is divided into pairs for some short training exercises such as a course in the grounds of the base, a local street orienteering course or a compass journey. Young people working out of doors are likely to be safer working in pairs than on their own. By working in pairs for orienteering, participants can share ideas and be fully involved in map reading skills.

Weather related activities

Weather conditions will always present problems, challenges and opportunities for outdoor groups. Extreme weather can often result in cancellation or modification of activities due to conditions such as dangerous winds in exposed places, heavy rainfall making streams into hazardous rapids, or periods of drought preventing access to areas because of fire risk. Some alternative plans are necessary In these situations, but less extreme weather conditions can provide some interesting and realistic problems. The 'windy day' exercise is a useful example that can be integrated into a navigation walk. This involves the construction of a homemade windshield to assist boiling a kettle of water in windy conditions. Other weather related activities could include the construction of bivouacs on a rainy day, a first aid initiative task dealing with dehydration on a hot day, a first aid initiative task dealing with hypothermia on a cold and windy day or a map and compass navigation training exercise on a foggy day.

Modifying and simplifying

By changing or simplifying a complex task we can often create an ideal training exercise suitable for beginners. An orienteering map of complex woodland would take the experience and determination of a dedicated orienteer to produce, but a small strip of the map within clear boundaries can be made by young people as a skills training exercise. This would involve practise with using map symbols, following directions and understanding scale. Even the formidable job of preparing a route card for a navigation walk can be simplified for training purposes. Although some prepared resources are necessary for this activity (see route planning), a high standard of achievement can be gained by using questions with an alternative answer style and a transparent overlay sheet with the route marked on to fit over an Ordnance Survey map. On a lighter note, the standard routine of pitching a tent and fly sheet can be modified into an interesting team problem solving task. If some of the participants are blindfolded then group co-operation and communication skills will be tested to the full. Competitive white water slalom work is best left to the experienced and highly competent canoeist, but a simplified slalom-training course can be set up on still or slow moving water for beginners. Long canes or posts are pushed into the lake or riverbed to create a suitable skills course within safe boundaries.

Spontaneous activities

Although we seem more and more restricted in our outdoor work by an ever-increasing burden of rules and regulations, hopefully there will always be room for spontaneous activities that may develop during the course of any planned day. Within safe boundaries and limitations there are many worthwhile ideas that suddenly become obvious and could be used to enhance an activity. Such situations may occur at a point along a walk or at a rest stop when there are a few minutes to spare. Sometimes a mini activity is needed to 'spice up' a dull period. This could be an opportunity for the group to talk about the country code, or to try a memory game where participants try to memorise, say, 15 items produced from pockets, rucksacks or the immediate surrounds. A brief simulation exercise can be a useful way to focus on a particular problem, for example, where volunteers from the group act out a conflict situation between landowner and hikers. Often, the layout of the landscape can unexpectedly stimulate an idea. A spectacular view may suddenly become visible as the group approaches

the top of a ridge. This can be made into an observation game where pairs are given sixty seconds to memorise as much as possible about the view. If the group is passing through an interesting area with slopes, fallen trees or large boulders, a mini assault course can be created within safe limitations, involving balancing along, jumping over, crawling through or snaking under natural features.

Ways of motivating

Although the adults working out of doors with young people may be totally enthusiastic, dedicated and addicted to their occupation, some of our students are occasionally less than enthusiastic. Individuals sometimes appear on an outdoor course that have been persuaded by parents or friends, or have been misguided about the activities. As we have responsibility to cater for the needs of all participants, including the reluctant members, some thoughts about methods of motivation may be helpful. As noted in the introduction of this chapter, one of my main fundamental aims in outdoor work has been 'to ensure that the participants have fun in their work'. If this fundamental can be kept as a central focus in our planning then many of the doubtful customers will hopefully be quickly transformed into happy and active members of the group. Participants are more likely to want to be involved if the activities are stimulating and interesting. It may be possible to use a game or puzzle to spice up a learning situation or to offer some sort of reward or prize, perhaps in the form of sweets or certificates. Many students may just need the satisfaction of a good grade or comment, especially if there is some planned follow up session or reviewing time. Realistic activities such as role-play exercises involving first aid or rescue tend to be very attractive to young people as they are acting out adult situations, but using a variety of important skills in the process.

Planning an appropriate level of challenge is always a finely balanced problem. If the task is too easy or too difficult, then many individuals will be turned off.

Games

Hopefully, outdoor games should not be seen as 'extra time fillers'. Their social value is obvious enough, but as a means of introducing or developing skills, they become an important part of any outdoor programme. Games can be adapted to suit almost any outdoor activity. Map reading becomes much more fun when it is presented as a trail with a set of puzzles as clues, or when an orienteering course in the grounds of the base becomes a sweet chase. A problem solving activity changes into an exciting situation when teams not only invent and construct an obstacle course, but also then take part in the blindfold event, organised as a timed relay game. There are many games suitable for beginner's canoe groups that are great fun and help in the learning of basic control skills such as turning, manoeuvring and stopping. Bulldog and tag are favourites, and variations of canoe polo or canoe ball provide useful training opportunities. On camp, after the day's activities have been completed, the whole group can look forward to some sort of wide game such as 'prisoner' where the whole group is divided into prisoners and guards. As with 'hide and seek', the guards come out of their prison for a given time to search for the escaped prisoners. Another version is the 'sentry' game, which can be played at night along a linear feature such as a wall, ditch or hedge. In this case, the sentries must remove a white wool armband from the spies to prove they have been caught.

Creative preparation work and follow up exercises

The process of working in outdoor environments with young people is stimulating and exciting, but enjoyment can be extended beyond the outdoor part by developing a range of interesting experiences before and after. The complete educational experience, including preparation work, main activity and follow up or reviewing, offers infinite opportunities for new or unusual ways of working and maximises individual involvement. Depending on the maturity of the participants, preparation work could range from map and compass training and route planning as a group exercise to paired or team tasks. Examples might include research work, making homemade equipment for the main activity or planning a menu. An interesting way of getting to know about new or unusual equipment before going out of doors is to simulate a camping shop experience, where small groups take turns to role-play shop assistants and customers. As a whole group exercise it can be useful to debate a number of 'what if?' situations before an expedition. Participants are given the opportunity to say how they would respond to a range of scenarios, possibly including adverse weather conditions or an accident. There are many enjoyable, practical ideas that can be used for follow up work. Displays including sketches, maps, graphs, photographs, three-dimensional models and written accounts all require teamwork and co-operative involvement. A scrapbook is a more visual alternative to writing up a diary or log of events. Some time may be set aside during or after the outdoor activity for discussion, either in small groups or altogether. Participants can talk about the things they liked and disliked or recap situations and offer improvements. By combining the practical and oral parts, a group presentation often makes a rewarding conclusion.

References

Smith, A. (1994) *Creative Outdoor Work with Young People*. Lyme Regis: Russell House Publishing.

15 Facilitation and Reviewing in Outdoor Education

Roger Greenaway

Abstract

This chapter outlines some of the main areas in which facilitation skills can be of value in outdoor education and raises some key issues along the way: such as the implications for facilitation style if you want to place learners' experiences at the heart of the learning process. The author draws on current and recent outdoor literature from different countries to illustrate the scope of facilitation and the issues raised by differences in language and practice. He concludes by urging outdoor educators to use the outdoors for reviewing and reflection as well as for activity.

Introduction

Teaching, in my estimation, is a vastly overrated function . . . I see the facilitation of learning as the aim of education.

(Rogers, 1969)

Going outdoors opens new horizons. It can be a journey into an unfamiliar world – a world of differences where norms and routines are left behind and where people dress, feel, think and behave differently. Going outdoors can also be a voyage of discoveries where people find things out about themselves, about each other and about the natural world. It is of course possible to venture into the outdoors and discover very little. Differences may not be noticed much, or if noticed may not be enjoyed. And even if enjoyed they may not have much 'educational' value. The process of discovery in the outdoors can falter if the visitors are not in the mood for discovery nor have the confidence to be discoverers. They may have forgotten how to discover, especially if they have become accustomed to being 'consumers' and 'recipients' and are unsure about how to be 'active learners'.

It is direct encounters with the natural world that generate the experiences at the heart of most kinds of 'outdoor education'. And it is the interaction between self, others and the environment that shape these experiences. Each of these three influences (self, others and the environment) can be very powerful. Add skilled facilitation to this dynamic mixture and you have 'outdoor education' at its best. You (as a facilitator) first need a reasonably clear picture of what it is that you want to facilitate. It could be:

- a meeting
- an activity
- group development
- personal development
- self-directed learning
- a learning climate
- a learning outcome
- learning skills
- self-esteem
- support
- an adventurous attitude
- a self-reliant expedition
- a commitment to sustainability
- curiosity about nature
- spiritual awareness
- independence
- interdependence
- or fun!

Once you know what it is that you want to facilitate, it is useful to consider any other facilitative forces that could be influencing how things turn out. Amongst these will be the personal attributes of participants, their individually different experiences, the group dynamics, the nature of the activities, and the influence of the natural environment. In outdoor education settings there are so many potentially facilitative influences around, that it makes sense to ensure that they are identified, appreciated and engaged. The value of doing so, and of doing so in a facilitative way, also happens to be well supported by research studies (Barret and Greenaway, 1995).

There is an enormous range of facilitation styles to be found in outdoor education. This diversity can be confusing. Despite much overlap in practice, facilitation is commonly understood to be less directive than teaching. A useful 'rule of thumb' distinction between facilitation and teaching is that in facilitation, the goal is usually for people to learn something that nobody knows at the beginning, whereas in teaching the goal is usually for people to learn what the teacher already knows. In most forms of outdoor education it is likely that both kinds of goal exist – so you may want to move between 'facilitating' and 'teaching'. But even when you have the knowledge or skill that others are trying to learn, it does not automatically follow that you abandon facilitation. There are many aspects of outdoor education (camp cooking, map reading, weather forecasting, first aid, and many environmental education topics) that are unlikely to be discovered without some assistance. But with imagination, even these very 'teachable' skills and topics can be learned by experiential methods and appropriate facilitation. For example, Joseph Cornell is an outstanding example of an environmental educator for whom direct experience is central to his philosophy and methods. In his foreword to *Sharing Nature with Children,* Cornell writes:

Each of the games creates a situation or an experience, in which nature is the teacher. Each game is a mouthpiece for nature – sometimes speaking in the language of the scientist, sometimes in that of the artist or mystic.

(Cornell, 1979: 8)

In *Sharing the Joy of Nature* Cornell (1989) describes the four stage sequence that he uses to facilitate what he describes as 'learning with a natural flow':

- awaken enthusiasm
- focus attention
- direct experience
- share inspiration

Cornell explains:

I call the fourth stage 'sharing inspiration', because sharing strengthens and clarifies our own deep experiences . . . After a successful Flow Learning session, each person feels a subtle, enjoyable awareness of oneness with nature and an increased empathy with all of life.

This is the challenge for all outdoor educators; to make students' own experiences central to the whole process: especially if we happen to believe that 'all genuine knowledge originates in direct experience' (Mao Tse Tung). Outdoor education is not just about changing the scenery. It is an opportunity for much deeper change, which facilitation can help or hinder.

Varieties of facilitation

Facilitation is often described as the art of making things easy for others, but if you make things too easy you risk returning to the spoon-feeding tradition in which learners passively digest whatever the educator wants them to. In essence, facilitation is an enabling role in which the focus is usually on what the learner is doing and experiencing rather than on what the educator is doing. Some of the facilitation styles that are used by outdoor educators are described next.

Non-directive facilitation

In his essay *Adventure Education* David Charlton (1980) provides an example of this approach:

The facilitator recognises the various signals given by the students indicating when and which way they want to go. The facilitator then creates the opportunity that enables them to go that way.

Even if you do not adopt a non-directive stance all of the time, there are situations where it can be an effective strategy: for example, where you believe that students can work things out for themselves and will find it more rewarding to do so. An impartial stance can also help to encourage discussion or defuse conflict or help students become more independent and responsible. But there are some issues on which you should not attempt to be neutral. These are your non-negotiable educational values, which you should be clear about to yourself and to others (Heron, 1999: 33–4).

Appreciative facilitation

Appreciative facilitation emphasises what works well and pays attention to success and achievement. At its simplest, it involves catching students at their best moments and providing positive feedback about what they did or said. Alternatively you can invite positive comments from participants for each other following a group exercise. Or just ask, 'What is working well?' Cheri Torres brings together her enthusiasm for appreciative facilitation and mobile ropes courses in *The Appreciative Facilitator* (Torres, 2001). Her handbook includes summaries of key research supporting appreciative facilitation, such as the 'Pygmalion Effect' ('As the teacher believes the student to be, so the student becomes') and how watching videos of your own successful performances leads to much greater improvements than watching videos of your mistakes. Appreciative facilitation draws on ideas and principles from appreciative inquiry (an approach to organisation development) and solution focused brief therapy ('Be careful what you attend to. What you focus on expands.'). Appreciative facilitation fits well with outdoor education, both as a source of techniques and as a philosophy.

Activity facilitation

This approach emphasises the facilitator's role during a group activity. Sometimes the facilitator may simply be enabling a group to achieve a task in the time available. But where the purpose of the activity is to generate experiences from which people will learn, the facilitator may want to intervene during the activity in order to influence what is experienced. This will typically involve changing the rules in some way, with or without consultation with the group. The Facilitator's Toolkit (Thiagarajan and Thiagarajan, 1999) is mostly about activity facilitation. The context is indoor training for adults, but much of this 'toolkit' can readily be adapted for outdoor education. Outdoor educators have less control over the many variables that influence what is experienced, but there are always plenty of ways in which 'activity facilitation' can enhance the quality of the experience. In *Learning Through First Hand Experience Out of Doors*, Pat Keighley describes many ways in which activities in the outdoors can be designed and adapted to provide experience-based elements of the National Curriculum in physical education, science, geography, maths and english (Keighley, 1998).

Group facilitation

Group facilitation can apply to any group situations: from the running of effective meetings (and keeping to the agenda) through to sensitivity group training (where there is no agenda). Like it or not, the group dynamics in outdoor education can have greater impact than 'the outdoors'. If the development of group skills is not a priority it may still be necessary to use group facilitation skills to redirect attention to 'the outdoors'. If the primary aim is social development or team building, group facilitation is clearly a must. But whatever your main purpose, you will at the very least want to ensure that the group climate is a highly favourable climate for learning and development. *The Zen of Groups* (Hunter, Bailey and Taylor, 1992) is a good introduction to the basics of facilitating group development. More advanced (and drawing on much of his experience working with groups in the outdoors) is Martin Ringer's *Group Action* (Ringer, 2001) which provides a psychodynamic perspective on group facilitation in experiential learning and adventure therapy.

Adventure programming

This approach to facilitation includes such techniques as 'Frontloading', 'Isomorphic Framing', and 'Paradoxical Symptom Prescriptions' (Priest and Gass, 1997: 190–221). This language implies a directive style of facilitation that leaves little to chance. Their emphasis on 'presenting' metaphors in advance of the activity puts the facilitator in the role of storyteller before participants have had the experiences to fit the story. This is an interesting mixture of drama and adventure in which participants are effectively improvising within the frame provided by the facilitator's script. It is a style of facilitation that has been comprehensively challenged by Johan Hovelynck who is concerned that 'adventure education is increasingly adopting the didactic teaching methods that it set out to be an alternative for' (Hovelynck, 2001). Priest and Gass appreciate the 'drawbacks' of framing. This is the last of six drawbacks that they identify:

> By narrowing the focus of a frame to a predetermined metaphoric message, you are dictating what will be learned in the activity. Even if you are on target with the frame, by

prescribing the way the experience will be interpreted, other metaphors may not be available for the group to interpret.

(Priest and Gass, 1997: 215)

Even when there is pressure to achieve particular outcomes, it by no means follows that 'predetermined' and 'prescribed' interpretations will be the most effective facilitation strategy. If interpretation precedes experience, the 'experience' is little more than an illustration in the facilitator's story. This is 'confirming through experience' rather than 'learning from experience'.

Choosing a facilitation style

Five styles of facilitation found in outdoor education have been outlined above. All have their advantages and disadvantages. In practice, facilitators often have a 'home' style that corresponds most closely to their values, and pick and mix ideas from other sources. If this sounds too haphazard, you will find excellent guidance in John Heron's *The Complete Facilitator's Handbook* about switching between different styles according to what is most facilitative for learners at the time. Heron's matrix of the dimensions and modes of facilitation can be used to help you decide when to take charge, when to negotiate and when to stand back. It can also be used as a self-review tool (Heron, 1999: 342–3).

Does research provide any guidance about choosing a facilitation style? Sivasailam Thiagarajan (Thiagi) spent 15 years in field research in what he admits was 'a futile attempt' to discover the secrets of 'effective facilitators' (who were rated highly by their peers and participants). Thiagi reported:

I did not find consistent, common behaviours among these facilitators. Further, even the same facilitator appeared to use different behaviours with different groups, even when conducting the same activity. To make matters worse, the same facilitator sometimes used different behaviours with the same group within the same activity at different times.

(Thiagarajan and Thiagarajan, 1999: 48)

Inconsistency appears to be what effective facilitators have in common! Thiagi eventually concluded that effective facilitators are flexible, adaptive, proactive, responsive and resilient.

Stuart Wickes came to similar conclusions when he carried out a study of effective facilitation in outdoor management development. Wickes' study highlighted (amongst other factors) the importance of personal commitment, the ability to work with 'feelings and intuition' and the ability to work with 'clarity of intention' (Wickes, 2000: 40). Such findings are consistent with this guidance from Dale Hunter and colleagues for group facilitators:

Be yourself. As a facilitator, you will be most effective when you are being your natural self and allowing your own personality to be expressed. People get permission to be themselves from the way a facilitator behaves: that is, through modelling. If you are stiff and formal, the group tends to be like that. If you are relaxed and self-expressed, the group tends to be like that too.

(Hunter et al., 1992: 54)

Search hard enough and you can probably find research supporting your own preferred facilitation style. Whatever that may be, the research reported above suggests that you should not be a slave to just one style. Such advice is particularly relevant in the unpredictable arena of outdoor education. You need freedom for manoeuvre, room for judgement, flexibility to respond and to make the most of unexpected events and experiences. The challenge is to develop a facilitation style or combination of styles that works for you and your students and that makes good use of the many facilitative influences that are found in outdoor education settings.

Facilitating reflection

Quality action and quality reflection on that action are of fundamental and equal importance

(Mortlock, 2001: 119)

Whatever style is adopted, one of the facilitator's primary roles in outdoor education is to facilitate reflection on experience. This process is referred to variously as 'reviewing' or 'debriefing' or 'processing'. Much of the advice in this area centres on the art of questioning. Clifford Knapp's *Lasting Lessons* is an excellent resource for helping outdoor educators develops their questioning skills (Knapp, 1992). But there are traps awaiting the unwary. After the stimulation of the activity, reviewing sessions can be an anti-climax. In *Islands of Healing*, Schoel warns:

> *Without the sense of action to the Debrief, it is often a lifeless, futile exercise . . . The experience can come alive in the Debrief. The experience can be relived. The discussion is not a static, safe, merely cognitive exercise. It has feeling, anger, frustration, accomplishment and fun.*
>
> (Schoel, Prouty and Radcliffe, 1988: 166)

What students experience during a review is at least as important as the experience that they are reviewing. It is not enough to expect that the stimulation of the activity will keep students alert and involved during a dull review in which the facilitator runs through a series of questions. Review sessions are an ideal opportunity for enabling students to be more active learners. Experiential learning is based on learners being active, curious and creative (Kolb, 1984). We should at least seek out learners' own questions. When reviewing in the outdoors there is no shortage of opportunities for active reviewing. The outdoors provides:

- A breath of fresh air and change of scene that can inspire a refreshingly new approach to learning.
- An abundance of visual aids, some of which are 'the real thing' rather than substitutes for it.
- A naturally stimulating environment for learning that is more 'brain-friendly' (and arouses more 'intelligences') than the most well equipped indoor classrooms.
- Space that is useful for more physical reviewing such as action replays, human sculpture, human graphs, or human scales.
- Privacy for solo reflection.
- Freedom from fixed or cumbersome furniture: you can move quickly between large group, small group, paired and individual reviewing activities.
- Opportunities for walking and talking – for paired discussions or for interviewing each other.
- Sand or soft earth for drawing anything such as a graph for showing ups and downs, a journey towards a goal, a force field, a flow chart, or a learning model.
- Natural objects and materials that can be collected and arranged as collages or sculptures or maps of a journey.

- Natural objects that can be arranged and moved to represent the changing group dynamics.
- Viewpoints from where participants indicate places that evoke thoughts or feelings associated with the experience being reviewed
- Opportunities for reflective exercises such as guided reflections or making personal gifts from natural materials (Greenaway, 1995).
- Opportunities for reflective drama inspired by the location or by environmental themes such as life cycles, the food chain, and the web of life.
- A *Canterbury Tales* journey where each review topic happens at a different location.
- The opportunities to 'walk through' what happened or perform an action replay.
- The opportunity to have a second go, and compare the differences between 'take one' and 'take two'.
- 'Teachable moments' or 'learning opportunities' which are best caught there and then as they happen.

Once you discover that you can abandon indoor teaching aids and exploit resources and opportunities in the outdoors for reviewing, you will become tuned in to spotting good reviewing locations and making the most of them. By making reviewing active, mobile and outdoors, the reviews themselves can be at least as memorable as the outdoor experiences being reviewed. This makes the learning as memorable as the experience in which it is grounded.

Who's voices?

Let mountains speak for themselves and students may only hear the echoes of their hopes and fears – or silence. Let facilitators talk too much and that is all that students will hear. Give students a chance to voice their experiences and you and they will find endless rewards in learning from experiences outdoors.

References

Barret, J. and Greenaway, R. (1995) *Why Adventure? The Role and Value of Outdoor Adventure in Young People's Personal and Social Development*. Coventry: Foundation for Outdoor Adventure.

Charlton, D. (1980) *Adventure Education*. North Wales: CELMI.

Cornell, J. (1979) *Sharing Nature with Children*. Watford: Exley/Amanda Publications.

Cornell, J. (1989) *Sharing the Joy of Nature*. Nevada City, CA: Dawn Publications.

Greenaway, R. (1993) *Playback: A Guide to Reviewing Activities*. Windsor: The Duke of Edinburgh's Award.

Heron, J. (1999) *The Complete Facilitator's Handbook*. London: Kogan Page.

Hovelynck J. (2001) Beyond Didactics: A Reconnaissance of Experiential Learning. *Australian Journal of Outdoor Education*. 6: 1, 4–12.

Hunter, D., Bailey, A. and Taylor, B. (1992) *The Zen of Groups: The Handbook for People Meeting With A Purpose*. Auckland: Tandem Press.

Keighley, P. (1998) *Learning Through First Hand Experience Out of Doors: The Contribution Which Outdoor Education Can Make to Children's Learning as Part of The National Curriculum*. Sheffield: National Association for Outdoor Education.

Knapp, C. (1992) *Lasting Lessons: A Teacher's Guide to Reflecting on Experience*. Charleston, ERIC/CRESS.

Kolb, D.A. (1984) *Experiential Learning: Experience as The Source of Development*. NJ: Prentice-Hall.

Mortlock, C. (2001) *Beyond Adventure*. Milnthorpe: Cicerone Press.

Priest, S., and Gass, M. (1997) *Effective Leadership in Adventure Programming*. Champaign, IL: Human Kinetics.

Ringer, M. (2002) *Group Action: The Dynamics of Groups in Therapeutic, Educational and Corporate Settings*. London and Philadelphia: Jessica Kingsley.

Rogers, C. (1969) *Freedom to Learn: A View of What Education Might Become*. Columbus, OH: C.E. Merrill.

Schoel, J., Prouty, D. and Radcliffe, P. (1988) *Islands of Healing: A Guide to Adventure Based Counselling*. Hamilton, MA: Project Adventure.

Torres, C. (2001) *The Appreciative Facilitator*. Maryville, TE: Mobile Team Challenge.

Thiagarajan, S. and Thiagarajan, R. (1999) *Facilitator's Toolkit*. Bloomington, IN: Workshops Thiagi.

Wickes, S. (2000) The Facilitators' Stories: What's it Like to Facilitate at Your Very Best? *Brathay Topical Papers*. 2: 25–46.

16 Teaching and Learning Strategies

Bob Sharp

Abstract

Good instructors need to fulfil a variety of roles. At various times they need to be technicians, communicators, scientists, social workers, administrators, trainers, managers, politicians and teachers. A key role is that of teacher/instructor. The present chapter examines some well-regarded principles central to the teaching/learning process. It does this by focusing on four key themes; practice, guidance, feedback and transfer. There are many aspects of practice which dictate the extent and nature of what is learned, all of which require careful consideration. For example, should skills be broken into smaller parts and if so, how? How long should practice last for and how should it relate to the learner's previous experience? To what extent should the learner be actively involved in the learning process? Guidance methods rely on use of the various senses. Each offers scope for presenting information in ways that differ in nature and application. Feedback is critical to learning and can arise from both within and outside the learner. How much feedback is available, what type is given and when are some key features? A fundamental requirement of education (and outdoor education especially) is its ability to promote transferable skills. Learners must be able to apply specific learning experiences to other situations in time and location. What are the conditions which allow this to happen? This chapter examines these matters through an introduction to key theoretical and practical principles.

Introduction

A clear expectation in outdoor education is that people will change in some way. A group of primary age pupils following a wayfinding course should know a little more about the forest environment and perhaps learn the rudiments of navigation. Someone involved in the mountain leader scheme will become more proficient in a wide variety of technical and leadership skills. And a party of youngsters on a weekend paddling expedition should find out how they relate to other people and how they respond to the absence of home comforts. Education in general seeks to impart information, inculcate values, develop skills and open people's horizons to interests, knowledge and opportunities beyond the immediate learning experience. The extent to which each of these is achieved depends on the subject as well as the learner, instructor and environment. A particular challenge for education is assessing whether or not aims have been achieved. Whilst this may be relatively easy in regard to technical skills (can the learner tie a knot or paddle in a straight line?), it is more difficult when assessing change in areas such as self-esteem, leadership and team spirit. The

difficulties lie in the adequacy of measuring instruments and the multi-faceted nature of human learning. The model shown in Figure 1 is a simplification but serves to highlight the complexity of human learning.

The affective dimension (to feel) concerns 'human' qualities such as emotions, attitudes and values. We reveal emotions when confronted with say a pleasant sight or hear of a terrible accident and we all respond differently to such situations. Thus, some might relish the challenge of righting a capsized kayak in a serious rapid whilst others would be quite fearful. The cognitive dimension (to know) is concerned with intellect, knowledge and memory – how intelligent we are, how capable we are at discussion and reasoning, how well we remember and make decisions. Understanding the features on a map and relating them to the ground is a cognitive skill. Judging the next sequence of moves on a rock climb is also a cognitive skill. The last dimension – psycho-motor (to do) – is concerned with physical movement and action. Climbing a rock face with precision and control is a psycho-motor skill. This three-way approach underlines the broad and complex nature of skill learning and shows that

Figure 1   A multi-dimensional view of learning

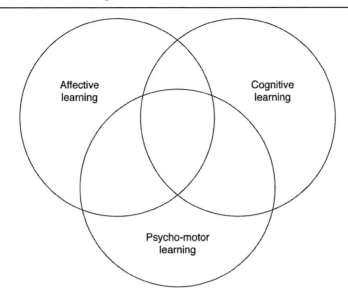

performance in any outdoor activity is an interplay between attitudes, knowledge and movements.

Characteristics of skill and learning

Learning is said to have taken place when there is a change in performance; it is implied and not directly seen. Improvement must be relatively permanent and not a transient change caused by a change in fitness, health or maturation. It is vital to note that lack of change does not imply an absence of learning; internal changes can occur (e.g., absorbing information, learning to recognise which cues require attention, understanding rules) which are not reflected in significant technical improvements. This accounts for the common experience of 'plateaus' in learning. There are four key features that define skill behaviour (Sharp, 1992; 2004). Firstly, skill is goal directed and has a clear outcome or end result – walking on a straight bearing, carving a ski turn, sailing against the wind. Secondly, skill is a learned characteristic requiring practice and experience for proficiency. This means that skill is not inherited nor does it result from changes in age or fitness. Thirdly, skill is reflected in movements which are economic and efficient in terms of their energy and time outlay. Skilled action is not clumsy to the eye. This is seen when, for example, a competent paddler negotiates a series of gates and rapids in a

competitive slalom event; movements are fluent, effective and well timed. Finally, skilled activity is the end result of a chain of central nervous system functions; it is more than just movements. For example, a skilled orienteer moves fluently through the forest, makes quick decisions about route choice, looks ahead to the next control and takes care not to give away any information to the opposition. Here there are elements of anticipation, decision-making, memory and deception as well as movement.

There are some important implications here for teaching and learning:

- Firstly, if skill is goal directed then instructors should be aware of the goals. Generally speaking, so too must the learner. This implies careful planning in terms of goal selection and learner involvement, especially as the reason for doing things is sometimes overlooked and assumptions made about what learners should or should not know.
- Secondly, instructors should consider what kinds of learning experiences are appropriate to given goals. What form should practice take? How long should practice last and how many unsuccessful attempts should be allowed before moving to something different? Should skills be practiced as 'wholes' or broken into smaller parts? Should physical practice be

balanced with other experiences such as watching others perform, discussing problems with fellow learners, critically evaluating one's own skill, mentally rehearsing and so on.

- Thirdly, learning should be monitored to evaluate what changes have occurred. Learning cannot be assumed to take place simply because the learner understands the task and attempts a skill successfully.
- Fourthly, if skilled activity is effective and economical then the instructor must know what constitutes 'good' performance; they need to be technically articulate. In this way they can effectively judge when something goes wrong and provide appropriate feedback. There should also be an understanding that skilled action does not always depend on following a well-defined, strict movement pattern. The outdoor environment is relatively 'forgiving' so that a degree of 'error' or variability in technique is usually possible whilst still allowing success. Thus, a sensitive instructor will acknowledge that in mountain navigation, there may be two or more ways to travel from A to B, all of which are equally effective. Similarly, a skier may adopt a style that is not textbook efficiency, but is still acceptable to the skier and recognises their stage of learning or body shape.
- Finally, it should be acknowledged that successful movements – kayaking a spate river, skiing off piste, surfing strong waves – depend on qualities such as perception, attention, confidence, motivation, decision-making and anticipation. Too often, instructors tend to get bogged down with movement techniques. They must be aware of which components to emphasise, which to attenuate and how to introduce them at each stage of an individual's development.

Transfer of learning

Practically all learning is based on the application of previous experience; new skills invariably arise out of previous learning. Indeed, an underlying premise in outdoor education is that experiences not only have transient worth, but they also have lasting influences in different situations. A central premise in education is that whatever is learned during practice will have a beneficial effect at a subsequent time. This is called positive transfer.

Sometimes negative transfer takes place; paddling an open canoe may prove rather tricky initially for someone used to paddling kayaks for many years. Similarly, a fear of heights may transfer itself to an aversion to rock climbing or hill walking. For instructors and teachers it is essential to know the conditions which maximise positive transfer and which minimise negative transfer. Research on this subject is considerable and has yielded a variety of theories. Gass (1990) describes three theories (specific, non-specific, metaphoric) that are relevant to outdoor education. Specific transfer takes place when previously learned skills are highly similar to those encountered at some later stage. An example would be when a novice climber translates belaying skills (e.g. feeding the rope through a friction device) to the task of abseiling. In both situations, highly similar techniques are required for success. Non-specific transfer takes place when principles or common ideas are taken from current learning to new situations. An example would be when an orienteer who has learned principles of fine navigation such as aiming off or hand railing, adapts them to navigate in the mountains. Another example would be when a youngster who suffers a fright when capsizing a kayak, transfers these negative feelings to other water sports. Metaphoric transfer takes place when principles are generalised from one situation to another, but in contrast to non-specific transfer, the principles are analogous or metaphoric. An example is seen when the principles of teamwork and co-ordination (as seen when two people paddle an open canoe) are transferred to different situations such as climbing together or expedition. The key to maximising transfer is to plan for it by designing appropriate learning experiences and adopting relevant teaching approaches. Gass (1990) and others (e.g. Sharp, 1992; 2004) describe a number of strategies that can facilitate transfer such as the identification of similarities between present practice and other situations, highlighting the similarities and differences (techniques and principles) between present and potential future learning, encouraging over learning, providing opportunities for learners to internalise and reflect (through verbalisation or visualisation) on their learning. It should be understood by learners and instructors alike that all skills and experiences are relevant within a wider framework; very little that is taught/learned happens in isolation. Attention should always be focused on what has happened in the past, where it fits into the present context and how it may be helpful in the future.

Methods of guidance

It is well known that practice alone leads to early plateaus in learning, the build-up of errors that go unnoticed and diminished motivation. There is no doubt that skill improvement is helped considerably through guidance from expert sources. There are three broad approaches each of which relies on different senses – visual, verbal and manual guidance (Sharp, 1992; 2004).

Visual guidance

Vision dominates the way we communicate with the outside world. Visual guidance can take three different forms – demonstrations, visual materials and display changes:

- Demonstrations take advantage of a very powerful principle in learning, viz., learning by imitation. They offer an immediate picture and also save the instructor the problem of expressing complex actions in words. They play a role at all levels of learning and the fact they take place in real time adds to their impact and motivational value. Demonstrations also allow advantage to be taken of other peoples' skills and expertise. However, demonstrations only work if a number of criteria are met; learners must attend to the demonstration, they must understand/remember the information conveyed, they must possess the ability to reproduce the movements, and be given the opportunity to practice. Furthermore, demonstrations must be relevant to the learners' needs, pitched at the correct level, technically correct, repeated and presented from the correct viewpoint. Showing someone how to tie a knot by facing them actually gives a mirror image of the correct technique!
- Visual materials which present static images such as wall charts, photographs and colour slides, are initially attractive and may brighten the learning environment but their inability to convey movement soon renders them redundant. Video is a better medium and is used increasingly by instructors for demonstration and feedback provision. Lightweight, digital technology makes this a very practical medium to use.
- Finally, vision can be used to focus the learner's attention by highlighting important elements in the display. The use of different coloured ropes for abseiling helps learners understand the mechanics involved; kayak paddles which are coloured on one side help the person grip the paddle correctly during a capsize; and the presence of chalk on a rock face may assist novice climbers locate the best handholds.

Verbal guidance

Verbal guidance is obviously very common and extremely important. Words can be used to tell a learner what something looks like (description) and how to do it (explanation). It is often simple to describe what a skill looks like, but more difficult to explain how it is carried out. To do so relies on in-depth knowledge of the skill and its composition, which is often based on personal experience. Thus, to describe abseiling as 'controlled sliding down a rope' only gives a superficial description; it says little about the elements on which the learner must focus, the actions required of the legs and arms, where the learner should look and how they should orient their body. There is an important distinction between direct and indirect verbal guidance. Direct verbal guidance specifies something clear about the task in hand, e.g., 'rotate the compass until the red arrow points north'. Indirect verbal guidance or hinting is a technique for achieving a particular movement without exactly specifying it (e.g., 'climb with your eyes'). Verbal guidance is particularly beneficial where discrimination, decision-making and perceptual judgements are critical. Further, 'open' skills that take place in a changing environment benefit more from verbal guidance than 'closed' skills where the environment plays little part. Verbal instruction is particularly meaningful at higher levels of skill where learners have the vocabulary to comprehend and motivation to concentrate. However, one should always be mindful of 'talking too much' and confusing learners with technical jargon.

Manual guidance

Manual guidance involves some kind of physical contact between the learner and instructor or between the learner and another device, e.g., use of a tight rope in climbing. It assists learning by highlighting or changing the internal sensations that accompany action. A major intention is to control movement and minimise or eliminate completely potential errors. Physical assistance by the instructor is useful where the learner lacks confidence or feels unsafe. Helping someone to roll a kayak in a swimming pool by assisting rotation of the kayak or holding on to the paddle are examples of manual guidance. Research shows that it can be an extremely valuable tool but should be withdrawn as soon as possible to permit the learner to take control of the actions.

Good instructional technique involves using and adapting each of these three methods as the situation fits. Some people respond best to a particular approach (e.g. they insist on seeing a demonstration before they practice themselves) whilst others learn best if helped in a variety of ways. Instructors too, often feel more comfortable with a particular approach (see Cross and Lyle, 1999 for a fuller examination of coaching and learning styles).

Providing feedback

To move skilfully and adapt to an ever-changing environment there is a need to monitor actions, their effect on the environment and react accordingly. Feedback is critical to learning and successful performance. Feedback can arise from within the individual (e.g. a walker sees the consequences of making a navigation blunder) or from outside (e.g. when an instructor provides praise for a skill performed well). Feedback has the capacity to help in three ways:

- It can highlight differences between what was achieved and what was intended.
- It can serve to reinforce good technique.
- And it can have a motivating effect.

Often, all three work together. From an instructional viewpoint, there are a number of key aspects. Firstly, for feedback information to be useful the instructor must have a 'model of correct performance'. Only then can they detect differences between desired and actual performances. The ability to do this well depends on good technical knowledge supported by sound personal experience of the activity in question. Secondly, instructors must be able to translate error information into positive guidance that motivates learners to improve. This is not an easy thing to do. It requires care and understanding plus a capacity to convert negative observations into positive experiences. Thirdly, instructors need to recognise that performance errors may occur for a multitude of reasons; the correct ones have to be identified and dealt with specifically. A youngster experiencing difficulty climbing a simple slab may have a number of problems: lack of fitness, low confidence, poor self-esteem, ill fitting footwear; lack of skill, slippery rock, etc. Problem solving like this requires extensive knowledge of skill breakdown and a sensitivity to respond accordingly.

There are a number of other factors that dictate the effectiveness of feedback. External feedback is most effective if it is given almost immediately after a performance. Furthermore, feedback is only relevant if practice follows straightaway to allow the learner to remedy any faults. It is generally agreed that learners should be encouraged to analyse their own learning by trying to identify 'what went wrong'. It is also considered that if individuals increasingly take responsibility for their learning then the degree of outside feedback from instructors can be reduced over time. Peer review and analysis may also be combined with instructor feedback. Finally, when a number of errors are noted in a learner's performance, the instructor should decide which is the most important to highlight. It may well be that correcting one error has a knock-on effect in solving a number of others. For example, a common difficulty with novice skiers is weight distribution. Correcting this often allows the skis to run together better, creates better control of speed and also allows for more efficient turning.

Practice methods

It is evident that practice is essential for skill improvement. Indeed, taking part is the essence of outdoor education. Practice can take many forms; it can be highly structured and well defined or it can be open-ended and individually determined. It can take the form of physical practice, mental rehearsal or even observation of others performing. A number of factors should be considered when designing practice – the role of making errors, how should skills be broken down, how much time and what resources are available, the role of mental practice and so on. It is vital to consider the learner's prior experience. Knowing the 'entry behaviours' of learners allows goals to be set which are attainable and leads to more informed and effective practice. Learners should be guided to focus on one or two essential points to avoid information overload; practices should be designed to highlight the points in question and guidance methods selected to emphasise those points. Consideration must be given to the nature of the skill being introduced; what are the safety considerations; is it physically demanding how complex are the movements; are they connected, etc? Asking such questions is a start to breaking skills down into manageable proportions. A useful framework is to adopt an information-processing approach to task analysis. Here, the individual/skill partnership is examined sequentially; what are the perceptual (input) demands of the skill, the decision-making aspects, the movement (output) requirements and the feedback possibilities. An approach like this helps give order to practice development and ensures that nothing important is excluded.

A particular problem of designing practice centres on whether relatively complex skills should be taught in their entirety or broken down into lesser parts. Traditionally, instructors use whole and part methods and various combinations to good effect. Whole methods expose the learner to all elements of an activity (e.g., a novice climber may complete a simple top-roped climb with little prior instruction or practice). The whole approach is desirable when skills contain parts that are linked to one another (e.g., forward paddling). In contrast, part methods typically focus on elements of a skill before linking them together (e.g., fitting a harness, tying on, climbing technique, etc.). They reduce the information load imposed on the learner, allow for more immediate feedback and quicker success. And, because part practices are simpler and less dangerous, they serve a useful role in eliminating fear that might otherwise block attempts at the whole skill. Combination methods centre on a whole-part-whole approach or a progressive-part approach where elements are taught individually and gradually built up into the complete skill.

A particularly important method of practice is called shaping. Shaping involves the acquisition of a complex movement through the gradual shaping or addition of simpler movements. Shaping is not unlike trial and error learning where some movements are eliminated and others steadily altered until the desired one is established. Shaping is often used to teach skiing. Most skiers aspire to perfect parallel turns but for most people this is too complex to tackle straight away. One approach is to teach firstly a simple snowplough glide. Once mastered, a turn can be incorporated first in one direction then the other. Following this, the element of unweighting can be introduced which allows the learner to bring the skis together for the turn. With practice the skis can be bought parallel earlier in the turn until both traverse and turn are accomplished with the legs roughly parallel. In this example, the whole skill has gradually been formed by successively developing simpler ones.

Practice variability and over learning

Research has shown that when skills that take place in a dynamic environment (moving water, changing weather, varied terrain, different rock types), variable practice results in greater accuracy and consistency than specific practice. In other words, if skill learning is concerned primarily with the acquisition of rules or principles (as with navigation skills) as opposed to discrete actions ('J' stroke in canoeing) then the richer and more diverse the practice the more effective it is. There is clearly a role in outdoor education for varied practice. Similarly, there is a key role for over learning. Over learning is the process of practicing repeatedly to a point where it appears unnecessary (e.g., practicing to role a kayak several thousands of times). If it is practicable to do this, then there are several benefits; learners may discover unrealised potential, skill becomes more resistant to error through stress and other outside influences and better recalled over time. Furthermore, over learning permits greater transfer to other skills/situations.

Figure 2   The learning gradient (Priest and Hammerman, 1989)

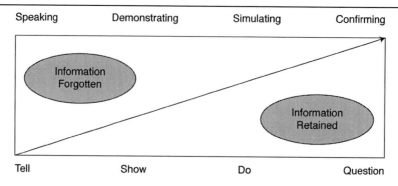

Active versus passive learning

There is a traditional dichotomy in education – didactic versus experiential learning. The difference hinges on the degree to which the learner is actively involved in their own learning. Whilst there are numerous examples in outdoor education where instruction needs to be authoritative, direct and relatively uninfluenced by the need to cater for individual differences (particularly in high risk situations) there is an overwhelming case to involve learners fully and permit them to take as much responsibility as possible for their own learning. Indeed, there is very strong empirical and theoretical support for experiential approaches to learning (see elsewhere in this book). The process of involvement includes a number of strategies, viz., use of trial and error practice, emphasising the value of mental rehearsal, provision of opportunities for learners to analyse their performance, sharing feelings, adoption of teaching styles which recognise individual differences in ability and interest, etc. Priest and Hammerman (1989) argue strongly for this approach to learning. In their model, the 'learning gradient' depends on the teaching style adopted (see Figure 2). They describe four different styles; speaking to the learner, demonstrating the activity, ensuring the learner practices the activity and questioning the learner about the activity. In their scheme, talking to the learner imparts little information as most is lost or forgotten. Showing learners what to do is better ('A picture paints a thousand words'). Practice is essential and leads to a fuller understanding. However, it is only when learners are actively involved through questioning their knowledge and analysing their performance that complete learning and understanding occurs.

Role of errors in learning

Most learners strive for success and instructors invariably direct learners towards the correct way of carrying out a skill. However, errors are an inevitable part of learning, especially in the early stages. Do people learn from making errors? Should learners be guided into error situations intentionally or allowed to repeat mistakes? A school of thought ('Schema Theory') argues that people can profit in several ways from their errors (Day and Sharp, 1993). For example, in sailing the learner picks up a lot of useful information about a boat's capabilities, the effect of wind on sails and emergency drills through capsizing a dinghy. Similarly, in orienteering, a novice learns important principles of navigation when mistakes are made for example, in pace judgement or walking on bearings. Errors add to variety in practice and also highlight the boundaries of good/poor performance. However, these benefits should be weighed against risks to safety and the possibility of bad habit formation through prolonged error practice.

Learning and teaching styles

This chapter has addressed some of the better known principles of teaching and learning that have wide application. However, it should not be forgotten that learners are individuals with different genetic make-ups, upbringing and life experiences. These factors produce differences in the way people perceive, process information and ultimately learn new skills. Various authors (e.g., Grant, 2002) have attempted to define and categorise the ways in which people learn – learning styles. Three distinctions are commonly cited – sequential/holistic, concrete/abstract and active/reflective. Sequential learners prefer progressive, part approaches to practice whereas holistic learners favour an attempt at the whole skill immediately. Concrete learners prefer direct experience – doing, seeing, acting – whereas abstract learners prefer to evaluate, observe and assess. Active learners tend to be concerned for the present and invest time/energy simply to enjoy the present. In contrast, reflective learners focus on understanding and judgement before action. Is it useful to know that people tend to adopt habitual styles of learning? Yes it is. Good teaching is rather like fitting together the pieces of a jigsaw; the more pieces fitted, the more complete the picture. In the same way, instructors seek to maximise their effectiveness by using all the information available to help each person learn. Knowing that people tend to learn in particular ways is a key part of the information gathering process.

It should be pointed out finally that instructors too, adopt characteristic ways of teaching. There are patterns in an instructor's behaviour that can be differentiated and represented in a particular type. One common distinction is that between autocratic and democratic styles of instruction. It is incumbent on all instructors to assess their habitual style of working with learners with a view to maximising their own potentials. Cross and Lyle (1999) discuss this matter in much more detail.

References

Cross, N. and Lyle, J. (1999) *The Coaching Process*. Oxford: Butterworth-Heinemann.

Day, L. and Sharp, R.H. (1993) Teaching by Error in Outdoor Pursuits Activities. *Journal of Adventure Education*. 10: 1, 7–10.

Gass, M. (1990) Transfer of Learning in Adventure Education, in Miles, J.C. and Priest, S. (Eds.) *Adventure Education*. State College, PA: Venture Publishing.

Grant, L. (2002) Learners and Learning. *Horizons*. 18: 27–9.

Priest, S. and Hammerman, D. (1989) Teaching Outdoor Adventure Skills. *Journal of Adventure Education*. 6: 4, 16–8.

Sharp, R.H. (1992). *Acquiring Skill in Sport*. Eastbourne: Sports Dynamics.

Sharp, R.H. (2004) *Acquiring Skill in Sport*. 2nd edn. Cheltenham: Sports Dynamics.

17 Duty of Care

Nick Halls

Abstract

The civil duty of care as expressed in common and statute law is described. How liability is judged and the implications for insurance are also examined. Reference is made to the law of contract.

Duty of care

In common law every person has a duty of care for themselves and others who may be affected by their actions. If somebody, or their property, suffers damage, believed by the person damaged to result from the action of another, they may raise an action against that person for recovery of the cost of the damage in a civil court. This is an action in the common law of tort (A tort is a breach of duty [other than under contract] leading to liability for damages, Oxford Dictionary, 1964). The plaintiff must prove the defendant owed a duty of care in the circumstances, and that the plaintiff was in a relationship of proximity such that the defendant should reasonably have kept the plaintiff's interest in mind. Lord Aitken (Donaghue v Stevenson [1932]) formulated a general principle for determining whether a duty of care exists – the 'neighbour principle' – which identifies foresight as an essential part of the duty. He said:

> *You must take reasonable care to avoid acts or omissions which you can reasonably foresee would be likely to injure your neighbour. Who then, in law, is my neighbour? The answer seems to be – persons who are so closely and directly affected by my act that I ought reasonably to have them in contemplation as being so affected when I am directing my mind to the acts or omissions which are called into question.*

Negligence

Negligence was defined in the case of Blyth v Birmingham Waterworks Co (1895) as:

> *. . . the omission to do something a reasonable man, guided upon those considerations which ordinarily regulate the conduct of human affairs, would do, or doing something a prudent and reasonable man would not do.*

The plaintiff must prove the damage caused was foreseeable and the actions of the defendant negligent in that they fell short of what is considered reasonable in the circumstances. This is usually evaluated in relation to evidence about good practice provided by expert witnesses, and guidance issued by authoritative organisations. During leisure activities, approved practice is based on recommendations for the safe conduct of the activity issued by a governing body of sport. Conformity to good practice is normally regarded as evidence that reasonable care has been taken, but this is not conclusive. Conversely, failure to conform to approved practice affords prima facie evidence of negligence but, again, this is not conclusive. The conduct of a defendant may reveal a higher quality of care than required by approved practice, or the failure to conform to approved practice may not have caused the damage.

It rests with the plaintiff to prove particular conduct on the part of the defendant which is both negligent and the cause of the damage. The plaintiff must show the damage occurred as a result of a chain of events to which the following principle is applied:

> *If the damage would not have happened but for the particular fault, then that fault is the cause of the damage; if it would have happened just the same, fault or no fault, the fault is not the cause of the damage.*
>
> (Lord Denning, Cork v. Kirby MacLean, 1952)

The proximity to the actions asserted to be the cause of the damage is taken into account. If they are distant in either time or place, this weakens the claim of causality. In the summing up in the case of Finlay v The Crown (British Mountaineering Council, 2001) in which Peter Finlay was charged with the criminal act of manslaughter of Jonathan Attwell, the jury was asked whether or not Peter

Finlay had breached his duty of care resulting in gross negligence. Sir Justice Richardson emphasised that what the jury must consider was what took place at the time and place of the accident, and whether this was the direct cause of the accident. Peter Finlay was found not guilty. Although things leading up to the incident did not conform to good practice, it was judged that these did not cause the death, which might have happened whether or not these other 'things' had occurred.

It may be that although a defendant was negligent, this conduct did not cause the damage. If an intervening event occurred which is not attributable to the conduct of the defendant, but caused or contributed to the damage, this will be taken into account. A person who fails to comply with good practice in the organisation of an excursion during which a participant is struck by lightning is unlikely to be judged liable, because the damage did not arise from the failure to organise the expedition properly. If the defendant acted in accord with good practice when the threat from lightning occurred, then other conduct will probably be regarded as unconnected with the death.

If the cause of an incident is unknown, the plaintiff may not be able to prove how actions of the defendant were a cause, in which case the plaintiff may rely on the maxim res ipsa loquitur ['the thing speaks for itself']. The plaintiff must show that an explanation as to how the accident happened is absent, that the 'thing' which caused the damage was under the control of the defendant, and that such an accident would not ordinarily occur without negligence. Whether the accident would not ordinarily have happened without negligence is judged in the light of common experience. This principle can give rise to unsubstantiated media comment immediately after an incident, often influenced by self-styled expert comment. For example, inexperienced or reckless people are unlikely to demonstrate foresight, and when involved in an incident the probable cause will be an action or decision which deviated from good practice. Inexperienced leaders may have difficulty in defending themselves from such reasoning, arising as it does from 'common experience'.

If the consequences of the conduct are unforeseeable, the defendant is not normally judged to be negligent, and it does not necessarily follow that the defendant will be liable, even for all foreseeable consequences. However, once a particular damage has occurred it is then regarded as foreseeable. In practice, the court evaluates the behaviour of the defendant in terms of risk. The defendant is more likely to be judged negligent if the conduct in question exposes the plaintiff to an unreasonable risk of harm. Risk will be scaled in terms both of the probability of damage occurring and the severity of the possible damage. The magnitude of the risk, the social desirability of the activity and the practicability of the precautions taken to eliminate risk, are all taken into consideration.

Social policy is considered. For example, a person voluntarily engaging in a leisure activity with well-known risks may be judged to have a low standard of responsibility in the event of damage to another, particularly in sports such as boxing or rugby. By comparison, the standards required of a person driving a car fall little short of perfection. In 1971 the Court of Appeal held that a learner driver must exercise the competence of a reasonably experienced driver. Leaders of outdoor activities are expected to meet standards akin to those required of drivers.

Inexperience, lack of understanding or lack of competence provide no defence to a charge of negligence. A reasonable person is expected to know those things that common experience teaches, and take their own inexperience or lack of competence into account. Whether the plaintiff, or anybody else, contributed to the damage which occurred will also be considered. Plaintiffs are expected to take reasonable care of themselves, in the same way as defendants must avoid negligence. In common law, a plaintiff whose injuries are caused partly by their own negligence can recover nothing. However, statute has ameliorated this, and since the Law Reform [Contributory Negligence] Act 1945, contributory negligence is no longer a complete bar to recovery but will result in a reduction of damages 'to such an extent as the court thinks just and equitable having regard to the claimant's share in the responsibility for the damage'. The defendant must show that the plaintiff did not, in their own interest, take reasonable care of themselves and thus, by this want of care, contributed to their own injury.

Consent

The consent of the plaintiff influences liability, and the principle of Volenti non fit injuria is applied. This maxim embodies the principle that a person who agrees with another to run the risk of harm created by that other cannot thereafter sue in respect of damage suffered as a result of the materialisation of that risk. Account is taken of whether the plaintiff consented to the actions which caused the damage, and whether this consent was an informed consent, based on an adequate knowledge of the risks involved. This is significant during voluntary participation in sport, for example, when a person agrees to go mountaineering or canoeing with a companion. Mere knowledge of a risk does not amount to consent. It must be found as a fact that the plaintiff agreed to incur the risk freely, with full knowledge of the nature and extent of the risk. Warnings of the risks of activities such as the participation statement of the BMC/MC of S that:

Climbing, hill walking and mountaineering are activities with a danger of personal injury or death. Participants in these activities should be aware of and accept these risks and be responsible for their own actions and involvement.

only inform of the dangers of participation. Such statements do not imply consent of participants to damage arising from lack of foresight, incompetence or negligence of a person whose conduct subsequently results in damage. For a leader of young people or novices, Volenti is not a useful defence. The lack of success of the volenti defence in a negligence action arises because the alleged consent usually refers to the general risk of the activity and precedes the defendant's breach of duty. In these circumstances, the plaintiff cannot be said to have possessed full knowledge and appreciation of the risk arising from the conduct of the defendant. Agreeing to go on a walk in the mountains with a friend does not imply consent to damage caused by negligence. However, getting into a car driven by a drunken driver does imply that the plaintiff consented to what is known by a reasonable person to be a risk, and thus any damage is likely to be regarded as partially arising from the plaintiffs lack of care for their own welfare.

Competence

It should be noted that in accord with the Unfair Contract Terms Act (1977), asking participants to sign disclaimers as evidence of their knowledge of the danger of an activity does not constitute an agreement not to sue for negligent behaviour on the part of providers.

People who present themselves as having a particular expertise or vocational ability should have the competence of a reasonably competent person exercising that skill or vocational ability. The standard of competence expected will vary according to risks involved. For example, a 'do it yourself' enthusiast fixing a cupboard door handle in their own home would only be expected to meet the standard of a reasonably competent carpenter, but not the standard of a professional working for reward. However, if the activity is of a technical or complex nature, and there is a risk of serious injury if it is not done properly, the defendant would be expected either to employ an expert or to display equivalent ability. Neither lack of experience or training, lack of a qualification, nor providing the vocational skill without reward, constitute a defence. The possession of a qualification reinforces the requirement to demonstrate the skill of an expert. Members of a profession or trade discharge their duty by conforming to the standards of a reasonably competent member of the profession or trade. People undertaking a leadership role during outdoor activities, even on a voluntary and informal basis, should ensure that they have the experience and skill of a reasonably competent expert.

Young people

An enhanced duty of care is owed to young or inexperienced people because their consent is less well-informed and lack of experience, competence and/or understanding renders them less able to recognise and cope with hazards, so their exposure to risk is regarded as higher. Consequently when young people are involved in outdoor activities, these should only be undertaken with the explicit and informed consent of parent/s. Part of the duty is to ensure that the experience and ability of young or inexperienced people matches the possible demands on them.

Lack of experience and maturity may lead to hazards both for themselves and others. In law, children and novices are responsible for their own safety and the safety of others and can be held responsible for contributing to their own damage. However, the degree of care expected will be in proportion to their age, maturity and experience. When a young person causes injury by conduct which, in an adult, would be classed as negligent, then a parent or other responsible teacher or leader may be held liable. This is a primary liability arising from failure to exercise proper supervision and control. When an employee of a provider of education, or a volunteer operating on behalf of a voluntary youth organisation, has responsibility for young people, then they should be well-supervised, and behaviour appropriate to the circumstances demanded of them.

In circumstances where education is provided for people below the age of 18 yrs, under statute and common law, responsibility for safety in maintained (supported by public funds) educational establishments rests mainly with the local education authorities. In independent educational establishments (privately financed) it rests with the governing bodies or proprietors. With voluntary youth organisations it rests with the governing council. Those acting on behalf of such organisations are deemed to be acting 'in loco parentis' and are required to show a standard of care similar to that of a wise and reasonable parent. This duty is onerous for, once assumed, it cannot be set aside until the young people are returned to the care of their parents, nor can it be delegated to other people. Government advice to local education authorities relating to the provision of outdoor education has become the standard of good practice. All who assume responsibility for the activities of young or inexperienced people should have regard to this body of advice, whether acting in an informal capacity or as an employee.

Liability arises not solely from the occurrence of an incident, but from not following good practice in the exercise of the duty of care. The duty of care requires all people, in every activity they undertake, to rigorously assess the consequences of their actions and responsibly assess the damage which could occur to themselves and others as a result of their conduct. Not to do so is to behave recklessly. If damage occurs attributable to reckless conduct, it may be treated as a criminal act, particularly if it results in serious injury or the death of another or if conduct contravenes statute law.

Civil liability insurance

People participating in a recreational activity during their leisure time may be involved when an injury occurs to another participant, or damage to property occurs. This may lead to them being pursued for damages. A benefit of membership of NGBs of sports is that they provide civil liability insurance for members while engaged in sport for recreational purposes. Liability insurance usually covers the insured for the costs of representation in court and for the cost of damages which might be awarded. Insurers take responsibility for defending and paying a claim on behalf of the insured. Insurers try to reduce their financial liability and are inclined to fight costly claims in court. Society is becoming more litigious, and it behoves anybody who participates in recreational outdoor activities to have civil liability insurance. Knowledge that a defendant has civil liability insurance may encourage a plaintiff to raise a frivolous action for damages on a no win no fee basis, although few lawyers are inclined to take on onerous work without a guarantee of recompense. As injuries and damage to property often occur during the course of recreational activity, it is prudent also to be insured for personal injury and damage to or loss of property. Possessing personal injury and property insurance may remove the necessity to pursue another participant to recover damages.

Employer's liability

Employers are regarded as having a duty of care for employees and those affected by employee's actions. An employer may be held liable, as master, for the actions of servants during the course of their employment. This is described as vicarious liability as the servant is deemed to act as deputy for the master. In addition to the common law duty there are statutory obligations cast upon employers for the protection of workers and others, for example, the Factory Acts, the Mines and Quarries Acts and Health and Safety at Work legislation.

The common law duty is threefold, as explained in the case of Wilsons and Clyde Coal Co. Ltd v English [1938], 'the provision of a competent staff of men, adequate material and a proper system and effective supervision.' The duty is not absolute but is discharged by the exercise of reasonable care and is thus similar to the duty of care generally. The employer's obligation is to see that care is taken by whoever is appointed to act for them.

Employers can be held liable for the actions of their employees as they have a duty to ensure they are competent. This embraces an obligation to ensure employees are trained for work activities. The employer may train an employee for the work required themselves, or employ people who are suitably trained. In the context of provision of outdoor activity experiences this has led to the growth of importance of leadership/instructional qualifications, as evidence of training and benchmarks of competence.

Employers have a duty to provide adequate plant and equipment and to maintain it in a state which is safe to use and fit for purpose. The duty extends to the provision of protective clothing and devices and when appropriate, instruction in how and when to use them. Employers can be held liable for any damage arising from inadequate machinery or equipment, and damage arising from not providing appropriate protective clothing and safety equipment.

A proper system refers to the organisation of work, the manner in which it is carried out, the number of employees required for particular tasks, the part each has to play, the taking of safety precautions, and the giving of special instructions, particularly to inexperienced workers. A proper system is one that accords with good practice and conforms to statutory requirements. The employer does not discharge this duty merely by providing a proper system unless reasonable steps are taken to see that it is put into operation. Although employers may have devised a safe system they may be found negligent if they fail to put it into practice, and monitor its effectiveness. Therefore, the duty includes effective supervision.

The duty of care, guidance from government and statute have all resulted in organisations providing outdoor activity experiences developing very elaborate operational procedures to help ensure competent instruction and the safety of employees and people who may be affected by employee's actions. The employee is bound by a contractual duty to comply with the instructions of the employer, and if they do not they may be found individually negligent.

Legislation

Duties of employers and employees have been given statutory force by such acts as *The Health and Safety at Work etc. Act (1974)*. This act was reinforced by *The Management of Health and Safety at Work Regulations* (The Stationery Office Ltd, 1999), which require employers to introduce arrangements for planning, organising, controlling, monitoring and reviewing their management of health and safety. This incorporated foresight in the form of risk assessment of work activities, combined with the identification of matching control measures and emergency procedures to minimise risks. These acts and regulations distinguished the formal approach to risk management required at work from the more informal approach usually adopted when participating in leisure activities. However, in both spheres of activity risk management should be essentially similar.

Safety of young people was further secured by *The Activity Centres [Young Persons' Safety] Act, (1995)* which established the Adventure Activities Licensing Scheme. While this only applies to commercial organisations and a limited number of activities which pose a particular risk of death or disabling injury, it reinforces the risk management approach of health and safety at work legislation. An accident during the conduct of outdoor activities may now be treated as a criminal offence, as in the case of Finlay v The Crown, (BMC, 2001) following the fatality on Snowdon in 1999.

Contract

An employee is regarded as having entered into a contract with an employer to use skills on behalf of the employer for the purposes the employer prescribes in return for remuneration. The legal relationship is that of master and servant. An employee owes a duty of service to the employer, and is deemed to have entered into an agreement to perform a job of work within the limits set by the employer. The employee is regarded as having a duty to comply with all the guidance, regulations and procedures laid down by the employer, particularly in relation to health and safety and the health and safety of people affected by an employee's conduct. If an employee steps outside the limits set by the employer it can be deemed to be a breach of contract, and criminal behaviour. *The Health and Safety at Work Act 1974*, states that it shall be the duty of every employee while at work:

- To take reasonable care for the health and safety of himself and of other persons who may be affected by his acts or omissions at work, and
- As regards any duty or requirement imposed on his employer or any other person by or under any of the relevant statutory provisions, to cooperate with him so far as necessary to enable that duty or requirement to be complied with.

The relationship of master and servant gives rise to vicarious liability. If leaders or instructors are thought to be negligent, the employer will be identified with that negligence if they were acting within the course of their employment when the negligence occurs. The plaintiff nearly always sues the employer (whom it can be assumed will be able to pay damages) rather than the employee (who often cannot) although the plaintiff can sue both or either. Some employers carry insurance which indemnifies both the employer and the employee, but this is not always the case.

A contract of service may be deemed to exist when operating in a voluntary capacity on behalf of a voluntary youth organisation or educational establishment. People working in this relationship should inform themselves of the understanding of the organisation on behalf of whom they act. It may be that the voluntary organisation will accept vicarious responsibility for the acts of the person operating as a volunteer, but they may not. When acting on behalf of an employer delivering outdoor education, outside working hours, or off the employer's premises, the employer should be informed and the activities officially authorised. The activities should be carried out in accord with the employer's requirements and good practice. An employee who acts outside the limits set by an employer and is responsible when an accident takes place is in a perilous position. Some leaders/instructors have become confused about whether the code of ethics and procedures of an NGB or those of an employer apply when

undertaking recreational activities, out of working hours or off working premises, but on behalf of an organisation acting in loco parentis. The employer's ethics and procedures always apply in the course of employment related activity. Those of the NGB only apply in the context of self reliant, leisure activity undertaken under one's own responsibility, unless formally adopted as approved practice by the employer.

Employers liability insurance

Employers usually take out public liability insurance to cover claims arising from the negligence of employees. In the event of an incident involving injury or other damage, an action may be taken out against an employer as being vicariously responsible for actions of an employee. Actions may be taken out by an employee or by a third party who has suffered damage arising from the conduct of an employee. Actions will be defended by the insurer and the proceedings will focus on the competence of the employee, the adequacy of any equipment involved, and whether proper systems of work were in place and whether all the employer's risk management procedures were carried out correctly.

Insurers acting on behalf of the employer, may argue that safe systems of work were in place but not adopted by the employee. This may result in the focus of attention being transferred from the negligence of the employer to that of the employee. In such circumstances an employee may have to establish that their conduct conformed to good practice, even where it deviated from that required by an employer. If conformity to good practice can be demonstrated liability will usually rest with the employer, as being negligent in respect of failing to ensure a proper system of work.

It is prudent for employees delivering outdoor activities to have independent liability insurance to enable them to defend themselves. This may be provided by a union or a professional association.

People working in a voluntary capacity should inform themselves of the insurance arrangements of the organisation on behalf of whom they act. Civil liability insurance provided by a NGB may be sufficient to cover activities of a volunteer or it may be that the voluntary organisation will accept vicarious responsibility for the acts of the person operating as a volunteer. In all cases it is prudent to be suitably experienced and trained and in membership of an appropriate NGB and professional organisation if one exists.

References

Blyth v Birmingham Waterworks Co. (1895) http://www.sixthform.info/law/0182modules/ mod3/12822tort82introduction/1282282282bre ach/1282282282182breach82of82duty.htm

British Mountaineering Council (2001) Scout Death Judgement. *BMC Summit*. 24: 5.

Cork v. Kirby MacLean (1952) http://www.ohscanada.com/LawFile/liable.asp

Department of Education and Science (1995) *Safety in Outdoor Education*. London: HMSO.

Donaghue v Stevenson (1932) http://www.kennedys-law.com/article/art . . . 91.htm

HMSO (1974) *Health and Safety at Work etc. Act 1974*. London: HMSO.

Law Reform [Contributory Negligence] Act. (1945) See world wide web: http://www.polity.org.za/ html/govdocs/discuss/apport1.html

National Association for Outdoor Education (1987) *Safety Principles in Outdoor Education*. Penrith: NAOE.

Scottish Education Department (1972) *Safety in Outdoor Pursuits*. Circular No 848. Edinburgh: Scottish Education Department.

The Stationery Office (1999) *The Management of Health and Safety at Work Regulations 1999*. London: The Stationery Office.

Tiernan, R. (1993) *Nutshells. Tort in a Nutshell*. London: Sweet and Maxwell.

Unfair Contracts Act. (1977) http:// www.john.antell.name/ucta1977.htm

Wilsons and Clyde Coal Co. Ltd v English (1938) [1938]http://melbourne.butterworths.co.uk/ journal/archive/2002/stresspoints.ht m.

18 Outdoor Education as a Vehicle for Integrated Learning in the School Curriculum

Patrick Keighley

Abstract

Outdoor education has a huge potential for fostering an integrated approach to teaching and learning throughout the formal and informal school curriculum. This chapter references some of the educational changes that have taken place in recent times. It proposes some considerations for teachers and lecturers in designing and in developing outdoor programmes, which are cross curricular in nature, but which have a huge potential for integrated learning when structured in an appropriate way.

Introduction

Events in recent times have illustrated very clearly that the world in which we now live is undergoing many dramatic changes. Advanced technology, worldwide political and social unrest, environmental pollution, cultural and religious tensions, inequality and hunger each highlight some of the issues facing the world at large. Within the United Kingdom, massive changes are being experienced in terms of demographic trends, employment, land use diversification and in the use of alternative technology. These changes, when measured against the relative complacency of the previous three decades, have sharply brought into focus the need for education to consider alternative approaches to teaching and learning away from the all too familiar traditional patterns. In order to equip young people with the necessary relevant and transferable skills which they will require in meeting the challenges of the future, the school curriculum will have to continue to adapt and change.

In recent decades, the evidence from many structured outdoor projects, coupled with the available data from empirical research, indicates very strongly that, as a direct result of immersing young people in first hand experiences out of doors, changes in personal characteristics, attitudes and awareness of the environment do take place (Heaps and Thorstenson, 1983). Well planned and effectively reviewed outdoor immersion experiences have led to changes in people's self-concept, in their attitudes to the environment, conservation, to global issues and to the wider issues that dominate our society and affect our planet (Department of Education and Science, 1983). Through experiences out of doors, young people are continually confronted with real live situations which enable them, with tutorial support, to begin to make sense of the complexities of the world in which they live and gain an insight into the ways of tackling some of the issues.

The introduction of the National Curriculum in the latter part of the 20th century, while causing much anxiety and consternation to many teachers in England and Wales, now appears, not to be so much of the straightjacket that it was first thought. Initially, many teachers felt that its prescription was a recipe for a narrow and unbalanced curriculum, and that it was totally inappropriate in meeting the needs of young people in helping them prepare for and take their place in a fast moving and changing society. Evidence has shown that most teachers have been both creative and enterprising in accommodating change (Schools Curriculum and Assessment Authority, 1997). Without either a denial of their legal responsibilities nor abdication of maintaining subject integrity, many teachers have been able to shape the curriculum and maintain much of what was always considered to be of value, in the face of major external constraints and professional pressure. Subtle changes to the legal requirements and something of a relaxation of the orders in very recent times has enabled many resourceful teachers to continue to adapt and modify the curriculum and at the same time meet the demands placed upon them (Her Majesty's Inspectors, 2001). For many teachers however, particularly those working in the primary sector, complex problems and constraints still exist. Many teachers, while facing the pressures of an ever increasing external expectation to deliver an even more prescriptive 'core' curriculum, find it extremely difficult to be able to justify those enriching aspects of children's learning. Thus, outdoor education, which though still considered being of value, has only modest reference in the National Curriculum (Department for Education and Skills, 2000).

This chapter has been written to offer frustrated, yet often enthusiastic teachers, a rationale, to encourage them to take curriculum risks. It attempts to suggest a number of ways of exploiting the more traditional approaches to outdoor activities in different ways, so that young people can benefit from learning and growing using the outdoor environment in an integrated way.

Integrated learning

The term outdoor education is now widely accepted to describe all learning, social development and the acquisition of skill associated with living out of doors. However, despite the fact that this area of the curriculum embraces not only physical endeavour, but also ecological and environmental understanding, many practitioners still believe that the underlying philosophy of outdoor pursuits is so alien to that of outdoor studies that both areas cannot and should not be integrated save at the most elementary levels (Drasdo, 1973).

In the past, despite several attempts to unify outdoor pursuits activities with outdoor studies projects in meaningful ways, both traditions have remained largely separate, discrete areas, regarded by some practitioners as unrelated. Leaders engaged in teaching certain aspects of outdoor pursuits have tended to use the adventurous activities as solely to develop a specific physical skill or as a vehicle for personal and social development. That is not to say that to undertake an adventurous activity for its own sake is not without value; quite the contrary. Research

into the impact of outdoor pursuits experiences illustrate quite convincingly that to embark upon a challenging venture, not only develops an individual's self-concept, but also enhances aspects of personal and social development and indeed broadens their knowledge and understanding in a range of subject areas (Keighley, 1984; Hopkins, 1986). One cannot and should not deny the value of such experiences. However, if outdoor education is to have a more relevant and important part to play within the framework of an integrated approach to the curriculum, practitioners will need to be prepared to rigorously plan and evaluate experiences, in order to ensure that curriculum objectives are met. In the context of developing an integrated approach to teaching and learning out of doors, all outdoor experiences should be regarded as having a valuable part to play. This applies not only in relation to its potential for personal and social development, but also for cross-curricular work as well as for the development of physical skills. In all approaches and focus, the setting of clear objectives is crucial to this process (Spragg, 1982).

Through almost any experience out of doors young people can be introduced to a wide variety of themes and activities, which can either introduce or reinforce other areas of the school curriculum. All outdoor education activities, being inter-disciplinary in nature, provide opportunities for integrated learning. Because they cut across the entire curriculum, they have many implications for a host of learning areas such as the sciences, humanities, social studies, languages, arts, health, physical education, music and mathematics. Some activities and projects for example, require calculation, measurement or an understanding of scale, which gives real meaning to difficult mathematical concepts. Similarly, respect for and an understanding of the principles of safety can be developed at the same time as the study of natural phenomena involving the skills of observation, recording, and prediction and testing. Adventurous activities and outdoor projects can provide a great stimulus for creative writing, art, drama, aesthetic appreciation and spiritual development. As a direct result of new challenging experiences, sensitivities to the natural environment are heightened as well as the implications of one's involvement.

Outlined in the following paragraphs are examples of ideas and suggestions, which can be used as opportunities for teaching and learning across the curriculum. A wide range of study projects and topics are listed. Many of these may emerge quite naturally from students' initial involvement in any of the traditional outdoor activities and can be further developed at some stage in the future, either in the field or back in the classroom.

Mountain walking

This activity helps young people to become acquainted with landscapes and the forces, which have shaped them, the study of wildlife, farming methods, settlement patterns and livelihoods. Issues to do with conservation and respect for the natural environment can be introduced as well as providing scope for ecology studies in flora and fauna of different areas. The activity develops the skill of navigation in unfamiliar terrain and provides a unique vehicle for the reinforcement of numerical concepts. Through expeditions, young people develop a social responsibility for one another, group cohesion is developed and opportunities abound for problems to be solved and decisions to be taken. Leadership, tolerance, sharing and compromise are important learning skills, which can be developed as a result of this activity.

Canoeing

Both flat water and white water canoeing create unique opportunities for personal, social and environmental awareness to be developed in addition to the acquisition of physical skills. Through canoeing activities, young people become aware of their own strengths and weaknesses and those of others. They develop a responsibility for themselves and others, group cohesion, team spirit and co-operation. Through this activity, groups can undertake many varied outdoor study projects to include recording and measurement of depth and flow, elementary surveying, the study of hydrology, flora and fauna of the area and of environmental issues. Canoeing not only strengthens interpersonal relationships but also develops self-confidence, self-reliance, initiative, and trust. It provides opportunities for the reinforcement of specific learning skills, particularly those of numeracy, communication, problem solving, decision-making and creativity.

Climbing and abseiling

Both of these activities provide opportunities for the development of personal characteristics, particularly self-discipline, self-confidence and self-awareness. Through climbing, a wide range of integrated learning vehicles are possible. For example, from the activity can develop a sensory awareness of the locations used in the form of textures, shapes, colour and diversity in art. Sites can lead to a study of geology, geography, mathematical concepts and biological studies, which include the fauna, and flora of the area. It can be used to enhance the specific learning skills of communication, numeracy, literacy, problem solving and decision-making.

Gill scrambling

Gills are fascinating habitats offering unparalleled situations for intensive adventure. They are also unique environments illustrating ecosystems of times past and of flora dating as far back as the last glacial interphase. This activity which involves a group journeying up and through a water worn gorge generates spontaneous excitement and challenge, providing unlimited opportunities for personal, social and environmental awareness to take place. Gill environments also provide opportunities for a range of outdoor study projects to be undertaken. These include stream studies, surveying, hydrology, plant biology and the study of small mammals. They can also enhance the learning skills of creative writing, science, numeracy and communication.

Cave and mine exploration

One of the most potent vehicles for personal and social development and for integrated learning in outdoor education can be found in the activity of caving and in mine exploration. Young people often find this activity very challenging and most rewarding. The potential exists for a host of skills to be developed. These may include creative writing, numeracy, science, communication, decision-making and problem solving. In addition, the subterranean environment provides unique opportunities for a range of studies and projects. These range from surveying involving mathematical concepts, to studies in geology, biology, hydrology, geomorphology and archaeology. Studies in flora and fauna may be contrasted between the entrance twilight and total darkness zone by the use of simple line and belt transects.

Sailing

Dinghy sailing provides wonderful opportunities for young people to develop aspects of their personal and social characteristics as well as an awareness of the natural environment. The activity can be used to reinforce the specific skills of scientific enquiry, verbal communication and of those connected with numeracy. Unlike many of the other traditional activities, sailing requires an intellectual understanding of wind direction, speed, and velocity. This activity may be used as a vehicle for a range of study projects to include surveying, measuring, navigation, lake studies, biological and geographical projects as well as being used to develop mathematical concepts. Dinghy sailing increases group cohesion, responsibility, co-operation and awareness. The activity helps to develop initiative, leadership, self-confidence, trust and self-reliance.

Use of 'adventurous journeys' as a vehicle for projects

By far and away the most interesting, exciting and enjoyable way of combining the elements of adventurous activity with undertaking a study project is by engaging young people in the whole idea of preparing for and undergoing some form of an adventurous journey. This can take place either on water, on land or underground. Clearly, there are enormous implications for leaders and young people alike in terms of attending to the necessary preparations, developing the necessary skills required and in considering the level of difficulty of the journey itself. Safety considerations cannot be sufficiently over-stressed. However, all would agree that to undertake an adventurous journey of whatever difficulty is one of life's most enriching experiences. Through such encounters with nature we learn a great deal not only about ourselves, but also about our fellow beings. It is my belief, that in addition to the potential for developing personal qualities, journeying can offer teachers unique opportunities of engaging young people with exciting curriculum opportunities,

which not only enrich their learning, but can have an impact upon the way they interact and develop their relationship with the natural world (Keighley, 1998).

Water based journeying projects

Throughout the country there exists an extensive network of rivers, canals, lakes and even the seashore from which groups might undertake a journey using either canoes, kayaks or sailing craft. Study projects might range from surveying and measurement involving a detailed study of part of a riverbank or shore, to compiling a waterways or coastal guide. Options might well include mapping a bay or island, taking soundings, recording temperature change or comparing the range of animals and plants along the route and with undertaking various land use surveys.

Exploring cliffs and outcrops

Although most cliffs, outcrops and crags lend themselves to a wide range of study projects, the activity of scrambling and rock climbing can realistically only provide opportunities for either surveying and measurement projects, or for a detailed study to be undertaken to compile a guide book of the area. Study projects to compare and contrast vegetation, geology, lichens and even fauna, while valuable and often fascinating are very difficult in practice, due to the precarious nature of the activity. Nevertheless, cliffs, crags and outcrops offer some wonderful environments for creative writing and for study of all descriptions.

Exploring the underground environment

To journey below ground provides opportunities for recreation, for study and for adventure. It enables young people to experience the mystery of the unknown and the ever-present possibility of making new discoveries. To explore the beauty of the underground environment gives rise to a sense of wonder, achievement and comradeship which arguably is unparalleled in any other form of adventurous activity. Exploration of a cave system provides unique opportunities for groups to record, collect data and observe, but also to record feelings and personal reflections. Groups may either wish to carry out a detailed study of a cave system or to record and observe the different species of flora and fauna of the various parts of the cave system (Duke of Edinburgh Award, 1996).

Teaching and learning

If experienced based learning out of doors is to endure the rigours of scrutiny and accountability in a climate that is increasingly hostile towards 'marginal' areas of the curriculum, teachers and other practitioners of outdoor education will need to carefully examine their styles of teaching and learning. Teachers will need to reconsider the methods by which they present adventure experiences and seek to develop alternative ways in which young people are better engaged in their learning through a plan-do-review approach. Teachers of outdoor education will need to consider using activities as 'vehicles' from which a wide range of integrated learning can take place, either to introduce or reinforce work, which is being developed in other areas of the school curriculum.

Integrated learning activities have a unique and invaluable part to play in providing a different, more relevant curriculum, based on experiential learning, enquiry and problem solving situations to enable young people to prepare for the needs of tomorrow's world. As outdoor education is very much an approach to learning rather than being a subject specific area of the curriculum of schools, it is my view that both outdoor pursuit activities as well as outdoor studies projects are equally relevant in providing an inter-disciplinary interrelated core of experience.

Teachers should be very aware that an integrated approach should be very carefully and sensitively managed in order to ensure that young people maintain a high degree of interest and enthusiasm. To expose young people to a specific area of study and neglect the adventurous element will almost certainly prove to be counter productive. For most young people the adventurous element will be the motivation to stimulate them to embark upon an integrated learning project. Teachers will need to structure experiences in such a way so as to encourage and facilitate maximum involvement, providing

where possible specific opportunities for individual and group exploration and discovery to take place.

The balance between activity and focussed project work will largely depend upon a number of factors. These will include the current constraints of the curriculum, the age of the pupils, their ability, motivation and levels of prior knowledge and experience. When introducing an integrated learning project, teachers will need to be very well organised, having clear aims and objectives, which are openly shared with the pupils. Teachers will need to have a fairly flexible approach and be adaptable to change in order that the projects/explorations meet with the differing interests and needs of the group. They should know when it is appropriate to restructure learning so as to maintain interest and involvement and never be too rigid, but where possible, allow pupil centred self-discovery to take place. Approached as a 'topic', it is generally believed that all experienced-based projects provide a unique and valuable vehicle for integrated learning across the curriculum. The importance for the teacher should not be so much in developing the activity itself, but rather in facilitating experiences in which learning takes place. Learning largely comes about as a direct result of pupils' active participation developed through a well-defined strategy of clear aims and objectives, which is followed up by a structured review of the activity. Clearly, there are many important factors to consider in this approach to teaching and learning. However, if an integrated approach to learning is to take place, it should be the first principle and overriding aim of any teacher to utilise the activity/project, primarily as a vehicle for learning and for curriculum enrichment. Shaped in this way, there is little doubt in my mind, that experienced-based learning out of doors, will continue to have currency not only in the context of a National Curriculum but for lifelong learning. In so doing, experiences out of doors will increasingly be regarded as a valued and enriching agent for a wide range of curriculum learning as well as realising its potential for personal and social development

Conclusion

While experienced-based learning in the outdoor environment has a huge potential to foster and engender effective learning in young people, there are major implications for education. Teachers cannot assume that through this approach learning will automatically occur. Learning programmes need to be carefully structured to ensure that young people develop in their levels of skill, knowledge and understanding. First-hand experiences are a very powerful medium to effect good learning, but effective teaching and efficient management of the learning process is a vital and crucial element in the whole equation. In devising programmes of integrated learning for the young people, teachers will need to be very clear about the following:

- Establishing clear aims for the session.
- Identifying particular learning objectives.
- Selecting appropriate tasks and activities.
- Effectively managing and facilitating the experiences and the reviews, to ensure learning outcomes are achieved.

Educators will need to develop not only effective teaching strategies which involve young people in planning and doing the tasks, but also create time and space and the opportunities for young people to reflect upon their experiences, in order to ensure that they learn and grow.

Outdoor education is a most potent vehicle not only for personal development but also for enabling young people to learn and grow in many diverse ways. By engaging young people in thinking more about the environments in which they journey and in encouraging them to undertake a level of study and enquiry about aspects of the natural world, it is likely there will be a spin off in terms of their greater awareness of the world in which they live. An integrated approach to learning out of doors, will by its very nature, not only raise young people's awareness of environmental issues, but also and perhaps more importantly, lead to and develop within the next generation a greater sensitivity of the real issues facing the natural world and also of the planet in general.

References

Department of Education and Science (1983) *Learning out of Doors. An HMI Survey of Outdoor Education and Short Stay Residential Experience*. Department of Education and Science.

Department for Education and Employment (2000) *The National Curriculum. A Handbook for Primary Teachers in England. Key Stages 1and 2*. London: Department of Education and Science.

Duke of Edinburgh Award Scheme (1995) *Exploration Resource Pack: Exploration Through outdoor Activities*. London: Duke of Edinburgh Award Scheme.

Drasdo, H. (1973) *Education and Mountain Centres*. Denbighshire: Caedean Press.

Her Majesty's Inspectorate of Schools (2001) *Ofsted Annual Report of Schools. Inspecting Physical Education. Report 312*. London: HMSO.

Heaps, R. and Thorstenson, C. (1983) Self Concept Changes. *Therapeutic Recreation Journal*. 7: 60–4.

Hopkins, D. (1986) *Self Concept and Adventure*. (Unpublished MEd Thesis). University of Sheffield.

Keighley, P.W.S. (1984) *An Examination of the Role of the Outdoor Education Centre in State Education*. (Unpublished MA Thesis). University of Keele.

Keighley, P.W.S. (1998) *Learning Through First Hand Experiences Out of Doors: The Contribution Which Outdoor Education Can Make to Children's Learning in the Context of the National Curriculum*. National Association for Outdoor Education.

Schools Curriculum and Assessment Authority. (1997) *Expectations in Physical Education. Key Stages 1 and 2*. London: HMSO.

Spragg, D. (1982) *Learning to Learn*. Cumbria: Brathay Hall Trust.

19 Learning Theory and Experienti<

Angus McWilliam

Abstract

This chapter is about learning theory and how it can help in outc
students of outdoor education become trapped, believing that b
grounded in the individual's experience, theories are at best irrelevant or at worst a barrier to
relevant learning. Others adopt a single theoretical model and apply it with uncritical
evangelical zeal. This chapter will attempt to persuade the reader of the value of theory as a
guide and critic of practice and introduce them to a selection of the learning theories that
abound.

Are theories useful?

Theories are helpful. Lewin (1936) said 'nothing is as practical as a good theory.' Tappen (1989) identified many of the ways in which we can use theory. Theories she says can help us organise our ideas, look at events differently, explain why events occur, predict what might happen and guide practice. Not all theories however are alike. Some may be good at helping us to look at life differently but not so effective in telling us what the result of a particular action will be. Others might tell us what will happen but leave us very little understanding of why. Broadly, theories may be split into three main groups, viz., those which break down the world into cause and effect events, those which help us make sense of the complexity we see around us and those that prescribe how the world should be and how we ought to behave. Scientific theories are typical of the first, interpretive theories of the second and ethics of the third. The value of scientific theory is its ability to predict consequences. The value of interpretive theory is its ability to create understanding and the value of ethical theory is the guidance it offers in telling us how we ought to behave toward one another.

Much social science theory, including that related to learning, teaching and education seems to slip, often on shaky logic and little evidence, from one kind of theory to another; starting perhaps as a description of how things are, and arguing therefore that this is how things ought to be. We have to be careful to recognise what kind of theory we are using and its limitations. In addition, it is important to remember that all theories are abstractions; approximations that

can't hold all the answers and that even good theories can mislead if they are misused. So, selecting theory is important. A useful guide is to ask:

- Does it make sense; does it appeal to your reason?
- Does it feel right; is it consistent with your values?
- Does it match your experience; is it supported by evidence?
- Does it provide useful guidelines for practice; is it practical and permissible?

Learning theory

What is learning? Learning is a concept that describes one of the ways in which people can change. It's like education, teaching and studying but different from each of these. For the most part it is used to describe the way in which we acquire and make sense of information and adapt to the world around us. The ways we change through learning are often categorised as learning outcomes. These include knowledge and understanding, skills, attitudes and behaviour. Knowing this can help us draw a chart of the learning process (Figure 1).

This is helpful as it allows us to describe what we expect our clients to learn and measure our success. Others have tried to describe learning in terms of the learning process and how it occurs by detailing the activities a person undertakes as they acquire a new skill. This does not help measure how much learning occurs but does give us an insight into how it occurs. The difficulty here is that we can't observe the learning. We can see the

Figure 2 Learning as a learning process

Figure 3 Learning as a purposeful activity

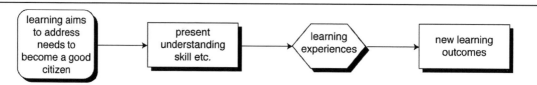

materials used, we can listen to the discussions that take place but the learning itself is invisible and internal, not capable of being described like a chemical reaction or the assembly of kitchen furniture. Learning processes involve a number of separate activities such as accessing information by reading, watching or listening, making sense of information by analysing or reflecting and testing out ideas skills and behaviours by practicing, experimenting and sharing. This can be seen in Figure 2.

Finally, learning can be defined according to its purpose, as the way in which individuals adapt to their environment, or the way in which communities create themselves. This does not allow us to measure learning or even understand the process but does allow us to make judgements about the moral justification of the process and its consequences. Again some of the many purposes of learning are concerned with satisfying the learner's needs or expectations and/or satisfying someone else or societies, needs and expectations. And again this can be used to expand the figure further (Figure 3).

With such an array of aspects of learning it is not surprising that learning theories have developed in a number of directions led in part by the fashions of the time and the disciplines of the researchers. Recently, many of these have been published on the web. For example, Kearsley (2002) has compiled a web based database (Theory into Practice) which describes more than 50 learning theories. For the sake of simplicity we will group these into the following categories: behaviourism, cognativism, humanism and social learning.

The behaviourist orientation to learning

Behaviourists shut their eyes to the internal process of learning or what its purposes were and focussed on the conditions that led to the attainment of specific learning outcomes. Much of the theory was developed using animal experiments. The advantage of this approach was that it allowed them to play with the external environment, changing the actions of the teacher or the sequence in which the information was made available. From this research, Thorndike (1932) and Skinner (1954) developed the 'stimulus-response' theory of learning capable of describing how the learning of a new behaviour was strengthened or weakened by the consequences of the behaviour. Thus, if the consequences of adopting a particular action were good for the participant then the participant learnt to adopt that behaviour rather than other alternatives. This notion was later refined by Skinner and used to develop a teaching strategy known as 'operant conditioning'. This proposes that you should reinforce what you want people to learn and ignore or punish what you want people to stop doing. In addition, it suggested that reinforcing the learning often and quickly further improves the learning.

Does an understanding of behaviourist theory help the outdoor teacher? Behaviourist research suggests that clear targets, frequent practice, successful outcomes, positive feedback and encouragement all seem to improve the effectiveness of learning and remind the instructor of the impact of their actions and the external environment on the motivations of the learner. However, there are limitations in the behaviourist approach. It tends to ignore the unique individuality of the learner; learners may be different in terms of their ability to learn and in terms of the learning strategies they adopt. Secondly, it ignores the fact that learning takes place in a social context where moral codes may or may not permit the use of specific rewards or punishments.

The cognitive orientation to learning and constructivism

The second group of theories focus on the internal process of learning or of coming to know. Everyone has a picture of the world they live in; a construct that makes sense to them. Learning involves creating and changing this construct as we find out more information about the (real?) world and experience the impact it has on us. Piaget (see Bybee and Sund, 1982) studying the way in which children learn, found that this changes as their understanding and experience becomes more complex. He identified four stages of mental growth ('sensorimotor', 'preoperational', 'concrete operational' and 'formal operational'). These describe the stages children go through as they move from simple playing with objects to recognising that objects differ in all sorts of ways, to playing with ideas and finally to creating and

evaluating new ideas. Expressed simply, this means that children and probably adults too, learn new behaviours more effectively if they start by playing and experimenting with real things in real situations with real outcomes. He also recognised that some new information is simple and discrete and can be easily 'assimilated' into our worldview without changing that view. Other information has to be 'accommodated' as it makes us realise that the way we thought things were is not adequate to allow us to make sense of the new information and so the structure of our worldview has to change.

These ideas have given rise to the school of thought called constructivism that in contrast to the behaviourist describes learning as the construction of meaning. Bruner (1966) explored further how an understanding of these mental processes could be linked to teaching, creating learning activities which involve doing things rather than reading and hearing about them and tailoring learning to the individual, taking account of each person's understanding and encouraging them to mentally explore and accommodate new ideas. This is sometimes called 'discovery learning'. Does an understanding of cognitive theory help the outdoor teacher develop student learning? Cognitivism suggests that how we organise instruction and teaching is likely to be important and it recognises that in designing learning experiences one has to take account of previous knowledge and experience, the structure and sequence of learning, opportunities to experiment and test our understanding in and on the real world as well as just thinking, individual learning styles and opportunities to make sense of new experiences.

The humanistic orientations to learning

Thirdly, we have those theories of learning that are not concerned so much with what we learn or how we learn as who should decide what we should learn and how we should learn. Here we are clearly concerned with ethical questions of the purpose and ownership of learning. Perhaps the best known example of trying to classify what we need to come to learn is Maslow's hierarchy. It indicates that we are motivated to learn in order to satisfy our:

- Physiological needs such as hunger, thirst, sex, sleep, relaxation and bodily integrity.
- Safety needs which call for a predictable and orderly world.
- Love and belonging needs which cause people to seek warm and friendly relationships.
- Self-esteem needs which involve the desire for strength, achievement, adequacy, mastery and competence.
- Self-actualisation which is the full use and expression of talents, capacities and potentialities.

Maslow (1998) suggests this should provide a way of identifying what each individual needs to learn. He claims that only when a person has satisfied their lower needs will they be motivated to learn the skills and understanding required to meet higher needs. This has been criticised as too mechanistic and simple as people are capable of making sacrifices if the end result is, for them, great enough.

Perhaps the most persuasive proponent of a humanistic orientation to learning came from Rogers (1969). Rogers' view is that giving the individual the freedom to choose both the content and the method of learning will result in learning which leads to the ability to exercise freedom competently and responsibly. Concerns are voiced about an individual's ability to know the future they desire and to take charge of the learning that will make that future achievable. Rogers is optimistic and calls for a learner-centred education which had the following characteristics:

- **Total personal involvement**: the whole person physically emotionally and mentally immersed in the learning event.
- **Self-initiated**: the motivation to overcome, the seeking for guidance and help, the grasping and comprehending comes from within.
- **Pervasive**: it changes the behaviour, the attitudes and perhaps even the personality of the learner.
- **Self-evaluated**: it is for the learner to judge how effective and relevant is the learning.
- **Its essence is meaning**: when such learning takes place it is an act of sense making.

What can outdoor education take from the humanist learning theory? Humanists tell us we need to respect the rights of the learner and that ultimately they should have the responsibility to decide what they need to learn and how they should learn. Being more pragmatic, the humanists have drawn attention to the importance of the learner's motivation and how that is regulated by their needs and expectations. Many of the proponents of outdoor education (such as Kurt Hahn) come from the tradition of humanist thinking. However, many critics of outdoor education question whether outdoor education in practice does offer its learners the freedom to choose what they should learn and how it should be learnt.

The social/situational orientation to learning

Fourthly, we have those researchers who think of learning as a cultural or social activity, concerned with how the individual survives in society and how society develops useful individuals. One consequence of this approach is the recognition that people learn from observing others. They observe the consequences of other's behaviours and they get some idea of what might result from acting in a similar way (Bandura, 1977). This process involves attending to behaviour, remembering it as a possible model or paradigm and playing out how it may work for them in different situations (rehearsal). However, the idea of social learning extends beyond a simple model of how people learn. Learning is not seen as the acquisition of knowledge by individuals so much as a process of social participation ('situated learning'). Lave and Wenger (1991) draw attention to the need to understand learning in context and take account of the kind of relationships that exists between the learner, teacher and society. Vygotsky (1978) can be included as a part of this group when he focuses on the strategic role the teacher plays in facilitating learning. Vygotsky recognised that the skill of the teacher lies in identifying and working with students in that '*zone of proximal development*' or in that space in which the student has the potential for learning but simply not the resources and skills to take complete charge of their own learning. The teachers' task is then to construct the minimum amount of support necessary ('scaffolding') which will enable the learners to achieve their objectives.

Social learning theory draws attention to certain areas of concern. Firstly, learning is in the relationships between people. It does not belong entirely to the learner, but occurs in the dialogue they have with writers, teachers or others. Secondly, learning occurs in communities and reflects the social norms and needs of these communities. Learning is also part of daily living. Further, social learning theory reminds the outdoor educator of the importance of the relationship between the learner and the social context in which the learning takes place and the impact of the teacher as a role model.

Key points

This brief exploration of a selection of the broad foundational fields of learning theory has identified the following characteristics of learning:

- It is characterised by a change in the participant in terms of knowledge skill or attitudes.
- It may be stimulated or repressed by environmental and social influences.
- It involves a change in the way we construct our understanding of reality.
- The difficulty of the process of learning may be influenced by the correspondence of the new information with our current construct of the world.
- It is a process by which we satisfy our needs and realise our potential.
- It is a social activity where we model ourselves on others.
- It is a social process in which society moulds useful participants.

Recent developments

Advances in our understanding of the cognitive sciences are beginning to have an impact on our understanding of learning. It is now thought that the brain develops and changes in response to learning and that the brain multi-tasks by carrying out complex activities simultaneously. Nummela and Caine (1994) suggest that this has important implications for teachers who should immerse students in complex situations as this will stimulate and help develop neural synapses conducive to learning. One can, it appears, learn to learn. It is also now understood that different parts of the brain are related to different functions; sensory, emotional and reasoning. This has reinforced the ideas of Howard Gardiner who suggested there are multiple intelligences and that

learners need to develop a wide variety of important skills and understandings, viz:

- **Verbal-linguistic**: the ability to use words and language.
- **Logical-mathematical**: the capacity for inductive and deductive thinking.
- **Pattern**: the ability to recognise series and sequences of events objects or ideas.
- **Visual-spatial**: the ability to visualise objects and create internal images.
- **Body-kinesthetic**: the ability to control physical motion.
- **Musical-rhythmic**: the ability to recognise sounds sensitivity to rhythms.
- **Interpersonal**: the capacity for person-to-person communications and relationships.
- **Intrapersonal**: the spiritual, inner states of being, self-reflection, and awareness.

Further, there is the observation that the left and right sides of the brain are associated with different functions and that these functions may be differently represented in boys and girls. This led McCarthy (1999) to claim that schools tend to favour left brain activities and make a plea for more right brain activities in the aim of developing whole brain individuals (Table 1).

Table 1   Right brain–left brain differences

Left	Right
logical	random
sequential	intuitive
rational	holistic
analytical	synthesising
objective	subjective
looks at parts	looks at wholes

Recent developments therefore seem to be extending the content of learning, into the affective domain, identifying that the skills of learning can and need to be developed, and identifying that there are significant differences in the population with regard to their approach to learning.

Outdoor education and learning theory

Is there a theory of outdoor learning? Other chapters of this book may have described outdoor education as an approach to learning. But if outdoor education is taken to include field studies, outdoor pursuits, adventure education and personal and social development, then can the approach be uniform? A unifying factor is the idea that in outdoor education, whether we are teaching about ourselves, the people we are participating with, the environment or the activities, we learn from direct experience in the outdoors. It is this that has attracted outdoor education to that field of theoretical literature that falls under the banner of experiential education.

I describe this as a group or field as it includes theories of a variety of different kinds – predictive, interpretive and ethical. It therefore includes arguments which propose that this is the way in which people ought to learn because it respects them as individuals as well as arguing that it is more effective in developing understanding. It includes theories that explore how the external environment can be shaped to stimulate and reinforce the learning and how experiences can be tailored to individual needs and learning strategies. From this brief statement it can be seen that experiential education has drawn from many areas of educational and psychological learning theory described above. Experiential learning is an approach to learning based on a number of assumptions, viz:

- The real world is more complex than theorists or teachers would have us believe.
- People's experiences are uniquely grounded in their individual past.
- People can best prepare for the future through personal, direct encounters with challenges in the real world.
- To learn from such encounters people need opportunities to make sense of them.

Though the idea that we learn from experience is probably as old as civilisation itself, it was not until the 1930s that Dewey proposed this as a principle around which education and learning should be organised. Dewey's ideas grew out of the Science in Education movement and his concept of education bears a strong resemblance to descriptions of methods of scientific enquiry. Thus, he thinks of learning as the process by which an individual creates concepts which give meaning to the world around them and develops the competence which allows them to participate.

But his major concern was not the creation of a psychological theory of learning but the creation of an education system in the USA that would develop citizens who were able to participate in democracy and question authority. In this way, they would subject policies and practices to the rigorous test of direct personal experience. He proposed that learning occurs when a person 'experiences' events that create doubt or uncertainty about their understanding or ability. To overcome this uncertainty demands a response; the 'conceptualisation' of the doubt as a problem capable of solution and the 'adoption' of a new way of thinking or the application of a new skill which overcomes that problem. These ideas were adopted by Lewin (1936) who, like Dewey, was driven by a sense of social purpose of education and the need to develop education programs in which professional groups could actively engage in the identification and resolution of problems in their places of work. Lewin devised the terms action learning and action research and followed Dewey in representing this as a cycle of learning. Lewin applied the idea of a cycle in his training groups where participants engaged in activities which were followed by debriefing discussions and the planning of future actions. This idea of a cycle of learning was taken up by Kolb (1984) who refined and simplified it into the icon which now defines experiential learning in all the forms it appears today. One critique of the model is the impression that its circularity leads nowhere. A more accurate model is that of a helix rather than a spiral. Researchers such as Argyris (1976) have taken this idea to explore the potential of double loop learning.

This conceptualisation of learning has been very influential. Experiential learning proposes an approach that brings together the ideas derived from several other research traditions. Proponents believe that experiential learning:

- Develops problem solving and learning skills.
- Promotes social and ethical ends and the development of empowered autonomous individuals capable of acting in democratic communities.
- Allows educators to organise ideas about what learning is, break it down into a sequence of actions or behaviours engaged in by participants and predict the impact of external

Figure 4   The double loop of learning of Argyris

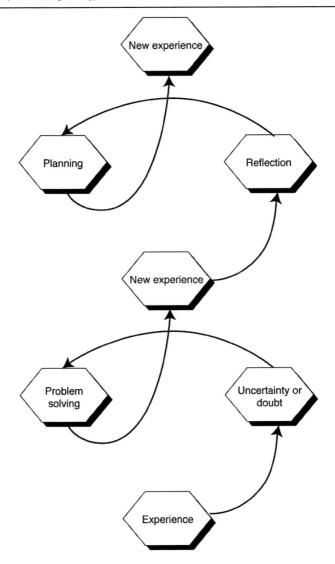

experiences and structured activities on learning.

Like his predecessors, Kolb believed that experiential learning was not just a series of techniques to be applied in current practice but a program for profoundly re-creating personal lives and social systems. It conceptualised learning as a deliberate act or sequence of acts over which we have some control. Associated with this was the idea that individuals are different and can develop learning styles based on preference and ability. Kolb developed a set of categories divergers, assimilators, convergers, and accommodators to describe these styles. In the UK perhaps more commonly used is the Honey and Mumford (1992) inventory which classifies learners into:

- **Activists** who favour active experimentation.
- **Reflectors** who take time to consider and go over what has happened.
- **Theorists** who search for meanings and explanations.
- **Pragmatists** who look for practical solutions to real situations.

The idea that people have a learning style has given rise to the hypotheses that individuals can be taught learning styles and that teaching which takes account of the learning styles of their pupils will be more effective. Little evidence as yet exists that these hypotheses are correct. It has also given rise to the mantra that experience without reflection does not lead to learning. Dewey (1938) described reflection as a process that 'transforms doubt into certainty'. Moon (1993) describes the possible stages of reflection as:

- The recognition of a need to resolve something.
- The clarification of the issue.
- A review and recollection of what has happened.
- A review of the emotional impact that resulted.
- The processing of the knowledge and ideas.
- The eventual resolution of the problem and identification of future action.

Others have more briefly but obscurely described it as; noticing, making sense, making meaning, working with meaning, and transformative learning.

Although many writers agree that there is an interweaving of all these activities, it may appear to readers that experiential education is a very pedestrian form of learning, endlessly cycling through experiences, reflections, future plans and then back to more experiences. Why does experiential education advocate that learning occurs in this way? Why not just pick up a book or ask someone? Proponents of experiential education answer this question in three ways. The first answer claims that this represents what actually happens not what should happen. What is described is a simple model of the way in which we behave; our brain processes new information, assesses situations and makes decisions about events, only most of the time it does it so blisteringly fast that we are unaware. When we stand at the side of the road needing to get to the other side, we estimate the speed of the oncoming traffic based on past experiences, question the reactions of drivers if we were to make a sudden move and make a judgement concerning the level of risk and move forward or stop. Depending on our choice we immediately begin to evaluate the consequences and decide whether to move faster or return. Finally, we make some evaluation of our actions judging whether

we acted wisely are not. All this happens within a couple of seconds. When problems are complex and the situation unknown we need to take more time and be more structured in our approach. Schon (1983) advocates learning in this way, particularly for professionals working in high pressure situations. He claims that learning in this way helps us develop habits and patterns of thought and 'reflection in action' that allows us to respond quickly and securely to new situations where good judgements followed by confident action is called for.

Researchers such as Moon (1993) and Entwhistle (1983) argue that learning in this way is a deeper approach in which we relate ideas to previous knowledge, look for patterns and underlying principles, check evidence and relate it to conclusions, examine logic and argument cautiously and critically, and become actively interested in course content. It also leads to a more secure understanding and better retention. Biggs and Collies (1982) develop the idea further by suggesting that the deep approaches utilised in experiential learning result in the development of understanding with a more logical and relational structure. Further, they take into account more influences and can adapt and transform meaning to more circumstances.

Finally, advocates of experiential learning propose this way allows learners to take responsibility for what they learn and to construct for themselves meanings and judgements they make about their future. It frees them from teachers, writers and the establishment enabling them to challenge oppression and develop independence. Friere (1970) advocates this approach as it empowers individuals and communities releasing them from the forces which oppress them.

Conclusion

Does or indeed should outdoor learning conform to the ideas of experiential learning? If we argue that experiential learning is simply a model of how we learn and that all learning is experiential, then by default it does. But learning as we have found is complex, situational, dependant on the aims of the learner and of the teacher. Individual learners are different with styles, competences and motivations which may be cultural or genetically derived. So the slavish application of one mode of structuring learning activities may not always yield the most effective results. If, on the other hand we take the idea of a cycle of learning as a strategy for engaging clients in activities, then many practitioners and programs have found Kolb's model to be an effective starting point for the planning and sequencing of activities.

Finally, if we view experiential learning as a process in which students learn to learn, learn to take control of their lives, learn to explore their potential and learn to act with rational care then perhaps these are goals which could describe good practice in outdoor learning.

References

Argyris, C. (1976) *Increasing Leadership Effectiveness*. New York: Wiley.

Bandura, A. (1971) *Social Learning Theory*. New York: General Learning Press.

Biggs, J. and Collies, K. (1982) *Evaluating The Quality of Learning*. Academic Press: New York.

Bruner, J. (1966) *Toward a Theory of Instruction*. Cambridge, MA: Harvard University Press.

Bybee, R.W. and Sund, R.B. (1982). *Piaget for Educators*. 2nd edn. Columbus, OH: Charles Merrill.

Dewey, J. (1938) *Experience and Education*. (Revised edn. 1997). New York: Touchstone Books.

Entwistle, N. and Ramsden, R. (1983) *Understanding Student Learning*. London: Croom Helm.

Friere, P. (1970) *Pedagogy of the Oppressed*. Harmondsworth: Penguin Books.

Gardner, H. (1993) *Multiple Intelligences: The Theory in Practice*. New York: Basic Books.

Gardner, H. (2000) *Frames of Mind: The Theory of Multiple Intelligences*. New York: Basic Books.

Honey, P. and Mumford, A. (1982) *Manual of Learning Styles*. London: P. Honey.

Kearsley, G. (2003) *TIP Theory Into Practice Data Base*. Http://Tip.Psychology.Org/Kearsley.Html

Kolb, D. (1984) *Experiential Learning*. New Jersey: Prentice Hall.

Lewin, K. (1936) *Principles of Topological Psychology*. New York: Mcgraw-Hill.

Maslow, A. (1998) *Toward A Psychology of Being*. 3rd edn. New York: Wiley.

McCarthy, B. (1999) *The 4-MAT System: Teaching to Learning Styles With Right/Left Mode*. Http://www.Funderstanding.Com

Moon, J. (1993) *Reflection in Learning and Professional Development*. London: Kogan Page.

Nummela, R. and Caine, G. (1994) *Making Connections: Teaching and the Human Brain Person Learning*. Los Angeles: Addison Wesley Long.

Rogers, C.R. (1969) *Freedom to Learn*. Columbus, OH: Merrill.

Schon, D. (1983) *The Reflective Practitioner*. San Francisco: Jossey-Boss.

Skinner, B. F. (1954) The Science of Learning and the Art of Teaching. *Harvard Educational Review*. 24: 2, 86–97.

Tappen, R (1989) *Nursing Leadership and Managemen.t* 2nd edn. Philadelphia: F.A. Davis Company.

Thorndike, E. (1932) *The Fundamentals of Learning*. New York: Teachers College Press.

Vygotsky, L.S. (1978) *Mind in Society*. Cambridge, MA: Harvard University Press.

Section 4:
Current Issues in Outdoor Education

20 Rewards from Risk: The Case for Adventure Activity

Marcus Bailie

Abstract

Whilst empirical research-based evidence concerning the effects on young people of taking part in adventure activity is difficult to find, there is almost universal consensus that it is beneficial in both health and sociological terms. Much of this benefit is perceived to stem from the co-operative undertaking of activities which have inherent risk

Introduction

In this chapter, I offer an explanation for why the concerns about young people in adventure activities are disproportionate to this risk and outline how properly managed adventure activities can be part of the solution facing young people, rather than part of the problem. My argument for the net benefits of adventure activity is reliant on proper management by providers. How society, its representatives in government or the outdoor industry ensure 'proper management' is not the subject of this article.

Nobody can or should be asked to tolerate death or other accident that stems from wilful action or negligent inaction, particularly in pursuit of economic gain. What is not reasonable is for society via the media to demand, on each and every occasion, a scapegoat on the grounds that 'tragedy has occurred, ergo someone must be punished.' Thus the level of the risk, the current control of the hazard, and the relation of these to the benefits achievable comprise the framework of this chapter.

Level of risk

Causes of death and society's reaction

Gathering statistics is difficult partly because causes are collected by different organisations, each of whom may have different interests and 'use' different categories. Thus, 'accidental' does not include suicides and murders, because it wasn't an accident; 'unnatural' does not include terminal illnesses and conditions; 'premature' is pretty close, but it's rather vague. Age categories also vary widely – under 14s, under 16s, under 18s etc. The statistics given later are intended to give as clear an overview as possible, but may not stand up to detailed statistical analysis.

The vast majority of us, over 98 per cent, do not die of accidents. Indeed, over 80 per cent reach retirement age and eventually die peacefully in bed of natural causes. Yet, society in general, and the media in particular are, in my opinion, so obsessed with the remaining 2 per cent that we allow this to completely dominate our lives. Even more illogically, we do not focus our greatest fears or efforts on where there is greatest risk. For example, 25–30 per cent of us will die prematurely from illnesses that result directly from our chosen life styles, yet we choose to do little to safeguard ourselves or our children from this awful level of devastation.

Analysing the causes of fatal accidents and other causes of sudden or premature death is difficult and distressing. Every death is a terrible personal trauma; none can be discounted as insignificant. Every such death is devastating for family, friends and others who may have been involved. The most painful and permanent of memories that change lives forever. We must not lose sight of this as we trawl through the records. If there is a single aim, it must be to reduce the total of these tragedies and not just make one aspect of our lives safer at the expense of another.

If we look at a comparison of the various causes of premature, accidental or unnatural death we find some surprises. The facts in Table 1 may be instructive.

If we now look specifically at the situation as it affects the UK's 13 million young people, i.e. 18 years of age and under (Table 2) we find that these

Table 1   Causes of premature and sudden deaths (data taken from National Statistics Office)

Number	Cause of death	Source	Category
130,000	All cancers	Dept of Health	Lifestyle
120,000	Heart attacks	Dept of Health	Lifestyle
100,000	All smoking related illnesses	Dept of Health	Lifestyle
30,000	Obesity and unfitness	National Audit Office	Lifestyle
20,000	All alcohol related illnesses	Dept of Health	Lifestyle
10,000	All accidents	HASS/LASS	Accident
6,000	Suicide	Samaritans	Non-accident
4,000	Asthma (rapidly increasing among the young)		Lifestyle
4,000	Accidents in the home (attracts so little attention)	HASS/LASS	Accident
3,500	Road traffic accidents		Accident
3,000	Asbestos stripping	HSE	Accident
1,200	Sunbathing (of the 1,400 deaths per year from skin cancer, 1,200 are from over-exposure to the sun)		Lifestyle
1,000	Allergic reaction to hard (class A) illegal drugs		Lifestyle
450	Drowning	RoSPA	Accident
350	Accidents at work (attracts so much attention)	HSE	Accident
200	Allergic reaction to aspirin	REC First Aid Training	Accident
130–180	All adventure activities/ages/contexts (accurate figures are hard to acquire)	AALA estimate	Accident
8	Train crashes or derailments	HSE Railways Inspectorate	Accident
5	Canoeing (all ages, all contexts. More people drown in their cars than do canoeing)	British Canoe Union	Accident
5	Toddlers who drown in the bath	HASS/LASS	Accident

are equally instructive. In total there are about 1,400 accidental deaths a year, 150 unnatural deaths (suicides, murders, etc.) and a further 1,800 medical conditions.

From these figures alone it is clear that the greatest risk to the future safety of ourselves and our children comes from lifestyles which we have chosen and which we could change. Ironically, some of the things which could keep us very much safer in the long term, e.g. adventure activity, are discarded because they are perceived as too dangerous in the short term.

On other occasions when we try to make things safer in one area we unintentionally make them more dangerous in another. Consider what happened after the Hatfield rail crash when four people tragically lost their lives. In order to make a comparatively safe means of transport (i.e. rail) even safer, tens of thousands of travellers turned, or were forced to turn, to a vastly more dangerous

Table 2   Accidental and sudden deaths each year – 18 yrs and under (data taken from National Statistics Office)

Number	Cause
700	Road traffic accidents (easily the biggest single cause)
200	Skin cancer caused by sunbathing
140	Suffocation
125	Poisoning
110	Suicide (not part of the 1,400 total)
90	Drowning
80	Fire (when did you last change the batteries in your fire detectors?)
70	Falls (kids fall a lot, but it is not often fatal)
50	Homicide (not part of the 1,400 total. The vast majority of them knew their killer very well.)
3	On school trips (the average since 1985)

Figure 1 The conventional model of risk

Figure 2 The triangle model of risk

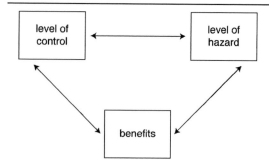

one (i.e. roads) during the improvements with the loss of an immeasurable number of lives, but certainly in the 100s. The 'Hatfield Effect' could be defined as inadvertently making the dangerous even more dangerous in an attempt to make the safe even safer! Risk and our reaction to it therefore is complex, and worthy of deeper examination.

The triangle of risk

Conventional theories about risk generally consider there to be a two-way balance between the hazard and the control measures; as the level of seriousness increases then ever more effective measures are applied to control them. In this model, control measures are adjusted until the residual risk is tolerable.

I argue that this model is fundamentally flawed. The key problem is that if any risk remains, there is always some further control which at least some people will want to see applied even if that control measure is total avoidance. Inevitably, this model leads society deeper into risk aversion, where we eventually lose the ability to identify, let alone manage everyday hazards around us. However, if we consider the balance to be a three-way dynamic equilibrium the picture changes dramatically. If we factor into the model what the benefits are, such as an increased chance of medium or long-term survival, then we may decide that they are sufficiently important to justify taking greater risks.

David Attenborough and Robert Winston both suggest that this is a fundamental factor in animal survival and was certainly so in early human development. If the benefits are big enough in terms of lives saved or lives enhanced we are prepared to accept the risks. The flaw in this evolutionary principle is the opinions of the few who pay the price for the benefits of the many (or their surviving loved-ones) are now disproportionately amplified by modern communications especially the media. However,

without this trade-off the benefits would be achieved by no-one. It leaves us with a considerable dilemma, the outcome of which lies in achieving maximum benefits for a minimum price.

Consequently, in properly assessing whether a risk is tolerable we must take into account the benefits. There are therefore, not 'Five Steps to Risk Assessment' as we are often told, but six. The first – 'identify the benefits' is frequently ignored. In Attenborough and Winston's terms this greatly influences the decisions about how much risk to take. In any given situation we cannot begin to quantify the level of risk which is acceptable without first knowing what the benefits are. Thus, when we describe having an involvement with adventure activities as part of the solution we are not suggesting it is a risk free solution; merely that it is substantially safer than not having one.

A fundamental observation from the tables of statistics above is that the risk of death from adventure activities is tiny compared to most other causes of death. However, if we are to decide if this level of risk is tolerable we must apply the triangle of risk, i.e. consider the benefits, in terms of lives saved or enhanced, from an involvement in adventure activities. For example, there is a broad acceptance that our children are worryingly unfit. It is considered by the National Audit Office that the biggest single cause of premature death amongst our current school leaving generation will be from obesity and unfitness. Already, it is society's third biggest killer, usually through the mechanisms of diabetes, hyper-tension and heart disease. It is beaten only by cancers and heart attacks. It is clear that young people need more exercise, not less. If we are serious about protecting our children we should ensure that they develop a healthy, active lifestyle which can be sustained through adult life. Clearly adventure activities offer an ideal opportunity to build in an advantageous process at a young age.

Consider another example. The second most common cause of death amongst 19 year old boys is suicide. Within this group the Samaritans tell us the highest occurrence is amongst those who leave school with no real sense of self-worth. Many children desperately need greater self-esteem. For some their lives depend on it. Society tends to measure success at school in terms of examination results, but not all children will be academic high fliers. Some won't, some can't. Given the inevitability of this, surely we ought to be ensuring that some of the other things which enhance self-esteem be given appropriate credence; sport, music, art and so on. There must be something within our schooling which a child can feel proud of, be good at and be praised for? Once again adventure activities have a proven record of success in this area.

Suicides amongst the young are twice as common as murders. This fact receives little attention in the media. Moreover, of the 50 or so murders of young people the vast majority (7 out of 8 some commentators say) are committed by someone very well known to the victim. When these facts are taken together there is no logic in our obsession with 'stranger danger' and our apparent disregard of teenage suicide.

Some categories are more difficult to quantify, but are no less real for that. The Society for the Prevention of Accidents to Children indicates that, 'Most accidents to children arise because they are children'. They are impulsive, preoccupied, and inquisitive and seem to consider themselves invincible. However, increasingly these days they have not learned how to look after themselves or not been allowed to do so. Adventure activity centres commonly observe that young people these days are noticeably clumsier, less hazard aware, more prone to having accidents.

On the other hand adventure activities enhance risk awareness and treat risk as something to be understood and managed. Logically, albeit counter intuitively, adventure activity is predisposed to reduce accidents, whereas the ultimately futile attempt to remove all risks to young people actually increases their susceptibility.

We could do similar studies on the positive effect of adventure activities (in terms of lives saved or enhanced) on, say, reducing the level of juvenile disengagement with school and the consequential increase in street crime, car crime, drug crime and the death toll which goes with it. At any given time there are currently 10,000 young people permanently excluded from school in the UK, representing the extreme limit of non-engagement. Adventure activities are a well tried and tested way of keeping many young people engaged and focused.

We could apply similar arguments to many other causes of death and show that an involvement with adventure activities can have at least some significant effect in reducing deaths from heart attacks, smoking or even alcohol. Moreover, we could even apply the same comparisons to the quality of life, not just the continuation of life, hence the use of the word enhanced in the paragraphs above. Whilst the numbers are vastly more difficult to quantify, we intuitively associate adventure activities with a fit, healthy lifestyle. Thanks to the publicity associated with the mercifully few fatal or disabling accidents, we do not so easily associate adventure activity with being intuitively safe.

Benefit relative to hazard and control

The role of adventure activities

There is a broad acceptance that it is not appropriate for our children's education to be totally focused on exam results. We expect our children to develop certain beneficial characteristics which will prepare them to deal safely and competently with their later years: the need to be able to interact with others, have good self-esteem, initiative, be able to lead or co-operate as the situation dictates, possess broad horizons, and be fit and healthy. Generations of teachers and pupils alike recognise the immense contribution which school visits play in this, and in particular the valuable role of residential-based adventure activities. I argue that adventure activities offer young people sustainable physical exercise which they can continue throughout life and at the same time enhance their sense of self-worth. Quite apart from the suicide issue referred to earlier adventure activities can help young people to learn how to look after themselves and provide a socially acceptable alternative to joy-riding, street crime and hard drugs. Properly managed adventure activities are much more a part of the solution than they are a part of the problem. Why then did they develop a bad reputation, is it justified?

Smoke without fire: the theory of moral panics revisited

I want to look now at how society can get itself into the myopic state where we focus totally on the short-term problems of the very few, whilst ignoring the short, medium, and long-term problems of the rest. The model of moral (or social) panics is not new and was outlined by Stanley Cohen in the 1980s. A typical moral panic can start with almost any issue which tugs at the heart strings of the nation. It is usually based on at least some evidence, albeit vague and inaccurate. The issue of child safety has an almost infallible ability these days to do this. This is not surprising since when presented with graphic detail of a tragedy involving a child; it is easy to extrapolate to, 'How would I feel if it was my child/grandchild/relation?' The media then respond with comment and criticism which as a society we devour with interest. One might expect the media to provide insight and analysis, but all too often they merely over-simplify very complex arguments into demons and victims; tabloid conclusions to complex social issues. Pressure groups form, either resulting from or giving rise to a further media campaign and the defining phrase becomes, 'Something must be done.' Sadly, conflict sells more papers than compromise and the media tends to fuel the arguments rather then seek realistic solutions. Arguably, that's not their job. More significantly, it would be inappropriate to blame the media alone, for it is we who buy the newspapers, we who influence news programme ratings and we who ultimately must accept responsibility. Our only mitigating claim is that we are easily led.

When we are advised of a hazard, common sense leads us to moderate our behaviour. However, if we can not identify, or are not told, or do not understand the extent of the hazard it is difficult to know how and by how much to modify our behaviour. If the consequences are reportedly serious, even if the likelihood is small, the situation is exacerbated, and we genuinely don't know what to do for the best. As a society, insidiously, we retreat into panic. This is the principle of modern terrorism. 'Beef on the bone' is another example of our over-reaction to a very small risk. 'Stranger danger' is another. The number of attacks on young people by strangers has remained relatively constant for the last 15 years. By comparison, our response to it has transformed out of all recognition, perpetuating the myth that the threat is growing. Individually and collectively we have become obsessed with it. Sadly, this reaction acts to the detriment of our children who are not allowed to become normally and healthily socialised.

'Something must be done'

At this point the 1960s 'theory of moral panics' simply states that 'the authorities react'. I now believe we have a bit more insight into how and why this happens. I see no master subversive plan in this, no conspiracy theory or hidden agenda. It's just that we can't see the woods for the trees.

Just as the media react to their readers wishes so too do elected authorities. Sometimes the result is that perceived imperatives have obscured the overview of the greater good.

'Reducing Risks, Protecting People'

In 2001 the Health and Safety Executive published a document entitled *Reducing Risks, Protecting People* (affectionately referred to it as R2P2). It is a sort of bearing of the soul; an insight into how the HSE views various problems and how it implements its solutions. It started off as merely a discussion document but a number of its phrases entered the lexicon of the public domain with its publication.

Tolerable risk

This states that as a society we are prepared to tolerate certain risks if the benefits to society are big enough. This fits in well with the triangle of risk model and with the views of Attenborough and Winston. Thus, for example, we tolerate an enormous number of deaths on the roads because of the benefits that the individual ability to travel over distance undoubtedly confers.

Societal concerns

If, as a society we have serious concerns about an issue then it appears that this, in itself, is sufficient grounds for preventative legislation. Even if it may not actually cause us harm it seems we have a right to be protected from it. At best it is democracy in action. At worst it is tabloid legislation; a sociological justification for the knee jerk reaction. Nevertheless the power of Societal Concern should not be underestimated. In the case of child safety it is only an exhibition of that most natural facet of animal behaviour – a desire to protect the young. This is deeply programmed in our genetic makeup, which explains why an apparently illogical level of concern overrides rational thinking in this field.

The precautionary principle

This one started off as a principle to be applied where a catastrophic outcome remained a possibility even though it had never actually happened. In essence it states that if you are not sure if it is dangerous then assume it is. The phrase may have come into HSE-speak from the nuclear industry where the control measures imposed are totally disproportionate to the number of accidents. That, however, is generally thought to be the right way to go with this particular industry since the potential exists for an accident to affect millions. Sometimes we approve of disproportionate solutions, provided they don't compromise the benefits.

Combining the above

The principle of societal concerns gives legitimacy to an authority exploring whether an issue is sufficiently serious to justify official government intervention. Moreover, the precautionary principle may persuade them to put legislation or similar control measures in place, even in the absence of statistical evidence. Taken together, these two principles can explain how 'the authorities react' in the context of the theory of moral panics. However and here lies the rub, there is a danger that we see government's reaction not as assurance but as reinforcement for our original concerns: if the government have decided to 'do something about it' then there must be problem! With moral panics

our concerns can be raised rather than lowered by the introduction of government control or legislation, and panic becomes self-perpetuating.

Current Control

Background to current controls

In March 1993, four teenagers drowned whilst kayaking at an adventure activity centre in Lyme Bay with their school. The centre was subsequently found to be negligent and the centre's manager was jailed. At his trial the judge, Mr Justice Ognall said that the potential consequences of adventure activities were too serious to be left to, 'The inadequate vagaries of self-regulation'. Two years later the Young Person's Safety (Activity Centre) Act (1995) was passed which paved the way for the Adventure Activities Licensing Regulations (1996) see below. In addition, National Governing Bodies of sport and individual providers not falling within regulations implemented a wide variety of safety measures, codes of practice and professional competences. Many participants in the field are also covered by the Health and Safety at Work Act, general duties of care and a range of specific regulations relating to food, accommodation and other areas that may accompany the provision of adventure activity.

The Adventure Activities Licensing Authority

The regulations required providers of certain adventure activities to demonstrate that they operated to nationally accepted standards of good practice. Not all activities were included. Only those specified as 'higher risk' required a licence and even then, only if offered in more remote or isolated environments. Not all providers were included. Exemptions were given to schools offering activities to their own pupils, to voluntary associations such as the Scouts, to 'family activities' where the parent would be present, and to most providers who offered activities free of charge. By 2003 there were nearly 1,000 licensed providers across England, Scotland and Wales. The aim of the Adventure Activities Licensing Regulations is:

. . . to provide assurances that good safety management is being practised so that young people can continue to have the opportunity to experience exciting and stimulating activities outdoors without being exposed to the avoidable risks of death or disabling injury.

This sentence is taken directly from the first paragraph of the Health and Safety Commission's guidance document to the Licensing Authority (HMSO, 1996). Interestingly it refers to 'avoidable risks'. The Health and Safety Commission (HSC) recognises that some risks are not avoidable without fundamentally undermining the benefits. There are clues in the structure of the Licensing Authority that these regulations were different from other HSE measures. In fact they are not the HSE's at all, although they draw heavily on the Health and Safety at Work Act. The original bill was sponsored by the Department of Education and Employment (DfEE), now the Department for Education and Skills (DfES). Consequently, the Licensing Authority is funded by DfES but operates under the written guidance of the HSC.

The structure is a not-for-profit private company; an independent watch-dog overseeing an increasingly private sector provision. When introduced, licensing was widely unpopular with many in the outdoor community and there was a real concern that the result would be a reduction in provision overall. This does not appear to have transpired as numbers of licence holders are currently some 15 per cent above the level seen at the commencement of licensing. Moreover, three years later in the first triennial review of the licensing scheme a large majority of the respondents were in favour of the continuation of licensing.

The DfES had (and continues to have) a real problem. We need only look at recent high profile tragic accidents on school visits to realise that on each and every occasion the cry goes up, 'Something must be done!' It falls to DfES to respond and society will not allow them to say, 'don't panic, these things are rare'.

Each local authority owes each of its pupils a duty of care which they are legally obliged to fulfil for as long as that child is in its care. Increasingly in this litigious society the imperative of the moment often obscures the bigger picture. Provision is threatened by the reluctance of local authority education departments, teachers and their unions to accept the liability in terms of finance, careers or adverse publicity. Short-term safety issues are imposed which ignore the long-term, and significantly more serious, threats. Moreover, I fear this will continue until we no longer separate accidents at work from accidents in the home, or road traffic accidents from suicides. We need to see all of these tragedies from a similar perspective, whenever the bell tolls:

Who by fire, who by water, who in the sunshine, who in the night-time, who by his lady's command, who by his own hand? And who shall I say is calling?

Leonard Cohen (songwriter)

Conclusion

I argue that if we want to maximise the overall safety of our young people we should:

- Argue vehemently that there are radical benefits for young people in taking part in adventure activity and that these benefits continue into adult life.
- Acknowledge that adventure activity is not without risk, but forcefully point out that the risk is small in both absolute and relative terms.
- Advocate that best practice is followed by all providers of adventure activities whether regulated or not so as to minimise risk and enhance public confidence.
- Accept that societal concern about young people is irrationally but understandably strong and that therefore controls will always be likely to be excessive in relation to the risk.

Adventure activity can help to extend life expectancy, enhance individual development and provide enjoyment for millions. It must not be allowed to be neutered by overreaction to the extremely rare tragedies that are the inevitable consequences of that much quoted goal – 'The right to life, liberty and the pursuit of happiness.'

References

Cohen, S. (2002) *Folk Devils and Moral Panics.* 30th Anniversary edn. London: Routledge.

Furedi, F. 2002) *Culture of Fear: Risk Taking and the Morality of Low Expectation.* 2nd edn. London: Continuum.

Health and Safety Commission. (1996) *Guidance to the Licensing Authority on the Adventure Activities Licensing Authority*. London: HSE Publications.

Health and Safety Executive. (2001) *Reducing risks, Protecting people*. London: HSE Publications.

National Statistics Office Web Site – http://www.statistics.gov.uk/

21 Outdoor Education and the Sustainable Use the Environment

Geoff Cooper

Abstract

This chapter considers the issues that can arise out of the use and misuse of the environment for outdoor activities. It identifies four types of impact on the environment and suggests how practical steps can be taken through codes of good practice to encourage awareness and alleviate these problems. The main argument however, focuses on our personal attitudes and actions and questions the philosophy and values of organisations and suggests how they can adapt their relationships to the environment and its sustainable use.

Introduction

There is sometimes an uneasy relationship between outdoor education and its use of the environment. Some groups may simply use the environment as a backcloth for their own aims. The environment can be treated as a gymnasium for physical activity or a laboratory for scientific investigation. The results may be similar and may lead to environmental damage and interference with the life of local communities. How can we encourage groups to interact with the environment in a more sensitive way? Hogan (1992) writing about wilderness programmes criticises many for using the environment as no more than a playing field. He argues that wilderness areas are very special places that can tap a spiritual dimension and transform people. He relates these environments to the psychiatrist Carl Jung's concept of 'Sacred Space', a place pervaded by a sense of power and mystery that can lead to positive empowerment. The environments leaders use with groups may not always provide a wilderness experience but they should still be presented as special places. Our groups are the guests, not there to abuse or compete, but to be made welcome and to feel at home. If leaders take this approach and at the same time encourage an awareness and understanding of the special places the group is travelling through, there is little doubt that the participants will benefit from feeling connected and the use will be sustainable.

The impact of outdoor activities

It is possible to distinguish a number of different kinds of pressure on the environment produced by outdoor activities:

Physical impact

At one extreme this could result from wilful damage to property or thoughtless actions such as climbing over walls, dumping litter or lighting fires. More commonly it is a result of the general wear and tear associated with group activities which may lead, for example, to footpath erosion and damage to surfaces by horse riding and mountain biking. It is important to keep this in perspective. Footpath erosion is not vandalism; it represents people enjoying the countryside. It sometimes produces visual intrusion but it can often be rectified by careful management, such as re-aligning footpaths and grading them up a hillside.

Ecological impact

This is often more serious and includes disturbance or damage to wildlife. Again this might be wilful, for example in collecting eggs or rare species of plants but it is more often a result of ignorance. Sometimes there is unnecessary trampling of sites with rare species of insects or plants or disturbance to nesting birds on crag, moorland or water. Ecological damage is not always obvious. It is often difficult to assess disturbance from outdoor activities on particular environments. A joint Countryside Commission and Sports Council study of 'Sport, Recreation and Nature Conservation' published in 1988 concluded that for a variety of outdoor activities disturbance and damage was relatively insignificant although local impacts can be serious. In contrast, studies of sensitive environments, such as moorlands of national ecological importance, suggest that group impact can be detrimental. In 1990 the Peak District National Park published a report by Anderson on 'Moorland Recreation and Wildlife in the Peak District' which found that several summer breeding birds, such as curlew, golden plover and common sandpiper are easily disturbed by recreational use particularly away from paths. The report also suggested that moorland plants, especially woody species and those growing on wet peat were susceptible to trampling. It argued that recreational use of some areas was exceeding the natural carrying capacities.

Social impact

This may represent the most significant impact of outdoor groups. The Hunt Report (1989) identified the following pressures sometimes faced by local communities:

- Noise, particularly at night, which may be exacerbated by drunkenness and foul language.
- Litter and occasionally thoughtless or deliberate vandalism.
- Fieldwork and surveys which involve questioning local people.
- Intimidating or aggressive behaviour and theft of property.
- Dangerous driving, either by students if they have use of personal transport, or by staff.
- Lack of understanding of, and respect for, the local culture or way of life such as failure to respect the Sabbath.
- Damage to the livelihood of farmers by leaving gates open, damaging walls and fences, disturbing stock.
- Wide games which are often carried out at night to test problem solving skills or map reading.
- Overcrowding of shops, inns and other local facilities.

This is a catalogue of disturbance, but the Hunt Report does point out that such difficulties are not widely experienced. They occur most often when

outdoor activities are based close to small communities and are poorly managed.

Psychological impact

This is a more difficult concept and harder to measure. It occurs when one group's activities affect the experience and enjoyment of other people in the outdoors. For example, a large noisy group paddling along a canal could impose themselves on people who had come to enjoy the tranquillity from fishing or bird watching. Some places, such as a cave or a deep narrow valley may quickly become crowded when several groups arrive together and this detracts from the experience. Walkers sometimes claim that the presence of mountain bikers on the fells affects their enjoyment. Large-scale events, such as orienteering, fell running or mountain marathons may be inappropriate in some environments enjoyed for their peace and quiet.

It is important to put environmental and social problems caused by outdoor groups in the more general context of wider pressures on the environment. Gittins (1990) makes this point clearly: ' . . . when put against the more general and fundamental environmental changes taking place globally, for example; climatic change, acid rain and the destruction of rain forests; and in the British countryside, in particular, such as the removal of hedgerows, loss of wetlands, the afforestation of moorland, the excessive use of pesticides and herbicides, the loss of green belt areas, rural depopulation and the loss of services in rural areas – the impact of young people participating in adventure activities is negligible'. Even the Council for the Preservation of Rural England, a strong conservationist body, states: 'the balance of advantage lies firmly in extending and enhancing the opportunities for young people to enjoy the countryside . . . through such experiences they will come to appreciate and care for the survival of our countryside'. It can be argued that those young eager feet eroding the paths belong to young people who will fight to protect the environment in the future.

Case study – the Lake District gills

The Lake District gills are a very special environment. They are the steep rocky valleys that descend from the mountains associated mainly with lines of weakness in the Borrowdale volcanic series of rocks. In total they occupy just 10 hectares of land, a tiny portion of the uplands. Unlike other areas they have not suffered the effects of sheep grazing and represent a remnant of the former upland vegetation. The ecologist, Bob Bunce, who has studied the gills for many years, points out that they have a very rich flora but their uniqueness is the variety of plants from different habitats found in close proximity. As you ascend the gills you find a succession of woodland, meadow and arctic-alpine species. Nowhere else in Britain does such a mixture occur. The nature of the gills, with their sheer sides, waterfalls and rock-strewn beds makes them dramatic environments to travel through. Gill scrambling is an exciting activity and one that has become popular over the last 15 years, especially with the publication of guidebooks and use by groups from outdoor centres. Concern over this growing use led to the establishment of a gill group who put forward a set of guidelines for outdoor leaders. These are now incorporated into a leaflet published by the Lake District National Park. There are five simple rules: keep to the rocky bed of the gill; groups should keep in line; leave plants for others to enjoy; avoid crumbling rock; and follow only established routes.

This raised awareness amongst outdoor leaders and many have been keen to convey the uniqueness of these environments to their groups. The adventure experience is enriched by this understanding. A study by Beasley (1997) concludes that 'the efforts of groups of interested parties over the past 15 years to raise awareness of users to the ecological and conservational importance of Lakeland gills has generally been successful'. This case study demonstrates how conservationists and outdoor enthusiasts can work together through mutual understanding and good communication.

Lessening the impact

The case study of the Lake District gills indicates that there is a growing environmental awareness and concern amongst outdoor leaders. This is reflected in an increasing commitment to conservation from the professional bodies involved in outdoor education and the national governing bodies of the various outdoor sports.

One organisation that has been active in this field for nearly 20 years is the Adventure and Environmental Awareness Group, which comprises representatives from outdoor education and national and regional recreation and conservation interests. The group argues that direct experience in the outdoors encourages an interest in conservation and at the same time greater awareness of the richness and interrelatedness of the environment enhances the outdoor experience. It tries to achieve these aims through workshops, talks, publicity and conferences and by forging links between outdoor enthusiasts and environmentalists. The group encourages outdoor leaders to place more emphasis on environmental education.

Sometimes there is a tension between adventure and environment. Adventure is about uncertainty and challenge. The environment, in the form of wind, waves, white water, crag, fell or forest may provide the challenge. If we pit ourselves against these natural elements, there is the excitement of real or perceived risk, we overcome the challenge and we enjoy the 'buzz' of success. At worst we are in competition with the environment, at best it provides simply the backcloth for our activities. How can the outdoor leader turn the self-centred 'buzz' into a more outgoing awareness of and interest in the environment? Here are a few suggestions for outdoor leaders:

- Recognise the link between personal, social and environmental education. If there is low self-esteem and little respect for others, there is unlikely to be much chance of developing environmental awareness and respect. The work of outdoor leaders in personal and social development is fundamental to environmental education that is concerned with changing attitudes and encouraging individual responsibility. Outdoor leaders can play a key role in this process.
- Introduce good environmental practice into the whole organisation and its programmes rather than through isolated activities. The outdoor leader is a powerful role model. Show enthusiasm for the environment and demonstrate through your own interest and practice.
- Help the group to appreciate the special qualities of each environment, encourage a

'sense of place' through an understanding of geology, ecology and history. Interpret the landscape but don't lecture. Focus on the detail of the environment – lichen, a rock, an eddy, a web, a leaf. Use different senses to explore the environment. Encourage a personal response through art, poetry, discussion or drama. In other words, help people to connect with the place.

- Outdoor experiences through climbing, caving, canoeing or sailing bring young people in close contact with the weather and the natural environment and help them develop a sense of awe and wonder. Such feelings can motivate and make young people more receptive to environmental education.
- Raise issues such as access, land use and conservation and consider the group's impact on the environment but don't concentrate unduly on problems. Be positive; remember this particular group hasn't caused all the problems. The aim is enjoyment, awareness and understanding.
- Adopt a more sensitive approach to activities. Promote the concept of journey and exploration rather than a hurried approach. Thrills may have their place, but avoid a programme based on a series of quick fixes.
- Reflection and reviewing can help young people put their experiences into the wider context of other people and the world around. Choose the time and place carefully, a quiet time for reflection and discussion after an active, exciting session can challenge attitudes and actions towards the environment.

Codes of good practice

One successful method of raising awareness of environmental issues and suggesting appropriate action is through guidelines and codes of practice. Drawing up guidelines is not always an easy task but it helps to focus attention on the needs of the environment and how we can use the outdoors sustainably. An early effort by a national governing body, the British Mountaineering Council, at producing environmental guidelines, is their joint publication with the Nature Conservancy Council published in 1988. Since then, other national bodies for outdoor sports, such as fell running, canoeing and caving have produced statements

and codes on their use of the environment. Recently some organisations have put forward 'charters' asking for stronger commitments from their members. One example of this is the Adventure and Environmental Awareness Group's 'Environmental Charter for Outdoor Users in the Lake District' which has been endorsed by the Lake District National Park Authority, the National Trust and Field Studies Council. This charter encourages outdoor leaders to take a positive lead in promoting education and awareness, for example, by giving groups 'an understanding about how the landscape, plants, animals and we are interrelated'.

Friluftsliv

In Britain we have a strong tradition of using the environment for adventure, scientific research and character building. In Scandinavia, a quite different tradition of 'Friluftsliv' or Outdoor Nature Life has developed over the last hundred years. This is a traditional and informal type of outdoor life more in tune with nature. Long walking and skiing tours throughout the year are a part of Norwegian culture. Tellnes (1992) argues that Friluftsliv can create a base for environmental consciousness, good health, higher quality of life and sustainable development. Repp (1996) also stresses the importance of 'good meetings with nature' in developing the whole person, physically, emotionally and intellectually. These experiences not only lead to a rediscovery of nature, in a sensitive way, but may bring about changes in attitudes and a deeper understanding of oneself and other aspects of life. The philosophy of Friluftsliv is people and nature in harmony, each benefiting the other. Tellnes believes that the deepest experiences result from the following considerations:

- Keeping the group small so that everyone can co-operate and take an active part in decisions as well as responsibility.
- Having people with a variety of backgrounds in the group.
- Choosing areas that are as natural as possible but try to avoid travelling too far to reach them.
- Having sufficient time for the experience.
- Keeping activities close to nature, for example in an open traditional boat, in a tent, around a campfire.

- Don't build unnecessary technological walls through use of equipment.
- Expedition according to ability but allow for progression. If circumstances are too demanding nature will not be considered as a friend.
- Learning from real situations.
- Allowing time for reflection, reviewing and discussion.

These ideas may be a long way from the outdoor sport enthusiast excited about testing out new machinery and gear and pitting their wits against rock, wind and water. But it should ring true with outdoor leaders interested in educating young people in terms of their broader personal and social development. Sometimes it is the approach adopted by the leader rather than the nature of the activities that is important. A mountain walk becomes a journey, an exploration rather than a dash for the top. There is time to experience detail – a rock, a tree, a bone, a view – and connect with the spirit of the place (Cooper, 1998: 99–102). The mountain walk is used to fire imaginations, introduce environmental issues and allow time for reflection.

Changing the organisation

As well as considering personal actions it is also important to determine ways of promoting environmental awareness and sustainability within organisations. The process of encouraging change through an environmental audit is well established:

- Start with an audit or review of current practice. This will involve looking at the whole organisation, all the staff and the work it undertakes with young people.
- Decide what changes you wish to make as a result of the audit. Draw up a list of priorities and a plan for action.
- Put forward a policy for environmental education and sustainability. Involve young people in drawing up this policy.
- Implement the policy and action plan.
- Evaluate its success over a specified period of time. Review and update action plans.

When considering an audit related to good environmental and sustainable practice it is important to consider more than collecting litter,

recycling cans and saving energy. The philosophy should permeate the whole life of the organisation, the attitudes and behaviour of the staff and their work with young people. The following guidelines may make this clearer:

- The aim should be holistic education. Personal, social and environmental awareness and skills are all part of the same process. This ethos should permeate the work of the organisation.
- Organisations should move away from narrow programmes based on academic fieldwork or outdoor pursuits. They should broaden their base to include other approaches, for example, through art, drama or problem solving, which encourage environmental learning.
- Organisations should question the importance they place on activities. Are they an end in themselves or used as a vehicle for learning? Are there opportunities to 'Plan, do and review'?
- Organisations should develop programmes in consultation with young people to give a sense of ownership and self-reliance. The ethos of the organisation should be conducive to this process.
- Teaching and learning styles should be varied and flexible depending on activities and situations. They should be designed to encourage all young people to achieve their potential. Leaders can help to 'unlock talent' which has failed to emerge through formal education.
- Organisations should address all aspects of environmental education from awareness, understanding and the development of skills to the discussion of attitudes and values and the ways in which action can be taken. They should tackle the major ecological concepts which govern all life on the planet. Through environmental issues they should also introduce economic and political systems and how they influence the environment. The aim should be to develop citizens who are environmentally competent and who wish to live more sustainably.
- Organisations should have an 'open' policy fostering links with the local community and other organisations and agencies working towards similar aims. They should look at ways of sharing expertise with other organisations

and encourage in-service development of their own staff.

- Organisations should try to improve their own environmental actions for instance in terms of energy saving, recycling and use of materials. They should examine their activities and use of sites and ensure these are compatible with their overall aims. There should be attempts to improve environments through practical conservation.
- Through their own example, organisations should discuss with leaders and young people ways to make improvements in their own actions and encourage them to adopt more sustainable lifestyles.
- Organisations should try to relate local issues to global patterns. This message should be positive, forward-looking and attempt to broaden horizons and foster international understanding.

Conclusion

The approaches and guidelines presented in this chapter set a considerable challenge to leaders and organisations. They question why we are using the environment as much as how we are using it. Sustainable use of the environment is not simply about reducing the wear and tear on sites but represents significant changes to our values both at personal and organisational levels.

References

Beasley, F. (1997) *A Study of the Recreational Impact of Gill Use Within the Lake District National Park.* Unpublished undergraduate manuscript.

Cooper, G. (1998) *Outdoors With Young People: A Leader's Guide to Outdoor Activities, the Environment and Sustainability.* Lyme Regis: Russell House Publishing.

Gittins, J. (1990) *Young People, Adventure and the Countryside.* Countryside Recreation Advisory Research Group, Annual Conference, Norfolk.

Hogan, R. (1992) The Natural Environment in Wilderness Programmes: Playing Field or Sacred Space? *Journal of Adventure Education and Outdoor Leadership.* 9: 1, 25–31.

Hunt, J. (1989) *In Search of Adventure: A Study of Opportunities for Adventure and Challenge for Young People.* Guildford: Talbot Adair Press.

Repp, G. (1996) Outdoor Adventure Education and Friluftsliv Seen From a Sociology of Knowledge Perspective. *Journal of Adventure Education and Outdoor Leadership.* 13: 2, 63–6.

Tellnes, A. (1993) Friluftsliv: Outdoor Nature Life as a Method to Change Attitudes. *Journal of Adventure Education and Outdoor Leadership.* 10: 3, 12–5.

22 The Contribution of Outdoor Education to Environmental Awareness and Sustainability

Geoff Cooper

Abstract

This chapter examines the links between outdoor education, environmental education and sustainability. It suggests a model for environmental education and considers four approaches according to whether the emphasis is placed on: appreciating nature, scientific knowledge, social or critical analysis or community action. The contribution of outdoor education to each approach is discussed and how outdoor education relates to the new education for sustainability. The paper attempts to re-position outdoor education within this framework and argues that it has much more to offer education for sustainability than an appreciation and understanding of the environment.

Introduction

The links between outdoor education and environmental awareness have long been recognised. The landmark conference at Dartington in 1975 (see Report of the Dartington Conference, 1975) suggested that the most important aims of outdoor education are to heighten awareness of and foster respect for *self*, *others* and *the natural environment*. Outdoor education was seen as a way of developing environmental awareness, valuing natural beauty, stimulating the imagination and gaining knowledge about the environment. Research has shown that many young people experience spiritual awareness in the outdoors (Barrett and Greenaway, 1995) and that experiences in the environment can influence attitudes and behaviour (Tellnes, 1993). Palmer (1992) conducted a survey of 232 environmental educators and found that outdoor experiences have been a major influence in developing their interests in the environment. From this work it is clear that the potential for environmental education through direct experiences in the outdoors is great. What is surprising is that outdoor educators have done little to develop these links. The last 25 years have seen many changes in environmental education and it is useful for outdoor leaders to appreciate these developments and consider how they can contribute through their own work.

A model for environmental education

Although the term environmental education was only introduced in the 1960s, in Britain its development can be traced to earlier environmental thinking in natural science, rural studies, fieldwork, countryside conservation and urban studies (Sterling, 1992). It is commonly accepted that environmental education should include opportunities for learning *about*, learning *in* or *through* and learning *for* the environment.

There are many definitions of environmental education but most are based on the one used at the UNESCO Intergovernmental Conference at Tbilisi in Georgia in 1977 which considered it as a process of learning which raised *awareness*, developed *understanding* and *skills*, clarified *attitudes and values* and led to *action* for the environment. These elements are considered below:

- **Awareness**: this includes awareness of our own connections with the environment as well as awareness of environmental issues. Raising awareness through feelings and personal response is a neglected area of environmental education and yet it may hold the key to changing our personal actions.
- **Understanding**: environmental education is underpinned by a body of knowledge which includes understanding ecological relationships but also understanding how we can be involved in decision-making through our own political and social system. There are two fundamental

questions: 'How are we connected to ecological systems?' and 'What can we do to improve this relationship?'

- **Skills**: a range of skills are necessary, from the scientific skills of observation, recording and analysis to more fundamental skills of effective communication. Personal and social skills which relate to taking individual and group responsibility for environmental action are invaluable.

- **Attitudes and values**: encouraging positive attitudes is essential for environmental education. Attitudes can be developed through experiencing a personal link with the environment and can also be explored through critical thinking about issues.

- **Action**: environmental education is about change, it is about improving our relationship with the planet and it should inevitably lead to personal and group action. This can include changes in our own behaviour, such as reducing our dependence on cars or saving water. It can relate to practical conservation, for example creating a wetland habitat or restoring a building. It can also involve political action, such as lobbying, joining a pressure group or taking direct action. Environmental education has failed if it does not lead to positive changes in our behaviour and lifestyles.

These five elements summarise the process of environmental education. They can be seen as a series of stages starting with awareness and leading to action. This is a logical progression but all the elements are interrelated and it is possible to start at any point (see Figure 1). For example a scientific or field studies approach may start with the skills of collecting information and analysing it. This could lead to awareness of an issue and further fieldwork to gain evidence or knowledge of the situation. Such investigation may lead to changes of attitudes and an attempt to seek a solution to the problem. In contrast, we might start the process with action for example with a practical conservation project. The task of cleaning up a stream may provoke questions on how the pollution occurred and this awareness and knowledge could lead to discussions of our attitudes and values which may lead to changes in our own behaviour.

Figure 1   A model for environmental education

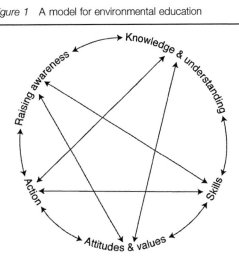

Approaches to environmental education

In Britain there have been four distinct approaches to environmental education. Each has had its own focus, methodology and proponents. Table 1 summarises these approaches.

Direct contact with the environment

This approach emphasises the importance of direct experiences of natural environments. These environments are places to explore our feelings, consider how we are connected to the rest of life, express our sense of awe and wonder and develop our imagination and creativity. The environment is viewed as home or as a sanctuary. Artists and writers have often used the environment in this way as a source of inspiration. Terry Gifford, a climber and poet, has for many years inspired children's writing at the Wigan LEA outdoor education centres (Gifford, 2002). Adventurers frequently comment on a spiritual awareness that results from harmony with their surroundings. For example, Colin Mortlock on a solo kayak expedition off the coast of Alaska in 1981 describes how he overcame his initial fears concerning safety and problems of loneliness:

What happened was totally unexpected. I was not only not lonely, despite the emotional intensity of a long solo, I felt totally at home, at least on the sea, a deep inner harmony with the surroundings, the ocean, the rocks, the birds, etc. This feeling persisted even when I was in

Table 1   Approaches to environmental education

Approach	Environment seen as	Focuses on	Methodology	Represented by
Direct contact with nature	Home Sanctuary	Feelings Values	First hand experience Personal response	Non-formal educators Interpreters Outdoor leaders
Scientific/knowledge based	Laboratory Classroom	Knowledge Scientific skills	Fieldwork Scientific study	Science teachers Field studies officers
Social/critical analysis	Resource for managing	Citizenship skills Attitudes Values	Discussion Issue-based learning Enquiry	Humanities teachers Environmental activists
Community action	Place to live	Citizenship skills Action	Forums Committees Action groups	Teachers Local and national campaign groups

danger of a capsize off a rugged headland in a gale. Since then I have felt a deep affinity with nature in all her forms . . . I am more aware, I have more respect and I love nature.

(Cooper, 1988)

Environmental educators such as Van Matre (1972), Cornell (1979), Henley (1989), Cooper (1998) and Knapp (1999) have stressed the value of direct contact with the environment and see this as a starting point in the process of environmental understanding. Their books offer many ideas and activities that can be used by outdoor leaders to encourage environmental awareness. Outdoor education can play a key role in this process. Michael Cohen (1989) is a pioneer in the field of nature-connected psychology and in his work he puts forward a strong argument for the restorative and developmental qualities that result from experiencing nature. Nature can reach the hearts of people but also produce clearer thinking and understanding. Direct experiences in the outdoors are great motivators; they can unlock talents that remain hidden in more formal situations. Direct contact with the natural environment, particularly in challenging situations, can be inspirational and lead to feelings of 'oneness' with the earth.

Scientific and knowledge-based approaches

The most traditional link between outdoor education and environmental education has been

through field studies in subjects such as geography, geology and ecology. It is important to understand the natural processes that relate us to other life on the planet. This will include knowledge of key concepts such as the water and nutrient cycles, food webs, habitats, adaptation, evolution and change over geological time. Some of these concepts can be introduced through scientific field investigation which might include aspects of observation, measurement, recording, analysis and hypothesis testing. Although outdoor leaders may not wish or be able to undertake field studies they can still introduce many of these concepts to their groups and use the outdoors to provide first-hand experience and examples.

Social or critical analysis

This approach places peoples' attitudes, values and behaviour firmly at the centre of environmental considerations. There are no such things as environmental problems, rather the problems lie with the way individuals and societies make economic, social and political demands on the environment. In this approach the emphasis is as much on the process of enquiry and critical analysis as on the understanding of any particular issue. It is about clarifying our own values and learning how we can be involved in effecting change through democratic processes.

Outdoor education offers many opportunities to introduce environmental issues through direct experience. Issues relating to land ownership, land use change, loss of habitats, recreational conflicts and access to the countryside are a few obvious examples. It is important to appreciate the range of opinions expressed by different interest groups, assess the arguments on each side before making a personal judgement.

Community action

This approach involves taking action to improve the environment. It is about being a more environmentally-conscious citizen. The action could include energy saving, recycling schemes, tree planting, renovating buildings, clearing litter etc. but may also include campaigning on environmental issues. Outdoor leaders can play an important role in encouraging good environmental practice. They often provide strong role models and their own actions will be significant. Furthermore they will often represent an organisation whose practice should also be seen to match the environmental messages it wishes to communicate.

Outdoor education clearly has a great deal to offer all four approaches to environmental education. It can address all aspects of environmental education from awareness, understanding and the development of skills to the discussion of attitudes and values and the ways in which action can be taken. It also has an important part to play in what has become known as education for sustainability.

Education for sustainability

The obvious link between sustainability and outdoor education is in terms of our sustainable use of the outdoors. Although this is important, there is great potential for outdoor leaders to contribute to the whole process of encouraging more sustainable lifestyles. The term *sustainability* has become increasingly important as a concept since the United Nations Earth Summit in Rio in 1992, when governments throughout the world drew up priorities for action on environment and development. Education for sustainability is likely to receive government support in Britain over the coming years.

There have been many attempts to define sustainability. An early definition and one often quoted is: 'development that meets the needs of the present without compromising the ability of future generations to meet their needs' (World Commission for Environment and Development, 1987). This definition was a starting point but is now considered to be too narrowly centred on the needs of people. More recent definitions have stressed the importance of improving the quality of our lives without harming the ecosystems we depend upon.

Sustainability is not just about environmental protection but also includes sharing resources more equitably and improving the quality of our lives in terms of access to health care, education, justice, work, leisure and democracy. Sustainability relates to people from all sections of society and countries of the world. It is concerned with both present and future generations. It implies the need for a new ethic based on co-operation rather than competition, quality of life rather than standard of living and community rather than individual interest. Education can play a key role in changing attitudes and behaviour.

Education for sustainability is a wider concept than environmental education and also includes aspects of personal and social education, citizenship, economic understanding and moral and spiritual considerations. A model for such an education is shown in Figure 2.

This framework is based on the three simple considerations below. Let's consider these a little further:

- I recognise the *need* to act – **Awareness**.
- I *know how* to act – **Empowerment**.
- I *will* act – **Commitment**.

Figure 2   The process of educating for sustainability

Awareness

There are two aspects of awareness. It is important to have a knowledge and understanding of issues influencing the environment and our quality of life. For example it is necessary to have some ecological understanding to appreciate the intricate relationships between plants, animals and ourselves. But it is also vital to have knowledge of political structures to appreciate how and why decisions are made which influence these relationships. The second aspect of awareness is concerned with feelings and having a personal connection with the environment. We have become separated from nature, we think of ourselves as apart from rather than a part of nature yet our minds and bodies still respond to rhythms of day and night, lunar cycles and the changes of the seasons. There is an urgency to develop this biological awareness through encouraging a personal response to the environment. Understanding comes through feelings as much as knowledge. This aspect of awareness could be the key to attitude and behavioural change.

Empowerment

There is a need to involve people, to give them responsibility and make them feel responsible for their own lives, to empower them. A basis for such empowerment is to develop self-esteem, confidence and motivation. Many people have poor self-worth, they have under-achieved in a school system designed to measure a particular type of intelligence and academic learning. They are given little responsibility in this system, there is a lack of identity and motivation can be low. The first step is to reverse this process, to develop self-esteem and to improve confidence. Empowerment also involves encouraging a range of skills and competencies. Effective communication is essential but for much oral literacy may be more important than the written word. Interpersonal skills are increasingly important in an age when knowledge can be acquired at the press of a button. Problem solving, lateral and critical thinking and negotiation will be valuable to young people involved in decision-making. Creativity and vision for the future are also required to inspire positive change.

These skills are often underdeveloped in formal education. Knowledge of ecological and political systems also forms a prerequisite for empowerment.

Commitment

Sometimes we are aware of an issue that needs addressing, we have the ability and confidence to take action but we still do not do anything about it. What triggers our commitment to act? This is a difficult question, we may change our behaviour because there are rewards or penalties. Rewards may be economic but can also come from the satisfaction that we are improving the quality of life for ourselves or others. Good self-esteem, tolerance, empathy and co-operation are attitudes conducive to action. People who do not value themselves or respect and co-operate with others are unlikely to show concern for the environment. Penalties such as fines or prosecution can alter behaviour, for example the dramatic shift in attitudes towards drinking and driving in Britain over the last 30 years. There is evidence to suggest that the development of personal feelings and strong connections with an environment may influence our commitment to act for its protection.

Awareness, empowerment and commitment are the building blocks leading to action. It is possible to summarise this by presenting ten competencies which show the necessary knowledge, skills and attitudes that are essential in educating for a more sustainable society:

Ten essential competencies

1. Self-esteem, confidence and motivation.
2. Co-operation, trust and empathy.
3. Communication skills including negotiation and decision-making.
4. The ability for critical thinking, lateral thinking and problem solving.
5. Self-reliance, the ability to take responsibility.
6. Futures thinking.
7. Feelings of belonging to the natural world.
8. Creativity, imagination and a personal response to the environment.
9. Knowledge of ecology and social and political systems.
10. The ability for reflection and evaluation.

This list is not comprehensive but gives an indication of some of the important skills and qualities needed to change the present situation. A quick glance at this list and many outdoor leaders will realise they are very much on home territory! We have long recognised the value of social and personal skills and know that these have not met with much success in formal education. Generally schools do not encourage creativity, problem solving and leadership, common outcomes of many outdoor education programmes. The acceptance of the current political inclusion agenda in education could strengthen the work of outdoor education by emphasising different methods of teaching and learning and their benefits to individuals.

Re-assessing the role of outdoor education

It has been shown that outdoor education has many links with environmental education. It is clear that it has a role to play in encouraging all the elements of environmental learning from awareness to action. It can be argued that outdoor education is even more important in the benefits it offers the broader field of education for sustainability. I think it has three major contributions to make:

1. It is a great motivator and helps in personal growth by developing self-esteem and confidence. It encourages self-awareness and personal responsibility.
2. It emphasises co-operation, teamwork and social skills such as discussion and negotiation which are essential for effective community involvement.
3. Through direct experiences of the environment it can offer a very powerful means of stimulating feelings and encouraging spiritual awareness. This is an area that begs research. It may offer clues as to how a commitment to a more sustainable lifestyle occurs.

References

Barrett, J. and Greenaway, R. (1995) *Why Adventure?* Coventry: Foundation for Outdoor Adventure.

Cohen, M. (1989) *Connecting With Nature, Creating Moments That Let Earth Teach.* Eugene, Oregon: World Peace University.

Cooper, G. (1988) *Approaches to the Environment: Towards a Common Understanding.* Ambleside, Adventure and Environmental Awareness Group.

Cooper, G. (1998) *Outdoors with Young People.* Lyme Regis: Russell House Publishing.

Cornell, J. (1979) *Sharing Nature with Children.* Nevada City, CA: Exley.

Gifford, T. (2002) Environmental Creative Writing. *English in Educatio.,* 36: 3, 37–46.

Henley, T. (1989) *Rediscovery: Ancient Pathways: New Directions.* Vancouver: Western Canada Wilderness Committee.

Knapp, C. (1999) *In Accord with Nature.* Clearinghouse on Rural Education and Small schools. Charleston, WV.

Palmer, J. (1992) Life Experiences of Environmental Educators. *Environmental Education.* 41: 5–9.

Report of the Dartington Conference (1975) *Outdoor Education.* London: Department of Education and Science.

Sterling, S. (1992) *Coming of Age: A Short History of Environmental Education.* Walsall: National Association for Environmental Education.

Tellnes, A. (1993) Friluftsliv: Outdoor Nature Life as a Method to change Attitudes. *Journal of Outdoor Education and Adventure Leadership.* 10: 3, 12–5.

Van Matre, S. (1972) *Acclimatization.* Martinsville, IN: American Camping Association.

World Commission for Environment and Development (1987) *Our Common Future (Brundtland Report).* Oxford: Oxford University Press.

23 Working from the Urban Environment

Archie Waters

Abstract

This chapter examines some of the complex issues surrounding the operation of outdoor education projects within the urban environment. The author has intentionally avoided entering into a descriptive dialogue detailing the types of groups to whom services are supplied or the style of course content. Rather he concentrates more on the structuring and economic requirements of urban organisations.

Whereas there are many types of organisations working within this environment, some with a specific remit such as personal development or employment training, the discussion focuses mainly on the community-managed project.

Introduction

In the mid 1980s Urban-Aid, in the form of massive grants, was being pumped into our cities in an attempt to reduce the adverse effects of mass unemployment, mainly due to the decline of the country's large manufacturing industries. Indeed, it was arguably a Thatcherist knee jerk reaction to the growing threat of social unrest heralded by increased levels of disturbance and rioting within the inner cities. At this time many urban-based outdoor education projects were formed, which in itself marked the beginning of a small revolution on how people perceived the methodology and supply of outdoor education services. Few of those projects survive today and I would argue that this had as much to do with a lack of knowledge and skills amongst members of the outdoor education industry, as with short-term social planning or the lack of local political will. My comments, please note, are not meant to be critical of those who took on the management of said projects. The situation was very different then. The projects were new, idealistic and created with an assumption that local authorities would ultimately find a place for them under the mantle of growing public service provision. The knowledge we have today has been gained through hard experience, but operatives in those early days were simply expected to hold management skills enough to ensure the competent delivery of safe activities. Working from the urban environment now requires a new breed of outdoor education specialist. Individuals who are aware of the broader political and economic environment surrounding them and are prepared to develop management skills far and beyond those required of their predecessors.

Characteristics of the urban project

Imagine you had carte blanche to develop an outdoor education project without the constraints of pre-determined policy or the need to target specific client groups. That *you* as a professional had the freedom to be pioneering, innovative and imaginative. Imagine further that you had the ability to take the activities directly to those who most needed them and to focus your efforts on making real cultural and social change. Well, I would argue that the community managed project is the nearest we can get to achieving this altruistic utopia, without the assistance of major social revolution. In truth, all things have their constraints and carte blanche models are only temporarily clear of these before they begin to emerge as a function (or dysfunction) of the developmental progress. To elaborate, let us draw an analogy with down-wind sailing. In sailing terms, this is the easiest point of sail and destinations can be targeted directly. However, progress can only be made as long as one has the resource of a steady wind. One can only sail as fast as the competing forces of air pressure and drag will allow, and only as efficiently as the helmsman is skilled. I would suggest that working in the urban environment, at least within the structure of the community managed project, is very similar. Where funding availability is to the wind, bureaucracy and local politics are to the drag factor; and efficiency is to management structures and the attitudes of personnel.

Urban projects are inextricably linked with politics. Offer any politician the chance to be associated with a project that is exciting, high profile and provides apparent benefits to the electorate, without a price, and they would be delighted. But the price is always an underlying concern and spreading what financial resources there are around and between many competing projects, each advocating the essentiality of its service, makes for difficult political choices. The astute reader will have already identified several aspects emerging that directly affect the ability of a project to operate freely and, indeed, survive within the urban environment. Political will and adequate funding are obvious factors. However, 'fit', validity and building a structure that will ensure sustainability are also crucial.

Fit and validity

Validity, I would suggest, is a point that we have to argue constantly in support of our profession. Often seen as a 'fun' aspect of any treatment or education process, or the proverbial 'cream on the cake', I believe that each of us needs to promote the very special innate and cognitive benefits that outdoor learning holds for individuals. As mentioned above, in the urban environment outdoor education needs to promote its value amongst many competing services, each with equally good arguments for their inclusion within the overall provision of public services. Take, for example, a project designed to assist with recovering addicts. Ask yourself where the greatest priorities lie for the individuals faced with having to re-build their lives. In kayaking, cycling, hill walking . . .? Or dealing with debts, depression, pending court cases and avoiding regression? I would like to believe that you are now thinking to yourself that outdoor activities do have their place in recovery strategies; and indeed they do, very often earlier in the process rather than later. However, I would contend that if our profession is to 'fit' at all as a bona-fide aid to a process of treatment or education, it must promote itself as part of the overall process rather than a substitute or stand alone provision. Forming partnerships is an essential part of the urban-based operation. These are generally with other 'third sector' organisations, public sector agencies, grant providers and private sector

companies; though the latter is usually related to some form of cause-related or match-funding relationship. Partnership working is, then, part of the economic structure of the voluntary sector. Isolationism and causal independence weakens organisations, as does adhering to single stream funding policies, which leaves them vulnerable to changes in political and economic priorities.

Economics

When people working in the urban environment hear the word 'economics' I fear that many think simply of money, grants or budgeting. Yet in the urban environment an understanding of economics, as a concept, is crucial for project development and survival. I would contend that funding, for urban projects in contemporary times, is about structure. It's about developing the organisation so it is able to evolve to fit the ever-changing economic and political climates in which it operates. It is not simply about being able to attract funding. It is also about promoting the validity of the product, maximising efficiency in terms of delivery and assuring purposeful service provision.

The growth of the voluntary and charity sector – referred to earlier as the 'third sector' – has become significant enough to catch the eye of governments throughout Europe. It works in areas of market failure, where the economy based on the 'price mechanism' fails to provide equality of income sharing and wealth. Groups working within it are now dubbed 'Social Economy' organisations and number (circa) 50,000 in Scotland alone, employing in excess of 107,000 people (SCVO, 2002). Laterally, much of this expansion has been promoted by the application of European Social Fund grant aid. However, as with many other sources of funding, this is provided on a sliding scale and it can be anticipated that funds will be reduced to significantly lower levels in the next few years. Third sector organisations are thus constantly required to find new ways of sustaining themselves, and individuals working in the sector have to remain aware of current developments and likely trends. For instance, one support mechanism being considered by government is the introduction of new tax breaks. Examples of these are the provision of relief on fuel for community transport vehicles and alterations in the laws surrounding trading by charitable organisations making it easier for them to generate income through trading on the open market.

Charities are now also being encouraged to consider 'social investment loans' in order to support new developments, as opposed to searching for grant aid. However, while there are some advantages in accessing funds more rapidly, there are also some potentially grave dangers particularly for the small and medium sized charities, which invariably have weak balance sheets and few, if any, assets. If a charity should find itself unable to repay a loan it could easily become embroiled in financial and legal difficulties, which could jeopardise its status and ultimately the very existence of its service. In a worst case scenario, a reversal of control may take place with commercial banks foreclosing on what assets charities have. This, as I'm sure you will have realised, has implications for the 'independence' of the third sector. Charitable status for urban organisations has, of course, meant greater access to the resources of grant giving trusts, but there are very strict laws governing the operation of a charity. For example, grants given must only be used for the purposes for which they were supplied. If used, in the Social Investment Loan scenario, to pay off a debt, the Board of Directors could be acting criminally.

The complexity of all this further increases the demand for those working in the urban environment to have a sound knowledge of the law as it applies to their organisation. It is imperative that nothing is done which would constitute an illegal action on its behalf. As mentioned earlier, in the past it was primarily seen as the urban outdoor education professional's job to ensure the quality and safety of the activity provision. It is now also their responsibility to maintain the integrity of the organisation and to protect its board members, often local people with no depth of knowledge of legal matters or organisational principles, from breaking either charity or company law.

Management

Management, in the urban environment, is not necessarily the sole domain of the professional. The community project exists on the ideal that it is 'owned', if not fully managed, by local people. The lack of knowledge spoken of in relation to the early projects was attributable as much to the community volunteers elected to run projects, as to the professionals they employed. Denial and displacement, two psychological phenomena arguably culturally innate within the urban environment, have led to the demise of more than one project. Management committees and boards of such projects carry the power of dictate over their employees. Subsequently, one of the major attributes of the professional is the ability – and preparedness – to enter into persuasive argument without alienating the layperson. Concepts such as deferred gratification and investment can be foreign to some committee members, as can the principle of entrepreneurialism. But political dogma is clearly understood and there is often a perception of honour in failure and dogged adherence to outdated restrictive principles. The professional may encounter considerable resistance to change against the background of such deeply held beliefs. In the urban environment, where poverty strikes hard, protecting the status that maximises personal or family income is crucially important (it is one of the fundamental forces controlling what we commonly term the 'poverty trap'). Advancement from dependency carries enormous threats, not only to one's financial security, but also to one's psychological well-being. Overcoming such deeply embedded values, allaying the fears that surround change, winning the argument and demonstrating the essentiality of moving on from first principles are hard tasks for the professional. Thus, negotiating skills and an ability to build rapport and trust with local people are also essential.

Flexibility

One of the great strengths of the community led urban outdoor education project is its flexibility. Many other styles of provision have pre-set programmes that are promoted or advertised to attract potential clients and the customer may or may not buy into these depending on suitability. By contrast, the urban project has no pre-determined programme and therefore it has the ability and the freedom to provide courses designed from bottom to top, to suit individual client and group needs. Such flexibility allows outdoor education within the urban environment to target specifics. It can easily adapt to help meet the aims and objectives of a wide variety of client groups. Such groups can include those working to prevent young children becoming involved in stimulant abuse, supporting the recovery of addicts, benefiting adults with mental health problems, improving the employability of trainees, working with children suffering from abuse problems, rehabilitation of offenders and those promoting education, health and recreation. This list, of course, is by no means exhaustive. Not being tied to the organisational structure of a residential centre or the demands of a pre-set programme also allows for great flexibility in course design. A course can last a few hours, a full day or even be planned as a regular series of events organised in a wide variety of permutations. In addition, venue choice is unrestricted other than by the limitations of travel and funding resources. As a result of being able to design courses freely, cost factors can be adjusted to suit individual group budgets. Importantly, this encourages wider participation which, in turn, increases social inclusion. These are valuable features of the peripatetic style of provision, which should not be underestimated, as they enable a close fit with the disparate needs of varying client groups working in the urban environment.

Growth and development

As previously mentioned, there are developing opportunities for social economy organisations in the urban environment to grow through commercial style investment. However, with the freedoms of movement that this promises, so too comes a high risk factor. I would argue the need for caution. As with the early urban-aid model, the 'boom and bust' funding scenario where large injections of cash are thrown at priority social problems can stifle long-term effectiveness. Rather than creating sustained provision and extended effect through consistency, this scenario encourages short-term thinking both in the minds of the suppliers and the clients. I would suggest that effective supply has to be rooted in the cultural growth of a community, whether it is urban, rural or otherwise. Active lifestyles and positive attitudes towards healthy and sociable

living must be encouraged across generations and initiated at a very early age, particularly if young people are going to accept the principle as part of the cultural norm. Furthermore, aspirations need to be supported within a real context. That is, individuals should never be told they can achieve what is blatantly unattainable to them and, if the aim of a project is the personal adoption of outdoor activities as a vehicle for improving the quality of life, then the project design needs to include the development of structures and facilities which allow for sustained involvement on a personal basis. Only in this way will cultural change and personal support mechanisms be effectively created and maintained. To achieve this, particularly in the urban environment, there needs to be agreement and policy cohesion between all the agencies and community groups involved with the provision of services. These would include local development and funding organisations, employment training groups, social work and health organisations, schools and libraries, local news agencies, youth services and leisure services. This obviously can be identified as another level of partnership working but, given the complexities of the urban environment, is one that is extremely difficult to co-ordinate or sustain. However, much more emphasis is being placed on common threads of policy with departments and agencies complementing the work of others in order to promote generic themes. Moves towards a more cohesive approach are being emphasised within government policy, and organisations at all levels will need to embrace this principle if maximum benefits are to be realised. Growth and development thus needs to be organic, with each new initiative working to build on the work of previous projects and older ones evolving to meet new and alternative challenges. This same principle applies to the physical growth of the urban project. Its development needs to be based on steady capacity building and long-term sustainability.

One of the problem areas for projects that are set up on a fixed term grant is sustainability over the long term. Such projects are generally given the task of providing a specific service, but once the particular allocation of funding which set them up has run its course, it is difficult for them either to re-focus their services upon other target groups or, in the case of local authority sponsored projects, to secure ongoing financial support from their political masters. Neither are they necessarily structured in a way that allows them to move easily towards independent control. This, I would argue, is partly due to the unwillingness or inability of some grant giving bodies to commit to long-term support, often because of fear of over-commitment or because of limiting criteria attached to the funding provision. It is also my contention that those projects that are singularly funded are doomed to inevitable failure, either through termination or through institutional entrenchment. Institutional entrenchment can exist in those organisations that have been funded from a single source for a considerable length of time and have not changed significantly in how they operate. Their continued existence is assumed, as is the idea that they are still providing an appropriate service. Ironically, they can become detrimental to the general supply of services by absorbing financial resources that could be better or more efficiently deployed elsewhere.

As adventurers we quickly learn the value of flexibility to cope with the ever-changing outdoor environment that we love. It is often essential for our survival. And flexibility, in terms of projects surviving in the urban environment is the essence of development. Capacity building, for example, is important, but most people will immediately equate it with growth. Too much growth can easily overtake capacity and result in a phenomenon known to the commercial sector as 'over trading'. For instance, good advertising campaigns will inevitably increase demand, but if an organisation cannot cope with all its new customers, it can then run into cash flow and credibility problems as a result. This has to be a particular consideration for community groups, as they generally hold few, if any, financial reserves (historically, holding reserves was frowned upon and possibly led to an end of year 'claw back' or subsequent reductions in grant support). Situations can therefore arise which leave them struggling to cope financially. For example, a project may have to lay out large amounts of cash to hire additional instructors, transport and equipment, long before receiving the payment of invoices for the services provided. Therefore, in lieu of the irregular nature of funding in the urban sector, capacity building needs to be controlled and include the *capacity* to reduce the size of a project as funding levels fluctuate, without risking damage to the core structure. In this way we allow for reduction of services and re-expansion as the environment dictates. Clearly maintaining an objective understanding of the processes involved in project structuring, and remaining aware of the factors influencing the development of urban funding, is paramount for any contemporary manager.

Conclusion

Of all the working environments available to the outdoor educationalist, the urban one is perhaps the most involving. It can offer the privilege of innovation, allowing dedicated workers to take chances and to try new styles of service provision, without the constriction of pre-conceived ideas.

As I hope this chapter shows, working from the urban environment is complex and those who wish to work in it have to be prepared to develop a wide range of skills and a high level of knowledge in order to deal with the intricacies involved in management and development. Such work is undoubtedly demanding, but the rewards can be truly satisfying. It is an environment where as well as exercising professional freedom one can achieve very real effect.

Reference

Scottish Council for Voluntary Service (2002) *Statistics*. www.scvo.org.uk/research

24 Professionalism, Quality and the Market Place

Randall Williams

Abstract

The author argues that professionalism and quality cannot be separated from market expectations. He illustrates the complexity of the market place and emphasises the need to balance the interests of the various stakeholders. He discusses the tensions that exist between being demand led, value led and funding led. He expresses concern over pressures to compromise expectations and challenges providers to reappraise continually the degree to which they are giving their clients maximum value. He identifies the key elements of professionalism and suggests how it might be recognised.

Professionalism, quality and the market place

It is not the employer who pays the wages. It is the customer.

(Henry Ford)

We have all had powerful, high impact, sometimes life changing experiences in the outdoors. That is why we are outdoor enthusiasts. When it comes to passing on that enthusiasm to others, we would naturally wish to do so in a professional way. But what does this mean? Is professionalism giving our charges the intensity of experience that we know is so powerful? Or is it giving them what they want? Or what their teacher expects? Or what someone will pay for? I suggest that it is impossible to ask what is professionalism without also asking who our customers are, what do they want, what do they understand by quality and what influences are there on the decision to buy? In other words, professionalism and quality cannot be separated from market expectations.

Before developing this argument, let us be clear that we do not have to be in a commercial environment to talk about purchasing decisions. Time is our most precious commodity and a young person's decision to invest time in an outdoor activity offered free of charge by a voluntary youth organisation is entirely analogous to the decision to buy a commercially packaged experience. Many volunteers are wholly professional in their unpaid work and the debate about quality and professionalism applies equally in a voluntary context.

Consumers in the market place

A simple model of the market place consists of suppliers and consumers. If only reality were as simple as that. Anyone who has organised a custom designed course for members of an organisation will recognise the tension intrinsic in the situation. The question 'Who is the customer?' is far from easy to answer. To what extent is it the organisation that pays for the course? To what extent is it the person who organised the course and may have defined the objectives? To what extent is it the unwitting participant who may turn up with quite different needs and perceptions? In reality, all three are stakeholders in the success of the course and the facilitator must tread a fine line between often conflicting interests in an attempt to satisfy all.

There are similarly varied stakeholders in educational provision. In simplistic terms, it might be that the young people want to have fun, their teacher wants to achieve educational outcomes, the parents want their children back in one piece, the head teacher wants to be confident that the school trip will not end up in the newspapers and the governors want it to enhance their position in the league tables. To complicate matters further, many young people's courses are funded by a government agency that will bring its own targets and monitoring criteria. We must add to the complexity of the market by asking what society wants.

Society appears desperately confused. Fed by a media which sells more copies on the emotional impact of a rare outdoor tragedy than on the infinitely greater waste of road accident deaths and suicides, it appears that society has a completely unrealistic appreciation of the true level of risk. At a rational level, society appears willing to accept huge statistical risks. For example, the Health and Safety Executive (2001: 46) suggests that an individual risk of death of one in a thousand per annum should be just 'tolerable' for any substantial category of workers. However, in the same document, the Health and Safety Executive recognises that societal concerns increase in the case of vulnerable groups such as children and that a tighter framework than might be rationally required is felt necessary for these groups. Whether or not this constitutes societal hysteria, I believe that, individually, parents have an intuitive understanding that adventure is good for their children. There is hope that this will continue to outweigh their concerns. Libby Purves (2002) wrote:

> I have spent the last 15 years nervously entrusting my children's lives to other adults as they confronted dinghies, canoes, horses, tall ships, campfires and the rest. I know the dread. But it has always seemed worthwhile, and reassurance has always lain in a belief in the high quality and knowledge of the people who lead them to conquer their fear and come through triumphant and capable. This ideal of high quality – whether in outdoor-adventure professionals or in ordinary teachers taking a class trip – is a gold standard to be cherished.

It was in order to encourage parents and society in general to balance risk and benefits that the English Outdoor Council launched the *Campaign for Adventure* (2001). However, underpinning any campaign for increased participation in the outdoors must be the sort of consistent professionalism that will reassure Purves and other parents.

Suppliers in the market place

There is of course one more set of stakeholders – those who provide the experience. It could be argued that their needs are irrelevant in the context that they are there to meet others' needs. However, I think it is important to consider the provider's needs and to ask whether they matter. My answer would be emphatically yes. This is because almost everything that is achieved in the outdoors is achieved through the skilful guidance of an enthusiastic, committed instructor or leader. To keep the freshness and spark that helps to communicate the real value of the outdoors, it is vital that the person who actually delivers the experience finds their job motivating and satisfying.

Each individual will of course have a different set of motivators. For some, one beginners' climbing group after another can begin to pall and they may need a variety of different activities or more advanced courses. Some others, who often achieve outstanding results, are able to maintain the freshness by such a degree of unconscious competence in activity terms that nearly all their attention can be on the individual participants and their learning and development. For me, in 35 years full time work in outdoor education, I have never been bored. Frustrated, tired and apprehensive yes, but never bored. Indeed, any of these negative emotions are rare in comparison with those positive factors that motivate many outdoor staff – the satisfaction of helping others to achieve and the privilege of working in such a special environment. As an employer, I consider it is really important to create conditions in which all staff can experience that same satisfaction.

We can neither deliver quality nor professionalism unless we are able to survive in the market place. To do so requires us to acknowledge that life in a few years' time will be very different to what it is today – to accept that change is endemic. As adventurers, we ought to be comfortable with the idea of working in a context where the outcome is uncertain. We should recognise that we cannot control the environment in which we operate but at the same time should realise that our decisions can nevertheless affect the probability of the survival of our organisation. A parallel can be drawn with white water canoeing or powder skiing – in neither of these environments do we have absolute control over our overall motion, yet by exerting small control forces, we can both survive and use our relative motion to get where we want to be. One such control force is to be continually responsive to our customers' needs, achieving consistent customer satisfaction.

The outdoor community is complex; statutory, voluntary, charitable and private sectors are all represented. Such a mixed economy has both strengths and weaknesses. A strength is that the sum total of provision is less affected by external influences that can impact negatively on one sector. A weakness is that it is less easy for the outside world to see the outdoor community as a coherent whole. Can we define a concept of professionalism that applies equally across these disparate sectors? I believe so – because the relationship between customers and providers is the same in each. No organisation, in any sector, will survive unless it consistently provides a service which will attract and retain users. It is clear that there is an extraordinarily broad range of stakeholders in what would appear to be a simple purchasing transaction. Quality and professionalism must be seen in the context of those many stakeholders. It must also be seen in the context of what we are trying to achieve.

What are we trying to achieve?

This should be relatively easy to answer. More difficult questions are what *should* we be trying to achieve and to what extent should we impose our beliefs and values? Not only is there a tension between trying to satisfy the needs of our various publics, but there is a tension between giving this 'composite' public what 'it' thinks it wants and giving it what we think it should get. Clearly, a provider offering highly subsidised courses can impose to a greater extent than one wholly dependent on market forces. Even so, too strong a 'product orientation' does not sit comfortably with the 'customer orientation' that is prevalent in today's market place.

A provider has a far clearer idea than the average consumer of the enormous potential of outdoor education and might be expected to influence the purchaser to buy a thoroughly worthwhile experience rather than a shallow one. However, there are real pressures to compromise the depth or breadth of what we offer, for a variety of reasons. I suggest that there has in general been some lowering of expectations in order to create a more controlled environment. Activities have been made safe but sanitised. It is easy to convince ourselves that a pool canoeing session allows pupils to progress faster than a session on open water. It is easy to argue that an indoor climbing wall is a more controlled learning environment than a crag. It is easy to let genuine

environmental concern restrict our activities to the grounds of a centre in order to minimise vehicle use. Does this represent best value for our clients? I suggest that, in general, our clients have a less adventurous experience than they had some years ago and contend that our taking the easy way of demonstrating compliance with current expectations is a significant factor in this.

Another 'easy' option is the way we choose to demonstrate competence in our staff. Although those on the steering group fought successfully at the time of drafting the Adventure Activities Licensing Regulations to allow providers to define competence other than by qualification, few do. It is easier to demonstrate compliance by requiring a qualification. It could be argued that we are now more consistently professional than we were a few years ago. We are undoubtedly better at the sort of processes that demonstrate to teachers, head teachers, governors and society that we are professional but do we give those in our care a better quality experience as a result? I doubt it.

Society clearly demands more than it did in terms of demonstrating that our approach represents good practice. Perhaps this contributes towards our tendency to seek an increasingly controlled environment and to be less adventurous ourselves in what we attempt with our pupils. It is a matter for personal regret that I see young people today being far more adventurous (or perhaps risk seeking) on their skateboards or in unstructured play than we allow them to be on an 'adventure' course. Should our expectations be higher? I suggest that we could be far more adventurous than we often are within a perfectly acceptable framework of safety. It does however require an effort both to set up more adventurous activities and to persuade others that the effort is worthwhile.

This is where we will inevitably (and rightly) bring our values to bear on the needs of our clients. 'Need' is arguably a mix of what our clients know they 'want' and what we know will benefit them. We *know* that to encourage young people to make a special effort to do something they are apprehensive about will have enormous benefits when they succeed. At the same time, we must be sensitive as to how far we go in that process of encouragement. I suggest that we have a responsibility to reassess such value judgements constantly. For example, a recent report (OFSTED,

2002) showed that the educational attainment gap between boys and girls is now clearly apparent at a far younger age than it was. Does this say something about an increasingly unsatisfied need that young males have for firm guidance and challenge to channel their intrinsic propensity to push at the limits? If so, does this have implications for our work?

Reducing expectations have been apparent in the 'Summer Activities for 16 Year Olds' programme, relaunched as 'Uproject'. During the first two pilot years of the programme, there was a great deal of innovative activity across the country, with extended community involvement by many residential providers. By 2002, changes to the way the programme was funded diluted the influence of the outdoor community and the adventure element was, in many cases, watered down into a standardised five day residential – packaged convenience rather than innovation. That programme illustrates well another tension that is evident in our response to the market. The market for the Uproject is effectively dictated by the government's funding criteria. When the scheme was first proposed, representatives of the outdoor community tried (unsuccessfully) to argue that the scheme should extend to a younger age group, on the basis that an intervention at age 14 would have more potential impact on a young person's behaviour. However, there has been no lack of providers willing to compromise maximum impact to comply with the criteria.

Why is this and to what extent should we respond to government agendas? There are many to which the outdoors can make a valuable contribution – for example, raising standards, active citizenship and social inclusion. Moreover, proposals by the Department for Education and Skills (Department for Education and Skills, 2002) for the 14–19 phase of education present us with enormously exciting new opportunities. Many individuals in the outdoor community welcome the fact that the potential of the outdoors to contribute to social policy has been increasingly recognised over recent years and feel an obligation to become involved in such initiatives in order to do their best to make them work. The success of the outdoor community in achieving this recognition can, however, bring its own problems. As more funded programmes come on stream, either the amount of provision must increase or providers must make choices as to how their resources should be prioritised.

Should we then simply accept market demand and cater for what the public or the funder wants or should we strive to influence the market to buy what we think we *ought* to provide? I should like to challenge providers to reappraise continually the balance between taking the easy option (by catering for that which is easiest to sell) and proactively creating demand for approaches that they feel will have maximum educational potential.

What is professionalism?

It has taken some time to lay out the argument, but the above considerations suggest that professionalism and quality are inseparable and that they are in turn contingent on the market place. The three are inter-dependent. The following three points attempt to define professionalism and its relationship with quality and the market place:

- Professionalism is the set of personal abilities, attributes and values that allow us to deliver quality experiences consistently.
- A quality experience for a given group of participants is clearly related to their individual needs.
- There must be a compromise between those individual needs and the expectations of the range of stakeholders that exist in our complex market place.

It may be surprising to see the demands of the market place positioned so prominently in a discussion of professionalism. However, there should be no conflict between our interests and those of our clients. Commercial transactions, as with other human transactions, are optimised by creating a 'win – win' situation. We will both maximise the probability of our own survival and delight our customers more consistently if we deliver quality services in a professional way. Kotler (1976: 15), an authority on marketing, defines the marketing concept as:

> . . . a customer orientation . . . aimed at generating customer satisfaction as the key to satisfying organisational goals.

Not only is the mutual benefit evident in this definition but customer satisfaction is rightly emphasised. Customer satisfaction is the outcome of a quality experience related to participants' needs. That should be the aim of professionalism.

Recognising professionalism

What then are the implications for the recognition of professionalism? We need to ask: how are quality and professionalism currently measured, would it be helpful to create a more commonly accepted form of recognition, who should do this and, what are the elements that make up professional competence? Quality is relatively easily recognised and measured. Client feedback gives a clear message. There are excellent networks where best practice is shared. Providers are subject to a variety of assessments, including National Governing Body approval schemes, licensing inspections and assessment against standards such as Investor in People. Professionalism is less easy to measure. A technical qualification guarantees a basic skill level but this forms only a tiny part of the totality of professionalism. A breadth of awareness gained from higher education will complement this. However, many people who have made an enormous contribution to work in the outdoors have done so through a vocational rather than an academic route and that alternative must be retained. Finally, skill and knowledge, however gained, are not enough. The essence of professionalism is how the individual applies these at the customer interface.

It would in my view be enormously helpful (to employers, employees and the public) to create a simple but comprehensive system that would give recognition to anyone who works in the outdoors. It is considered that the Institute for Outdoor Learning is an entirely appropriate organisation to administer this. At the time of writing, the Institute was in the process of developing a system for supporting and recognising professionalism by creating a Continuous Professional Development and Accreditation Scheme.

In drafting the requirements, the working group considered the range of attributes that outdoor employers are looking for in their employees. This clearly varies from sector to sector; the Outdoor Workforce Development Plan (SPRITO, 2002) lists these. Competence in some areas (such as technical and facilitation skills) is relatively easy to

measure. Attributes (such as enthusiasm) are less easy to measure but no less essential. Values such as the personal integrity to deliver consistent quality are arguably even more important. The new scheme must attempt to measure the whole range of abilities, attributes and values that constitute professionalism. Time will tell whether the accreditation of professionalism achieves the benefits for the profession that is hoped for. I for one look forward to the time when it is clearly understood what it means to be professional, when professionals are trusted to give those in their charge a quality experience, when they themselves consequently have the confidence to re-expand their ambitions, when they consistently give their clients real adventures (in relation to their needs) and when society has renewed confidence in the outdoor community. I also look forward to the recognition of outdoor professionals by the outside world and the added ability to influence decisions that this will create.

References

Department for Education and Skills (2002) *14–19: Extending Opportunities, Raising Standards.* London: Department for Education and Skills.

English Outdoor Council (2001) *Campaign for Adventure: Balancing Risk and Enterprise In Society.* Exeter: English Outdoor Council.

Health and Safety Executive (2001) *Reducing Risks, Protecting People.* London: HSE.

Kotler, P. (1976) *Marketing Management.* London: Prentice/Hall International.

OFSTED (2002) *National Literacy Strategy: The First Four Years 1998–2002.* London: Office for Standards in Education.

Purves, L. (2002) Common sense and a spirit of adventure. *The Times.* 12th March: 22.

SPRITO (2002) *The Outdoor Sector: Plans for Growth.* London: SPRITO (National training organisation for sport, recreation and allied occupations).

25 Technology in Outdoor Education

Bob Sharp

Abstract

Developments in clothing, equipment and footwear have had an impact on all outdoor activities in the past 25 years. Changes in materials and design have led to improvements in safety, comfort and technical performance. In the last 10 years, significant developments in information and satellite technology have spawned a variety of electronic devices such as altimeters and global positional system receivers. These have enhanced the availability of information and communication ability of those involved in outdoor activities. Most of these devices have been adopted almost automatically by the outdoor community without, apparently, thought as to the limitations and implications. This chapter summarises the nature and function of these devices and also examines some of the key issues relevant to outdoor educationalists. The conclusion is drawn that, despite the obvious advantages, there is a critical need to consider the implications in terms of reduced safety, diminished technical competence and degradation of the outdoor experience.

Introduction

Progress in research, technology, design and new materials results in improvements to our safety, comfort and overall lifestyle. In daily life there have been vast changes over the years in, for example, security, heating, transport, communications and general comfort. Vehicles are safer, better equipped, more accommodating to individual needs and environmentally friendly. Travel is faster, communications are more effective and workplaces are safer and ergonomically more efficient. Changes are equally apparent for those involved in outdoor activities. For walkers and climbers, the past 25 years have seen significant changes in clothing, footwear and equipment. In all of these there have been improvements with regard to materials, design, safety, versatility, durability and comfort. For example, a comparison of today's shell clothing using soft, breathable fabrics with the nylon-coated materials of 20 years ago shows just how far manufacturers have progressed in aspects such as comfort, insulation and durability. The same is true of climbing hardware where there have been dramatic developments in protection systems, rope materials and design of climbing tools/crampons. There have also been significant developments in other outdoor sports such as skiing (carving skis) and kayaking (polyethylene boats).

Developments like these have been aided through computing technology to assist the design (CAD) and manufacturing (CNC) processes. However, in recent years, computer technology has actually become the basis of the product itself. Notable examples are mobile telephones and global positioning system (GPS) receivers. Products like these have been designed to enhance the availability of information useful to those involved in outdoor activities and to aid communication between individuals. The following section examines some of these new products and also looks at the issues they present for outdoor education. Bartle (2000) gives a full account of technology and how it influences the outdoor experience.

Electronic instruments

Mobile phones

The popularity of mobile phones has increased at a phenomenal rate in recent years. In 2000 there were over 25 million subscribers compared to 1 million in 1990. Over half the UK's population now owns a mobile phone and numbers are continuing to increase. Communication between mobile phone users is made possible via base stations or cells located in strategic positions across the country. The number of cells has increased in recent years (and continues to increase) and this has resulted in improved coverage for users. There are currently four networks or providers in the UK each offering different levels of service and coverage. Level of coverage is a particular issue for outdoor enthusiasts in remote areas. Generally speaking, signal coverage in the Scottish Highlands and the interior of remote areas such as the Cairngorms mountains is poorer than elsewhere in the UK, which is generally good, even in areas such as the Lake District and Snowdonia. Handsets have reduced in size in recent years whilst at the same time the number of features they can support has increased – internet access, text and image messaging to name a few. The potential to identify the location of someone making an emergency call is available through triangulation of cells receiving a call, but this feature has yet to be developed as a commercial proposition. In contrast, a recent development is the mobile phone that incorporates a GPS receiver. When used in conjunction with a web-based mapping system (subscriber service) the user's position can be identified within seconds of a 'panic' button being depressed (Griffiths, 2002).

There is no doubt that a significant number of outdoor people (professional instructors and participants alike) take mobile phones with them as a back-up safety device. The question is, are they being used sensibly to help save lives and eliminate unnecessary danger, or are they being used selfishly by unprepared people to make unnecessary nuisance calls? These positions are clearly the end points of a spectrum. What is the evidence and what exactly are the advantages and limitations? There are some very obvious practical limitations – they can be lost, suffer damage or water ingress or lose network coverage; communication may be good one way but not the other. Limited battery life is a major problem, especially if the user is benighted on a remote mountain. Basically, mobiles are not designed to be used in cold and wet conditions when their efficiency is severely reduced. Beyond these problems, there are major concerns about how people use them and their perceived applications. There is a view that many outdoor people (particularly hill goers) see mobile phones as the all singing and dancing saviour which will rectify almost anything that goes wrong – from being lost, injured or late off the hill. It is also felt that possession of a mobile may inspire confidence beyond the user's technical ability. Many involved in outdoor education and the

rescue services believe that mobiles may actually deter people from acquiring basic safety skills and knowledge essential to self-sufficiency. There is evidence of walkers and climbers alerting the emergency services via a mobile phone when a solution to their predicament was well within their capability. Indeed, there have been instances of careless, unnecessary use – although very few malicious calls. A further problem is the widely held view by many hill goers that an emergency call from a mobile will result in an instant rescue. This is patently not the case.

What are the advantages? Mobiles carried by professional outdoor educationalists can give assurance to parents and colleagues by providing up-to-date information on location and time of return, particularly if there is a change of plan. They can also be used to alert rescue services in the event of a genuine incident that necessitates outside help. There is evidence from the mountain rescue service that call-out times have been reduced considerably which, in turn, has been of significant benefit to injured casualties. In some cases, lives have been saved. In addition, there have been incidents when lost walkers have been guided off the hill by rescuers with local knowledge. A major advantage is that mobile phone communications permit dialogue between those is distress on the mountain and experts who can inform and advice on treatment or other important actions. Used sensibly, there is a strong feeling that mobile phones make a valuable contribution to mountain safety and can make the task of the rescue service a lot easier. Waller (2000) discusses the use of mobiles in more detail.

Private mobile radios

The Radio Communications Agency has recently issued a radio band (PMR 446) which is license free with no call charges. Units are normally sold in pairs with a retail cost between £50 and £150. The receivers are very compact, water-resistant, weigh less than 200 grams and have very low running costs. They are designed for short-range communications in both business and leisure contexts. The typical communication range in an open space with good visibility is around three kilometres. This can reduce to around 100 metres in built-up areas. They have excellent potential in a mountain environment when walking or climbing groups are out of sight or sound and wish to communicate with one another. They suffer the same kinds of limitations as mobile phones such as damage, loss, low battery life and poor reception. Further, they are prone to interference from other radio channels. It is possible they may generate a false sense of security and lead to a reliance that is not mirrored by sound skill in navigation, planning, etc. Users need to fully appreciate their operational limitations, but in the correct context these devices have great potential to enhance the safety and communications of users.

Global positioning systems (GPS)

The United States has placed 24 satellites that have an orbiting altitude of 20,000 kms above the Earth. The GPS system is one of the major benefits left over from the cold war. It was conceived and is controlled by the US Department of Defence. It was initiated during the 1960s and fully implemented in 1995 at a cost of $10 billion. The satellites continually broadcast position and timing information to every point on the earth. Each one contains an extremely accurate atomic clock and transmits information on two frequencies that a GPS receiver can decode to provide position (latitude and longitude) and altitude at any location on the earth's surface, night or day in any weather. To obtain two-dimensional position information the receiver must register signals from three satellites. If a fourth signal is registered, altitude can also be displayed.

GPS receivers are exploited in many aspects of commercial, military and everyday life. One of the most important advances made is as an aid to navigation (Wale, 1999). Prices of receivers have plummeted in recent years (as little as £100 in 2003) and they are significantly smaller and more readily available than in the mid-1990s. When GPS receivers were first available to the mass market they were relatively inaccurate. Selective availability refers to the error applied to the satellite signals that civilian GPS instruments received up to 30th April 2000. The accuracy achievable at that time was within 100 metres. On the 1st of May 2000, the US Department of Defense switched off selective availability. The accuracy now is within approximately 15 metres, which is

good enough for the vast majority of navigators on foot. Most popular units provide a wide variety of functions. They can guide one to a position entered previously, store locations along a route to allow retracing and provide details of speed and distance to a feature. Some receivers have multi-functional capability (altimeter, electronic compass, mobile, etc.). They can be used in conjunction with dedicated mapping software to download and upload routes and have proven particularly valuable to rescue services in recording areas covered during extensive searches. A particular feature is the use of waypoints. Waypoints are positions on a route (grid references) entered into the receiver's memory during a trip to assist route finding. They can be added at various points on the route by pressing a sequence of buttons. If there is a need to backtrack and the weather is poor, the receiver leads the walker back by giving distance and directional information from one waypoint to the next.

Given these features, it is clear that GPS receivers are a significant aid to navigation, particularly when there are few land features to identify position and when the weather is inclement. However, there are numerous limitations. Considerable knowledge and practice is required to get the most out of GPS receivers. The user must be in a place where enough satellites can be 'seen' by the unit – no roofs, overhangs or trees in the way. GPSs cannot see around corners; they will not work in thick forests and deep valleys between mountains. Their accuracy can vary and this accuracy can be degraded at the whim of the US government by manipulation of selective availability. They are fairly robust and water resistant, but dropping and water ingress may be disastrous. It takes time to acquire a fix and most are generally hard on batteries (they may not work at all in sub-zero temperatures). They are not easy to manipulate in extreme weather (e.g., changing batteries, pressing small buttons) and it is easy to make mistakes when cold or wearing gloves. Spare batteries must always be carried. In addition, their ability to provide altitude information is considered to be variable; they are considered to be inferior to traditional altimeters that rely on barometric pressure information.

GPS receivers are marketed vigorously in the outdoor press and they are certainly here to stay.

Prices too are not outside the pockets of most hill goers. There is a risk that future generations of hill goers will adopt GPS receivers at the expense of traditional skills using map and compass. The view adopted by most outdoor authorities is that whilst GPS receivers are an extremely useful support to traditional navigational skills, they are not a direct substitute (Townsend, 2002).

Electronic compasses

Electronic compasses are relatively new devices that use magnetic sensors (magnetic flux gate) to display information digitally on a small screen. They are designed to give all the features of a traditional compass, plus several others such as memory of course being travelled, automatic reversal of a route and the facility to follow a previously planned course. Some serve as barometers and watches and others include a GPS receiver to provide positional information. Electronic compasses are variable in their accuracy depending on make/model, but an error of around 1–2 degrees is typical. On the surface they would appear to have few advantages over a traditional magnetic compass and several limitations. Batteries tend to discharge quickly because the units have very high power consumption. Batteries also tend not to perform so well in very cold weather. Like traditional compasses, they are prone to magnetic distortion. Generally they are not as simple to use, reliable or robust as a magnetic compass. Further, they tend to be bulky and do not sit easily in the hand. Further, they are not easy to read in bad weather or snow as a magnetic compass and some are slow to respond. It is impossible to take a bearing from the map as with a traditional compass and extensive time is often required to understand the various functions.

Multi-function instruments

There is a current trend for electronic instruments to serve a variety of functions and not just one (e.g., altimeter). Some instruments can now be purchased which serve a variety of functions – GPS (usual functions such as current position, record of journey enabling backtracking), compass, altimeter, mobile phone, personal organiser (phone book, calendar, etc.) barometer (historical trend over 24 hours to enable weather predictions), electronic maps, etc. Not all units embody all of these features but some contain several. Multi-function instruments avoid the need to carry several items of equipment and they use the same battery for a variety of functions thus avoiding the need to carry multiple sets of spare batteries. Some instruments permit the downloading of map sections to their internal screen. On the downside, these devices are generally heavier and bulkier than single-function instruments. They are also more costly. Their use may take a lot of time and patience because of the software complexity and multi-purpose use. There is the added problem that if the unit malfunctions or is lost then all of its functions are also lost! It remains to be seen whether multi-function instruments will replace single-function products. The feelings of outdoor authorities at the present time are the same as for other electronic devices; they can be an extremely useful support to traditional navigational skills, but are not a direct substitute.

Altimeters

Altimeters have developed from the traditional aneroid mechanical barometer that does not use batteries. Although based on the aneroid barometer, the information is converted into electronic visual information. Altimeter 'watches' indicate altitude by measuring differences in atmospheric pressure then calculating and displaying this information as altitude above sea level. Battery failure is not so usual and the units are generally reliable, robust and durable since they are made for hostile environments. Most provide only altitude information, whilst some can accumulate altitude to give total height gained. Some have a chronograph facility, backlight, alarm, etc. Some can also be used as a barometer to monitor barometric pressure changes over time. When displayed graphically, the picture gives an indication of weather trend and from that, predictions can be made. Accuracy varies around 5 metres, but top quality units are accurate to 1 metre. They can be a useful aid to navigation when used in conjunction with an Ordnance Survey map. For example, when moving along a linear feature (e.g., a ridge or forest edge) knowledge of height (and therefore contour) can provide a positional fix on that feature. Similarly, knowledge of height can be used to confirm position as given by other information such as a GPS grid reference or topographical features. However, weather fronts and rapid changes of pressure can play havoc with these devices. There is a need to re-calibrate (from a known height) often if the weather is changing quickly. They are also of little value if the user is unfamiliar with maps or doesn't possess a relevant map of the area.

Avalanche transceivers

Avalanche transceivers are highly dedicated items of equipment. Climbers and skiers carry them when moving across avalanche-prone slopes. They send signals that can be monitored by people close by to quickly locate the position of an avalanche victim. In practice, they are a group safety item; someone has to be close by in order to receive signals from the individual trapped in an avalanche. Consequently, when in use, they should all be switched to transmit mode. There are two different kinds – analogue and digital. The latest digital versions speed up the search process by displaying directional and distance information about the trapped person. They have a proven record of speeding up the search process significantly, but they do have limitations. Batteries can discharge quickly (especially when in transmit mode) and although fairly robust, they are sophisticated items of technology that can malfunction. There is some evidence that mobile phones which are switched on and in close proximity to a transceiver in receive mode can distort the received information. Transceivers can go off frequency and substantial training is required to get the best out of them. Their use in the UK is very limited but most ski tourers in the Alps carry transceivers.

Personal locator beacons

Personal locator beacons (PLBs), when activated send a signal which is received by a geostationary or polar-orbiting satellite. The transmissions are relayed by the satellite to Rescue Co-ordination Centres (RCCs). There are many RCCs located around the world. After analysis, and if seen to be valid, the receiving RCC passes the information to the appropriate search and rescue agencies. PLBs are not authorised by the Radio Communication Agency for use on land in the UK,

but they are a mandatory requirement for any maritime craft venturing more than 25 miles offshore. PLBs are available in combinations of three frequencies, each of which provides different kinds of features. Those used for maritime applications transmit signals containing information about the user and their precise location (½ mile accuracy). Cheaper versions (which can be hired from some outdoor retailers) only provide very crude positional information (error in the order of 100s miles). The chief problem is careless or accidental activation. They have to be 'seen' by a satellite and, as with other items listed before, they contain sophisticated electronics that can breakdown, suffer frequency drift and battery discharge. Their use on land is highly questionable and perhaps illegal.

Wind watches

Wind watches are portable wind gauges. They are light and can be handheld to yield a variety of measures such as peak speed over a measured period, plus average speed, current wind speed, wind-chill temperature, etc. They are sensitive to position and therefore have to be held as per the manufacturer's instructions. Some offer multi-function capability (wind speed, temperature, altitude, barometer). They are robust, not a big drain on batteries and also float. Their accuracy is typically within 2–4 per cent. As most outdoor users would use the 'felt' wind strength to make decisions about their travel or route, wind watches are probably of little practical value.

Issues for outdoor education

There are several issues and many questions for outdoor education in regard to the impact of the devices just described. Is technology gradually being 'absorbed' by the outdoor community without conscious and balanced analysis of costs and benefits? To what extent is technology influencing the values and skills currently held in high regard by outdoor educationalists? Is technology making things possible that were previously impossible or impractical? Is technology making things safer or less safe for users? There seem to be three broad areas of concern – safety, skill and adventure.

There is as strong view that increased use of items such as GPS receivers and mobiles may lead people to underestimate the risks of outdoor activities or incorrectly perceive their own levels of competence (e.g., Bartle, 2000). For example, the possession of a mobile phone may be interpreted by the owner (perhaps unconsciously) as an insurance policy for taking greater or more risks. Bartle considers their use may detract from reliance on knowledge, skill and experience that would have prevailed before the advent of such devices. Furthermore, because there is no guarantee they will work (batteries may fail, electronics malfunction, devices are lost) there is always a need for back-up skills. There is no direct evidence to support the proposed link between technology and safety, but the concern is a genuine one. This is an area that deserves close research attention.

A second point concerns the degree to which technology detracts from the richness and intensity of environmental experiences. Keay (1995) argues that developments in technology have the potential to destroy an individual's sense of isolation, self-reliance and dependence on their own resources. Bartle refers to 'technological filtering'. He suggests that new clothing, equipment and communications equipment essentially reduces peoples' interaction with the environment; sights, sounds and experiences all become simplified. Of course, the opposite argument can also be made. It could be reasoned that new equipment actually makes it possible for people to visit places, endure weather extremes and take on more challenging adventures, than was previously possible. It may be that adventure is augmented and new activities develop through the availability of sophisticated equipment. The questions as to which of these two views is valid may well depend on the individual and their level of experience. The danger is that those with less inexperience and others seeking a quick 'adventure fix' will adopt technology more to protect and control their movement in the environment rather than to extend challenges and enrich experiences.

There is no doubt that advances in equipment and clothing in recent years has helped improve the technical standards in many outdoor sports. This is positive because it means that many people have realised untapped potentials whilst others have been stimulated to more challenging goals and higher levels of technical performance. However, many outdoor professionals feel that some of the new developments in technology may give people the impression it is unnecessary to acquire and use skills previously considered essential for safe and purposeful practice. A consequence is that future generations of outdoor enthusiasts may fail to acquire fundamental skills (Wild, 2002) and fail to acquire the self-sufficiency and resourcefulness that is central to the spirit of the outdoor involvement. Technology may degrade effort and minimise commitment (Bartle, 2000). The consensus (certainly within the world of mountaineering) is that people should not rely on any form of electronic aid but should acquire the fundamental skills. Electronic aids should only be seen as a back-up or supplement to basic skills (MacNae, 1997). It remains to be seen whether ideals such as this hold well over time.

The essential consideration for outdoor education is well expressed by Bartle (2000). He says:

The point is not to despise the use of technology or to remain ignorant and distant from it, but to question how to embody technology within the educational aims sought.

References

Bartle, M. (2000) Technology and Outdoor Education. *Horizons*. 7: 56–9.

Griffiths, G. (2002) The First GPS Mobile Phone Receiver. *Navigation News*. Nov/Dec, 17.

Keay, W. (1995) *Land Navigation*. Southampton: The Ordnance Survey.

MacNae, A. (1997) *BMC Position Statement on the Use of Mobile Phones and GPS System in the Mountains*. Manchester: The British Mountaineering Council.

Townsend, C. (2002) Staying on Track. *The Great Outdoors*. February, 76–80.

Wale, T. (1999) Where are we Going? *Summit*. 13: 30.

Waller, R. (2000) It's Your Call. *The Great Outdoors*. March, 36–41.

Wild, R. (2002) The Global Positioning System. *The Scottish Mountaineer*. 13: 35–7.

26 Women Working in the Outdoors: Still a Man's World?

Kate O'Brien, Nina Saunders and Peter Barnes

Abstract

This chapter discusses the introduction and engagement of women to outdoor activities and outdoor education as well as the nature of women's employment as leaders in the outdoor sector. The point is made that many of the issues associated with women and the outdoors are symptomatic of wider sociological and socialisation issues within society. The chapter concludes, however, with a note that outdoor education is, in many ways, ahead of wider society, particularly with regard to the pace of change and the increasing participation of women.

Introduction

To any observer it is apparent that women still represent a minority of those currently working in the outdoor industry. Although there has undoubtedly been significant academic interest in the area of gender studies and outdoor education, this chapter can provide little more than a snapshot of this work. Little of this has, so far, transferred to practitioner levels. Humberstone (2000a: 21) comments:

Despite the considerable research over the last twenty years which has identified gender as a central concept in explaining human behaviour, and organisational and social structures, areas of the 'outdoor industry' seem frequently ignorant of this knowledge.

Most outdoor education providers and policy makers are white, male, heterosexual and middle class. Humberstone adds there is, 'little representation by women and black people on the teaching staff.' (2000a: 23).

Women can find it difficult to participate in outdoor pursuits and consequently they then find it very hard to pursue a career in this area. Warren (1996) talks about several myths that exist for women in the outdoors. One of these is the 'Myth of Accessibility' in which she suggests that outdoor activity opportunities are relatively unavailable to women due to social and economic factors that they feel may limit them. Women generally have lower earning power than men and so are less likely to invest their finances in outdoor pursuits. They perceive it as a risk, despite the

benefits and enjoyment they will gain in return. Instead, they spend their money in other ways, such as clothes for their children.

The outdoor industry has been dominated by men in the past (Saunders and Sharp, 2002) reflecting the social conditioning that women have been bought up to believe in. Warren discusses women's social conditioning, noting that, 'The moment she steps into the woods her femininity is in question' (1996: 12). Many people are brought up with the view that physical activities involving a high amount of risk are for men only. It is not, therefore, seen as appropriate for women to take part in outdoor pursuits. Giddens (1997) describes the gender differences and socialisation processes that exist in society today. From a young age children are constantly subjected to different types of gender role behaviour through processes of socialisation. It is widely accepted that adults will treat boys and girls differently from when they are born; other sources such as relatives, education, role models, peers and the media further enforce such stereotypical characteristics. For example, children's television shows, comics and storybooks often portray a dominant male character showing strength and independence. When female characters do appear, they tend to play a more traditional or subservient role. Giddens (1997: 95) sums this process up well in the following:

Clearly, gender socialisation is very powerful, and challenges to it can be upsetting. Once a gender is 'assigned', society expects individuals to act like 'females' and 'males'.

Guthrie (2001: 132) puts this point into the outdoor context, stating that, 'a woman outdoor leader is in a gender-role incongruent position which automatically has her facing biases'.

Outdoor pursuits offer opportunities to develop androgynous individuals and androgynous individuals therefore may be well suited to leadership positions in the outdoor industry. Those expressing traits considered as androgynous tend to display characteristics that are considered both male and female, conforming neither to stereotypical male or female traits. Stereotypes can cause barriers (Friedrich and Priest, 1992). Therefore, those that tend to be androgynous may be more open minded and suited to experiences and careers in the outdoors and perhaps help to break down stereotypes.

As well as the question of femininity, some women often feel guilty leaving family members behind while pursuing their own leisure activities (Pottinger, 1994). For women, their family commitments will often be more important than their need for adventure, and this is very much what is expected by society. Consider, for example, the media's reporting of the tragic death of Alison Hargreaves in 1995. She was described by the media as being, 'irresponsible as a wife and mother' (Loynes, 1996: 56) simply because she pursued her personal outdoor interests. Compare this to the treatment of David Hempleman-Adams. The national newspapers heralded his success upon return from his expedition to be the first person to walk solo to the geomagnetic pole, despite the fact that he had told his wife he was going on a skiing holiday (Hann, 2003). Moral standards are unfairly applied to men and women involved in high risk activities and adventures, to the disadvantage of the female sex.

Outdoor education has its roots in male ideologies. Not only are modern outdoor courses based on these ideas, but courses are often taught solely by men. This can have a negative effect and discourage females from continuing involvement in outdoor pursuits and they can further maintain the impression that these activities are not feminine, by having to complete courses more suited to male philosophies. Fischer (1985) suggests that female role models can have a positive influence on women and girls for continued participation and undertaking careers in the outdoor industry. However, Warren (1996) identifies another difficulty with becoming a female instructor in the outdoors and talks about the 'Myth of the Superwoman'. She suggests that once a woman becomes highly qualified in the outdoors others are no longer able to relate to her as a woman as her status is unrealistic and beyond her clients' reach. Participants will struggle with their pre-existing stereotypes and sexist conditioning, believing that a woman does not belong in the outdoors. She comments that:

> . . . with superior abilities, she becomes the superwoman, a woman unlike the rest of the population. Her students no longer have to view her competence for what it is – the ongoing struggle to gain parity in a male-dominated profession.
>
> (Warren, 1996: 15)

Rather than becoming a positive role model the superwoman becomes almost the opposite. Those involved on her courses may feel that they can never be as good as her and therefore leave feeling disillusioned or de-motivated. Significantly, women viewed as role models in the outdoors can lose their identity as first class sports-person in their own right. Ellen MacArthur, for example, is widely lauded as the fastest female trans-world sailor ever but she is rarely praised as one of the finest single-handed sailors in the world, irrespective of her gender.

Stereotyping and socialisation

There has been much written about the stereotypical characteristics of men and women as participants and leaders in the outdoors. Knapp (1985) in Kiewa (2001: 4) describes typical male characteristics as 'competitive, dominating, achieving, initiating, assertive, active and task orientated'. Conversely, women are considered to be:

> Nurturing, co-operating, expressive of feelings, self sacrificing, yielding in conflict, dependent or interdependent . . . gentle, emotional, passive and intuitive.

It has also been documented by Humberstone (2000a: 23), that women are closer to nature due to their biological predisposition to be able to carry a child. Women have also been described by Kiewa (2001) as being more focussed on the inner journey and the experience; therefore building relationships while men will focus strongly on the challenge of the activity and succeeding at it.

Gender socialisation processes influence our expectations of the traditional leader and, subsequently, outdoor leaders are expected to be male. Research in leadership has traditionally been based on studies that ask the question, 'What makes a good leader?' concentrating, for example on personality characteristics and traits (Stodgill, 1974). As the subjects of these studies were nearly always male leaders, the data revealed unsurprisingly that common characteristics such as being visionary, decisive and charismatic were common leadership traits and 'masculine'. Since these first studies were undertaken, other theories have been developed. One contemporary model in particular, the 'Transactional Leadership Model', emphasises aspects deemed to be more suited to the female stereotype, 'Working within relationships to motivate and lift others to higher levels of drive and performance (Hitt, 1990 in Jordan, 1992: 62). This type of leadership is thought to be more applicable to the experiential field of the outdoor industry. Despite developments in leadership theories and ideas, Jordan (1992: 61) notes however, 'The expected and accepted traits of leadership tend to (still) be associated with white males'.

Participation levels and employment

There are a far lower proportion of women than men involved in all aspects of participation and leadership in outdoor activities. According to Humberstone (1994) quoted in Allin (2000: 51):

> *Outdoor education as a career area is also predominantly male, with women particularly underrepresented in the higher levels of outdoor leadership and management.*

In one study carried out by Allin (2000) twelve women who had pursued a career in outdoor education were interviewed to gauge their views on their experiences and careers in the outdoor industry. It was found that many of these women lacked physical confidence due to societal stereotypes of women in the outdoors. The issues of pregnancy and childbirth were examined and how they affected the subject's careers. Many of the women felt that they had been held back, forced to put their careers on hold, or chose

between a family or career because of family commitments. A career in the outdoors and a family were seen as incompatible.

Sharp (1998) specifically talks about some of the barriers that women face when pursuing a career in the outdoor industry. He remarks:

> *Their coaching responsibilities conflict with family life, the need to travel [to work] and prepare courses etc.*
>
> (Sharp, 1998: 233)

Furthermore, he found that due to extra commitments required, for example, gaining qualifications, women tend to perceive problems such as, spending extended periods away from home and getting time off work as stronger barriers than men do.

One of the approaches that has been used to address some of these barriers is the controversial idea of women only courses and in particular women only leadership courses. It has been argued by Lynch (1999) that these types of courses can lead to a situation of exclusion rather than inclusion, or even that women only courses are a retreat from the reality of working in the outdoors. However, in defence of single sex courses, both Henderson (1999) and Robinson Pottinger (1994) argue that such courses can allow women to participate in a supportive environment free from physical and psychological gender role constraints and stereotypes. Collins, quoted in Barnes (2002), notes from her own work how it is sometimes important for young girls to be able to work separately from boys who may tend to dominate activities and create a 'competitive culture' which detracts girls from participating and reinforces their stereotypical perception of outdoor activities being a male domain. Rea and Slavkin, quoted in Barnes (2000) also highlight the way in which young girls may feel constrained to act in such a way that they maintain a socially acceptable 'feminine' identity. Clearly, it is not possible to examine gender issues within outdoor education without taking into account a much wider sociological and psychological perspective.

Having gained employment in the outdoors, research has indicated that male and female leaders can be perceived very differently by their clients (Clemmenson, 2002). In one study investigating the reactions of clients to male and female challenge course instructors, it was found that men received feedback regarding their technical skills, concrete skills and information giving. In contrast to this, women generally received positive feedback concerning the 'soft' skills of leadership, such as supportiveness, good facilitation and relationship building. Interestingly, when a man and a woman shared the leadership role, the woman was not acknowledged at all for her technical ability and often all questions were directed towards her male partner. Clemmensen comments:

> . . . participants . . . have a need to perceive someone in a leadership role in terms of technical, concrete skills and knowledge. When there is a man available he is attributed these qualities.
>
> (Clemmenson, 2002: 214)

Recent research by Saunders and Sharp (2002) indicates that numbers of male leaders actively working in the outdoor industry in Scotland are still greater than numbers of female leaders. Their paper discusses differences in leadership styles between men and women and examines whether or not this should be reflected in the way National Governing Bodies programme their courses. Although this hypothesis was not supported, their research indicated that there are 'many barriers (social, practical and biological) that women face'. There is also:

> A critical need for female leaders who work in the outdoors to be accepted into what is very much a male dominated community.
>
> (Saunders and Sharp, 2002: 92)

O'Brien (2003) interviewed a number of women who had undertaken careers in the outdoors and found that their experience supported previous research by Loeffer (1995) and Allin (2000). In her study, women talked about various issues when carrying out their jobs including, for example, how they feel when working predominantly with men. One remarked that, '. . . quite often you're the only lady working in a centre.' This theme was continued by another interviewee, commenting, 'It was more perceived than anything, I felt like an outsider.' Clients' perceptions were also considered. One woman stated that, 'there's always the perception that you're not the expected.' Another suggested that frequently, 'the girls want the guys and the guys want the guys as well.' She also thought that as a leader, 'you have

to constantly prove your abilities more than men.' Furthermore, she emphasised that, 'I have to be more confident so that I can give the girls a good time as well as the guys'.

Paradoxically, it is evident that being a woman can be a very positive attribute when looking for work, and possibly promotion, in outdoor education. Most, but not all, of the women interviewed by O'Brien had found that being a woman was of benefit when applying for jobs, for a number of reasons. One interviewee thought this was because there are so few females in outdoor education; more are required in order to deal with female issues. Other reasons were also described. It was suggested that some centres like to have a 'token female' to show that women can do things as well. It was pointed out however that all applicants for employment must have the required qualifications. Of course, many of the reasons for specifically employing women can be seen as both positive and negative. One woman in a study by Loeffler (1995) described her gender as a proverbial double-edged sword; gaining promotion to senior positions based on her gender rather than her qualifications and experience.

Some of the women interviewed by O'Brien (2003) identified many negative comments made to them by clients, as well as insensitive reactions to them as leaders when working in the outdoors. One woman related an incident when taking a group of children from one place to another in a minibus; one of the group had asked who was going to drive and when she said it was herself the boy retorted, 'But my dad says women can't drive'. Another woman had a similar reaction when a client she was teaching said to her 'I can't take this from a woman'. Another went on to say, 'I have found sometimes if I'm skippering a yacht, which I do commercially, that occasionally someone will ask who is the skipper and they seem a bit surprised when you say it is yourself'. Similar incidents were related by one woman who talked about teaching climbing – 'I could feel them thinking, will she be able to hold us?' While another had comments from men such as, 'You're fit for a bird ain't ya!' when she was leading a physical activity in the outdoors.

Whilst many of these comments may have been innocent remarks made by younger clients and perhaps said in jest or ignorance by adult clients, they can become a serious issue for women working in the outdoor industry if they occur on a regular basis. Whilst women may be working in supportive environments with their colleagues and employers, these types of comments are based on the general public's stereotypical views that they have grown up with in today's society. The use of sexist language on outdoor courses has, for example, been broached by Jordan (1996). Examining the attitudes and perceptions that others have of female outdoor leaders and how this impacts on their careers was also identified as an area to be investigated and developed by Saunders and Sharp (2002).

O'Brien's study raised the topic of physical strength. A few interviewees had found their levels of strength to be a problem when working with men in the outdoor environment. They suggested strength was an issue and sometimes lack of strength meant tasks could not be achieved that would be possible by men (e.g., carrying heavy equipment). This matter is, of course, not specific to outdoor education but relates to society's wider idea of gender and stereotypical gender roles (Lugg, 2003; Humberstone 2000b in Barnes, 2000). Even so, it does not detract from the fact that such issues are real and genuine areas of concern for those currently involved in the outdoor industry.

It is evident, even from this limited overview, that there are a number of fundamental areas to be examined with regard to women in the outdoors. Perhaps most noticeably, and most problematically, women who enter the outdoors as instructors but who leave after a short period need to be traced and reasons for their withdrawal investigated. Likewise, younger girls who participate in outdoor activities but fail to maintain an interest and women who start the qualification process but drop out should be questioned to examine the causes. Furthermore, tracing women from ethnic minorities, a significantly under-represented group, involved in outdoor activities and the outdoor industry could also be an important theme of research. All of these groups may provide important missing indicators about the relationship between women and their role as participants and leaders in outdoor activities.

To end on a positive note

In conclusion, however, it should be emphasised how much has changed in a relatively short period; for example, as recently as the 1980s, Outward Bound was still operating two centres in Wales one for men and boys and the other for girls and women – the latter with a distinctly more 'feminine' curricula. The field of outdoor education is actually leading society in many aspects regarding participation, with gender in particular being one such area. Whilst as little as a decade ago many centres, and indeed outdoor clubs, were still all-male preserves this has changed significantly. Equally important, it is now considered appropriate to consider and debate gender issues with a view to resolving some of the key issues. The challenge is to maintain the momentum and ensure that outdoor education embraces full and equal participation, and employment at all levels, for all.

References

Allin, L. (2000) Women in Outdoor Education: Negotiating a Male-Gendered Space – Issues of Physicality. in Humberstone, B. (Ed.) *Her Outdoors: Risk, Challenge and Adventure.* Eastbourne: LSA.

Clemmenson, B. (2002) An Exploration of the Differences and Perceptions of the Difference Between Male and Female Challenge Course Instructors. *Journal of Experiential Education.* Spring. 25: 2.

Collins, D. (2002) Working With Young Women in the Outdoors. in Barnes, P. (2002) *Leadership with Young People.* Lyme Regis: Russell House Publishing.

Fischer, M.L. (1985) On Social Equality and Difference, A View From the Netherlands. *Management Education and Development.* 16: 2, 201–10.

Friedrich, M. and Priest, S. (1992) Developing Androgynous Individuals Through Outdoor Adventure Experiences. *The Journal of Adventure Education and Outdoor Leadership.* 9: 3, 11–2.

Giddens, A. (1997) *Sociology.* (3rd edn.) Cambridge: Polity Press.

Guthrie, S. (2001) The Profession of Adventure Education Leadership. *The Journal of Experiential Education.* Winter 24: 3.

Hann, M. (2003) Gentlemen Prefer Mountains. *The Guardian,* Friday April 11th.

Henderson, K.A. (1999) *Should Gender-Specific Programs, Such as All-Women Courses be Offered in Adventure Education? (Yes).* in Wurdinger, S.D. and Potter, T.G. (Eds.) *Controversial Issues in Adventure Education.* Iowa: Kendall/Hunt.

Humberstone, B. (2000a) The 'Outdoor Industry' as Social and Educational Phenomena: Gender and Outdoor Adventure/Education. *Journal of Adventure Education and Outdoor Learning.* 1: 1, 21–35.

Humberstone, B. (2000b) Added and Contested Values: Femininity, Masculinity and the Environment. in Barnes, P. (Ed.) (2000) *Values and Outdoor Learning.* Penrith: AfOL Publications.

Jordan, D.J. (1992) Effective Leadership for Girls and Women in Outdoor Recreation. *Journal of Physical Education, Recreation and Dance.* 63: 2, 61–4.

Jordan, D. (1996) Snips and Snails and Puppy Dog Tails.The Use of Gender Free Language in Experiential Education. in Warren, K. (Ed.) *Women's Voices in Experiential Education.* Iowa: Kendall Hunt.

Kiewa, J. (1997) Transformational Leadership: Not Just for Women. *The Journal of Adventure Education and Outdoor Leadership.* 14: 4, 3–5.

Kiewa, J. (2001) Stepping Around Things: Gender Relationships in Climbing. *Australian Journal of Outdoor Education.* 5: 2, 4–12.

Loeffler, T.A. (1995) Factors Influencing Women's Outdoor Leadership Career Development. *Melpomene Journal.* 14: 3, 15–21.

Loynes, C (1999) Adventure in a Bun. *Journal of Adventure Education and Outdoor Leadership.* 13: 2, 52–7.

Lugg, A. (2003) Women's Experience of Outdoor Education: Still Trying to be One of the Boys? in Humberstone, B., Brown, H. and Richards, K. (Eds.) *Whose Journeys? The Outdoors and Adventure as Social and Cultural Phenomena.* Penrith: The Institute for Outdoor Learning.

Lynch, J. (1999) Should Gender-Specific Programs, Such as All-Women Courses be Offered in Adventure Education? (No). in Wurdinger, S.D. and Potter, T.G. (Eds.) *Controversial Issues in Adventure Education.* Iowa: Kendall/Hunt.

O'Brien, K. (2003) *Careers in the Scottish Outdoor Education Industry: A Gender Issue?* Unpublished research project; Glasgow: University of Strathclyde.

Pottinger, R. (1994). Mountain Leader Training, Why Women Only Courses? *The Journal of Adventure Education and Outdoor Leadership.* 11: 1, 15–6.

Rea, J. and Slavkin, M. (2000) The Gender Based Relationship of Girls to Their Natural Environment. in Barnes, P. (Ed.) (2000) *Values and Outdoor Learning.* Penrith: AfOL Publications.

Saunders, N. and Sharp, B. (2002) Outdoor Leadership: The Last Male Domain? *European Journal of Physical Education.* 7: 2, 85–94.

Sharp, B. (1998) The Training of Mountain Leaders: Some Gender Concerns. *European Journal of Physical Education.* 3: 229–38.

Stodgill, R. M. (1974) *Handbook of Leadership.* New York: MacMillan.

Warren, K. (1996) Women's Outdoor Adventures: Myth and Reality. in Warren, K. (Ed.) *Women's Voices in Experiential Education.* Iowa: Kendall Hunt.

Index